W9-AUY-231

THE
GHOST HUNTER'S
GUIDE

THE GHOST HUNTER'S GUIDE

PETER UNDERWOOD

*President and Chief Investigator
of The Ghost Club (founded 1862)*

BLANDFORD PRESS
POOLE · NEW YORK · SYDNEY

For
BEN and ADAM UNDERWOOD
two of my grandchildren
who may one day be
Ghost Hunters

First published in the UK 1986 by Blandford Press
Link House, West Street, Poole, Dorset BH15 1LL

Reprinted 1987

Distributed in the United States by
Sterling Publishing Co, Inc,
2 Park Avenue, New York, NY 10016

Distributed in Australia by
Capricorn Link (Australia) Pty Ltd
PO Box 665, Lane Cove, NSW 2066

British Library Cataloguing in Publication Data

Underwood, Peter, *1923-*
 The ghost hunter's guide.
 1. Ghosts
 I. Title
 133.1'072   BF1461

ISBN 0 7137 1860 9

Typeset by Best-set Typesetter Ltd, Hong Kong
Printed in Great Britain by
Mackays of Chatham, Kent.

Contents

Acknowledgements 6

Introduction 7

1 The Different Kinds of Ghosts 14

2 Ghost Hunting Equipment and its Uses 24

3 The Investigation of Hauntings 38

4 The Photography of Ghosts 61

5 Useful Forms of Questionnaires, Word-Association Tests and Instruction Leaflets for Ghost Hunters 75

6 The Problem of the Poltergeist 95

7 Mediumship and Exorcism in Ghost Hunting 107

8 A Step-by-Step Investigation of a Haunting 121

9 Britain's Most Haunted Areas 129

10 Ghost Hunting in Europe 147

11 Ghost Hunting in North America 161

12 Ghost Hunting in Australasia and the Far East 173

13 A Ghost Calendar 184

Useful Addresses 202

Recommended Books 206

Index 215

Acknowledgements

I am very grateful for all the help I have received from many people in researching, writing and illustrating this book, and in particular I am indebted to Matthew Alexander, Jay Anson, Professor Hans Bender, Dr John Beloff, John Birch, Chris Bonington, Tony Broughall, Tom Brown, Mr and Mrs B.B. Brown, Tony Cornell, John Cutten, Sir Peter Garron, KCMG, Dr Alan Gauld, Mrs V.M. Govan, Dr Peter Hilton-Rowe, Air Commodore R. Carter Jonas, OBE, Andrew Jupp, William H. Jebb, Richard Lambert MA, John Mallor, Information Officer, City Hall, Toronto, and City of Toronto Archives, Mrs Sheila Merritt, John Mitchell, Miss Eleanor O'Keeffe, Dr A.R. George Owen, Tom Perrott, Arthur Peters, Donald Ross, Keith Siggins, Mr and Mrs G. Stringer, Chris Underwood, Alan Wesencraft; also The Ghost Club, the Society for Psychical Research, the Harry Price Library at the University of London, *Psychic News*, the College of Psychic Studies and the staffs at the British Museum, Farnham Public Library and Alton Public Library; and especially my wife, Joyce Elizabeth, for her patience, help and encouragement.

Peter Underwood
The Savage Club, Berkeley Square, London W1X 6JD.

Introduction

What ghosts are is a problem that has puzzled mankind since the beginning of recorded history. Stories of ghosts and ghostly happenings have been reported from every part of the world, in every civilisation and environment, throughout all recorded history. But no one has yet discovered the complete answer to the question 'What are ghosts?'

There are many interesting theories and it seems likely that some of them, which we will look at in a moment, may well be the answer to some ghosts; but certainly not all. As yet there is no single theory that can explain all reported ghostly appearances, and there is overwhelming evidence that there are different kinds of ghosts. One of the ghost hunter's first problems in studying a case of haunting is to establish the kind of ghost that he is dealing with – after he has thoroughly explored the possibility that the ghost is not a ghost at all.

False ghosts, 'ghosts' that for one reason or another are not what they seem, are not all that rare. Perhaps the person or witness has been mistaken by natural objects; perhaps someone is purposely attempting to mislead others into thinking that a ghost is haunting a particular place; perhaps someone is 'ghosting for a giggle' – whatever the reason, it is always important to explore all likelihood of the reported ghost being a fake or not really being a ghost at all before attempting to define the type of ghost that may or may not have been seen. In other words always look most carefully and sympathetically for a normal explanation before considering the possibility of a supernormal one.

Some reported ghosts, perhaps the majority, are subjective; that is they have no objective reality outside the minds of those who 'see' them. They are figments of the imagination, thought forms, creations of the unconscious, dreams, hallucinations, illusions, the results of wishful thinking. Many people believe that 'it's all in the mind' and that that is the complete answer to the question 'What are ghosts?' But it is not as simple as that. True, as I have said, many 'ghosts' can be explained in this way, but certainly not all of them.

Before we leave the important question of 'subjective'

ghosts, however, there is an intriguing theory that also needs to be explored when a ghost hunter hears about a ghost or visits a reputedly haunted house. We might call it the 'electrical impulse wave theory'. It has been established that during a period of extreme stress, physical or emotional, brain waves (which can be recorded on an electro-encephalograph) become considerably more active; it may be that when these reach a certain level they produce a telepathic image which is transmitted, and this image may be picked up by someone who happens to be in the right place at the right time. It has been suggested that such an image or telepathic picture may remain for years, available to anyone, long after the death of the person who unintentionally transmitted the image.

Thus, let us suppose that a person was deeply distressed or in great pain, and that his or her brain waves may have increased to the extent that a telepathic image was transmitted, and let us suppose that the image transferred itself to a house some distance away. Then, according to this theory, anyone who is in that house, at any time for years afterwards, may pick up the image.

The person unconsciously transmitting the image may be thinking of a happy period in his life when he stood at a window and thought how beautiful the world was, or an unhappy period when he was sad and walked in despair up and down his room. Then a suitably receptive person, viewing the house at any time – or perhaps at a certain time – may see a telepathic image or 'ghost' standing by the window or walking through a room.

An interesting aspect of this theory is that it is one that could account for the many reports of 'ghosts' walking through closed doors and through walls; and for ghost figures being seen where there is no visible means of support, and above or below the existing flooring. This is because structural alterations may have been made to the house or building after the telepathic image settled, and the ghost would be seen in the position or moving along its precise track irrespective of any subsequent walls that may have been built or new flooring or any other alteration.

It is a theory that could account for many ghosts but by no means all of them. Of course it is only a theory, and one that is, as yet, impossible to prove or disprove; but it could explain how some ghosts of people, animals, objects and possibly sounds are produced in much the same way as electrical waves are transformed into television pictures or sounds reach a radio. It might even explain why most ghosts are no longer seen after a number of years; perhaps depending upon the intensity of the transmission or the climatic conditions prevailing; the image eventually fades, almost like a battery running down. There is the additional theory that people witnessing these kind of ghosts 'feed' the battery, and so the more people who experience the impression the longer the image lasts; an alternative idea is that witnesses have precisely the opposite effect and the more people who see the ghost the sooner it will disappear altogether!

Let us leave the idea of subjective ghosts for the moment and look at other types of ghosts that do not appear to be the result of telepathy or mind activity, and see whether we can find out what ghosts are if they are not telepathic images.

Spiritualists believe that ghosts are the spirits of dead people; that when people die their spirits continue in another world or dimension, and that under certain conditions these spirits return to the land of the living and can be seen by and even communicate with people who are particularly gifted or psychic. Spiritualists often regards ghosts as earthbound spirits, an undying part of a person that has for some reason, often in cases of sudden death, become attached to a certain house or part of the earth where it can sometimes be seen and occasionally heard, and more occasionally felt, by certain people. Spiritualists believe that ghosts need to be contacted by specially trained psychic people, mediums, who can communicate with them and who then convince such ghosts that they are really spirits of dead people, that they are not of this world, and can send them away to their rightful place. Evidence suggests that this explanation is not one that covers all or even many spontaneous ghostly appearances.

Ghosts of the Living, Ghosts of the Past, Modern Ghosts, Periodic or Cyclic Ghosts, Poltergeists – that are not really ghosts at all – Animal Ghosts, Family Ghosts, Haunted Objects; there is conclusive and well-attested evidence for all these categories and others – all different kinds of ghosts; so, what are ghosts?

The honest answer is: we don't know. But we do know, from

available evidence from all sorts of people in all sorts of conditions and in all countries and at all times of the day and night, that ghosts are seen and heard and felt and smelt. In fact it has been estimated that everyone has a one-in-ten chance of seeing a ghost sometime during their lifetime. And since ghosts do not usually appear as wispy, transparent figures but as apparently solid, naturally dressed and normal people in practically every way, it may be that many people see ghosts without knowing that they are seeing them!

All over the world serious people are studying ghosts and ghostly phenomena, perhaps more today than at any time in history, and the likelihood is that one day we shall know what ghosts are, why they appear, why certain people see them and not others; and each responsible and methodical and thinking and honest ghost hunter can contribute to the fund of knowledge and information that is already available. One day we may even be able to manufacture a ghost. Indeed that may have already been done, but we are not yet able to produce a ghost at will, a repeatable experiment demanded by science before ghosts can be accepted scientifically.

Some years ago I organised an international enquiry into the possibility of anyone producing 'physical phenomena' – or ghostly appearances – under test conditions before a distinguished panel of experts in various fields; with a prize of £25,000 for the winner. There was no winner and very few offers that were worthy of serious consideration; but this was not altogether surprising. Apart from the fact that evidence that is satisfactory to one person is unsatisfactory to another, it is not yet possible to reproduce a ghost to order; although there was a very interesting experiment conducted in Canada that lends weight to the theory that it is possible to manufacture a ghost of sorts.

In 1972 a group of members of the Toronto New Horizons Research Foundation decided to attempt to construct a ghost, following considerable discussion on the nature of ghosts and speculation as to whether most ghosts were in fact conjured up from the minds of those who saw them. Accordingly an entirely imaginary character was decided upon: an aristocratic Englishman, living in the middle of the seventeenth century, married and having an affair with a beautiful gypsy girl, and so on. It was decided that the imaginary character, named Philip, made no effort to defend the girl when she was accused of witchcraft and eventually burned alive; that he had been reincarnated several times, and that once every hundred years or so his ghost was seen at his home, pacing the battlements in remorse and despair. It was theorised that if he could materialise and be reassured that the gypsy girl had forgiven him, he would be at rest.

The group, five female and three male, spent a lot of time inventing and elaborating the story and then started holding sittings in a circle around a table and meditating on the mythical Philip. In the summer of 1973 it was decided to try a different approach, and an atmosphere of jollity and relaxation was introduced. Soon table raps were heard when certain songs were sung and these raps became progressively louder and more obvious after the group addressed the table as 'Philip', and after the procedure of one rap for 'yes' and two raps for 'no' had been adopted.

Questions were asked regarding Philip, his likes and dislikes, his habits and customs, and the table responded; nearly always in accordance with the invented personality of Philip. Later, some four weeks after the raps had first been produced, the table began to move around the room in random fashion. It would, on occasions, shoot across the room at great speed; and when the experimenters, catching up with it and standing round it, continued their questions, raps would come from the table with force and apparent intelligence. Once a member of the Society not associated with the experiment came into the room and witnessed a loud rap, and once the vice-President of the Society also heard the rapping, which was also witnessed by many sceptical people not associated with the project; as was the movement of the table. Everyone was satisfied that the raps and movements were produced paranormally. In fact 'Philip' even demonstrated in bright light in front of television cameras. Other reported incidents included cool breezes, metal bending and an upward thrust of more than twenty pounds, measured on a strain gauge and recorded on videotape.

For a good number of years now I have been President of the oldest organisation in the world that is seriously and objectively interested in this subject. The Ghost Club, founded in 1862, has had a long and honourable history with past and present members including Sir William Barrett FRS, Donald Campbell CBE, Sir William Crookes, Charles Dickens, Sir Arthur Conan Doyle, Air Chief Marshall Lord Dowding, Kathleen M. Goldney MBE, Sir Julian Huxley, Sir George Joy, Arthur Koestler, Sir Shane Leslie, Beverley Nichols, Dr A.R.G. Owen, Harry Price, Sir Osbert Sitwell, Dennis Wheatley and W.B. Yeats. I have long ago lost count of the haunted houses I have visited, the cases of haunting that I have investigated, the 'most haunted rooms' in allegedly haunted houses that I have spent a night in (usually quite uneventfully); but I am convinced that the information I and other investigators – ghost hunters if you wish – slowly and carefully gather is very important, and that one day we shall discover the cause and *modus operandi* of ghosts, and in the not-too-distant future there will be a breakthrough.

I shall not disclose all our findings in case the knowledge may suggest ideas to less serious people who might mislead us in future investigations, but I am quite sure that some ghosts are the results of a natural activity; they are not supernatural, i.e. outside nature, but supernormal, within nature but as yet not fully understood. After all none of us has ever seen a wireless wave or an X-ray, yet we know they must exist from the results that are evident. We have overwhelming evidence that ghosts exist, but as yet we do not know how or why they 'exist' in certain places, at certain times; sometimes only in the presence of certain people and at other times in the presence of everyone there at the time.

The already available evidence suggests that ghosts *do* exist. There may be a lack of evidence to show exactly what they are, and we cannot claim to understand much about them, but that should not cause us to give up. Investigations into all aspects of this subject are difficult and often tedious, but extremely important, and the results could add significantly to human knowledge with fascinating possibilities. It is an exciting prospect that has lured me on through fifty years of ghost hunting; and I am always pleased to receive responsible reports of investigations from responsible people.

What makes a sincere and responsible ghost hunter? Well, I suppose, to put it simply, he or she should be a mixture of the best kind of detective and the best kind of investigative reporter with something of the scientist and something of the psychologist thrown in. He should seek to discover and record as objectively as possible what people have experienced or believe they have experienced and seek by experimentation to establish scientifically or demolish the reported phenomena. My hope is that this book will help and encourage more people to become the best kind of ghost hunters.

1 · The Different Kinds of Ghosts

In half a century devoted to the study of ghosts, the people who see them, where and when they are seen and the conditions under which they are seen, there is only one thing I am totally certain of, and that is that there are many different kinds of ghosts, although sometimes one type intermingles with another type and there are mixed hauntings where the haunting influence cannot be easily categorised.

ATMOSPHERIC PHOTOGRAPH GHOSTS

There is most certainly considerable evidence, from all parts of the world over many, many years, to suggest that certain events, often but not always tragic or violent events, occasionally imprint themselves in or on the atmosphere of the place where the event occurred. Possibly climatic conditions at the time play a part in this strange recording, possibly the presence of a certain type of person is necessary, or it may be that such events remain as light-particles, imprinted and vibrating for many years, possibly for ever, to be sensed or seen or otherwise experienced by some individuals who happen to be in the right place at the right time. I have noticed that such ghost imprints are very rarely reported in a high wind; such manifestations might be classed Atmospheric Photograph Ghosts.

It may be that on rare occasions a particularly distressing, poignant or traumatic occurrence releases an electrical impression which remains, and it has been noted that such ghosts are always seen in the same place, doing the same thing, they are completely oblivious to the presence of human beings, and when they are approached – thereby perhaps altering the angle necessary for observation – they disappear.

Such Atmospheric Photograph Ghosts or Mental Imprint Manifestations may be unconsciously fed with whatever is necessary for their appearance by people seeing them and/or by the drop in temperature that those who see such appearances almost invariably experience. Often such visual ghosts

14

are accompanied by appropriate sounds: footsteps, the swish of garments, the clank of armour, etc. Interestingly enough these types of ghosts eventually fade, sometimes appearing misty or transparent before finally disappearing altogether, but often the sound that accompanied the apparition lingers on for some years before it too grows fainter and finally ceases. Sometimes such ghostly appearances form a Large Scale Replay, such as a phantom army in action or marching soldiers. In most cases they tend to become dimmer and eventually disappear over the years, rather like a battery running down.

HISTORICAL OR TRADITIONAL GHOSTS

These are usually associated with old and historic houses where uninterrupted occupation of the premises for many years seems to help to perpetuate the ghostly figures that are recognised as the forms of real people who once lived there. Such ghostly forms walk or seem to glide through rooms and passages that would have been familiar to them in their lifetime. They appear to be solid, seemingly dressed in the clothes of their time, and they usually act more or less naturally, although when structural alterations have taken place they will appear to walk through walls and closed doors that were not there during their lifetime; and if floors and ceilings have been altered the ghosts appear where they would have appeared before such alterations took place, so that sometimes, when flooring has been raised, for example, the ghost appears only from the ankles or knees upwards. In common with practically all spontaneous ghosts they never speak and rarely show any sign of being aware of the presence of a human being, although, once they have been identified, it is often found that they have suffered in some way during their earthly life. They seem to have a kinship with the Atmosphere Photograph or Mental Image Ghosts, but are 'place-centred' and confined to ancient properties, and apparently continue to appear for many, many years, perhaps for ever. Often they come to be treated as part of the family and fixtures, for they never harm anyone.

CYCLIC OR RECURRING GHOSTS

These come into a separate category because they return (or are alleged to return) at regular intervals. By far the commonest cycle is twelve months and we will be looking in Chapter 13, entitled 'A Ghost Calendar', at the truly remarkable number of ghosts that are reported to return annually, almost as though they require twelve months to build up sufficient power to manifest once again.

One of the difficulties about ghost sightings and ghost hunting is the mystery and the power of the human mind. If we visit somewhere that we know is reputed to be haunted and a ghostly figure of say, a monk, has been seen there each 30 March, when we go on that date we are half-way towards seeing such a figure before we even get there! The human brain being what it is prepares us for the unexpected by telling us what has, we know, been seen before, and our imagination does the rest. It is only too easy to see what we (unconsciously) want to see and to hear what we (unconsciously) want to hear. In any investigation of cyclic phenomena it is essential that the investigator takes with him an independent observer who has no knowledge of the reported ghost or the date or time it is supposed to appear. Even then a sighting is not foolproof for it may well be that the investigator thinks about the ghostly appearance and telepathically, but unconsciously, transmits such thoughts to his companion. Perhaps the best plan is to visit the site with the companion or companions a couple of nights *before* the reputed appearance date and then arrange for the observer to re-visit the site with another observer who has no knowledge of the haunting. Even then of course telepathy between the observer and the original investigator is possible, but then it is never possible to eliminate telepathy completely from ghost hunting; for all we know some ghosts are nothing more than telepathic recordings that are conveyed from one mind to another. Recurring Ghosts or Pattern Hauntings offer considerable scope for investigation, and if persistent research seems to substantiate the cyclic element every effort should be made to enlist the co-operation of an established organisation, so that permanent, acceptable, authentic and scientific records can be made of the event.

MODERN GHOSTS

It is a common misconception that all ghosts are misty Grey Ladies or shadowy monks of long ago; there are many modern ghosts and ghosts of modern people and present-day occurrences. For years a ghost bus was seen in North Kensington and many accidents were reportedly caused by other road users swerving to avoid the racing bus, hours after regular buses had ceased to run, only to find the brightly lit bus had completely disappeared. After one fatal accident (some say there were several) the dangerous corner at the junction of St Mark's Road and Cambridge Gardens was structurally altered and thereafter the ghost bus was not seen again.

In December 1972 an Eastern Airline Tri-Star, Flight 401, crashed in a Florida swamp, killing 101 people. According to reports the ghosts of the pilot Bob Loft and his flight engineer Don Repo were seen on more than twenty occasions after they had crashed to their deaths. They were reportedly seen by crew members on other planes of the same airline, especially it seemed when those other planes incorporated parts of the crashed plane that had been salvaged. The ghosts were seen by male and female air crew who all said the figures were lifelike; some of the witnesses had known the dead men and recognised them, others recognised them later from photographs. When an account of the ghostly appearances appeared in the airline newsletter John Fuller made a thorough investigation of the case and produced a mass of testimony that seemed to establish the authenticity of this Modern Ghost. I have met and talked with John Fuller about the amazing story of the ghosts of Flight 401 and there is no doubt that it is a most interesting case. Ghosts are no respecters of time and place any more than they are respecters of people; anyone, it seems, may see a ghost at any time of the day or night and that ghost may be of someone long dead or someone very recently deceased, perhaps only hours – even perhaps not dead at all – and that leads us to ...

GHOSTS OF THE LIVING

Prince Rupert led his cavalry into the first major battle of the English Civil War at Edgehill in 1642. For months afterwards people claimed to see a ghostly re-enactment of the battle, and among those reported to take part was Prince Rupert himself – but he was still alive at the time. There are thousands of such instances: people passing a friend in the street and later discovering that at the time that person was undoubtedly elsewhere; people waking suddenly and seeing the unmistakable form of someone they know only to learn that that

17

person was at the time miles away. Under this heading we must also consider the experimentally induced apparition, the ghost not of a dead or dying person but of someone alive and well who has deliberately made his or her image visible to someone else. G.N.M. Tyrrell (President of the Society for Psychical Research 1945–6) relates sixteen successful attempts of this type in his admirable study *Apparitions* (1943 revised 1953). This apparently repeatable experiment has been almost ignored by successive researchers and although there has been recent study in the realm of 'out-of-the-body' experiments good evidence of self-induced visibility at a distance is rare.

CRISIS APPARITIONS OR DEATH BED VISIONS

These post-mortem appearances take place at or soon after the death or near-death of the person seen and do not seem to be related to any particular place or event. They are quite common but are ghosts of limited duration and rarely occur more than four days after the death or crisis in illness of the person seen. A typical example would be of a man in England who had a daughter living in Australia. At any time of the day or night the daughter would be aware and usually see the form of her father standing quietly looking at her, and subsequently it would be established either that he died or reached a crisis of an illness at the time his figure – or ghost – was seen, or shortly before or after. Such single appearances were common during both the World Wars when wives and mothers 'saw' their husbands and sons, only to learn later that they had been killed at the time they had appeared to their loved ones. It seems likely that such figures are 'thought forms'. In a moment of crisis or danger a person is likely to think with considerable feeling of a loved one and, in picturing their wife or mother or father or son or daughter, it may be that they telepathically transmit a likeness of themselves to that person. A Ghost Club member used to meet a friend frequently at the old Sesame Club in London until a period of several weeks when he did not come. One day, he saw his friend again, sitting in his usual chair; he was about to go over and have a word with him when he was distracted. When he looked again there was no sign of the person he had seen and the chair was empty. On making enquiries he learned that the man had died several days earlier.

FAMILY GHOSTS

These are ghosts which are attached to certain families; often their purpose seems to be to warn members of the family of approaching death. In general they seem to be more common in Scotland than elsewhere, while the *Banshee* (a wailing sound that heralds a family death) is exclusive to those descended from the ancient Irish.

Perhaps the interesting family ghosts associated with the Pomeroys and the Townshends are among the best-known English examples, manifesting at Berry Pomeroy Castle in Devon and Raynham Hall in Norfolk respectively. The former seems to have its roots in a murder, but in the case of the latter, the famous Brown Lady, there is no definite story to account for the ancestral ghost. It was reportedly seen by, among many others, King George IV and Captain Marryat. Some people think the ghost is that of Lady Dorothy Walpole, the second wife of Charles, 2nd Marquess Townshend, and that she met a violent end on a staircase where her ghost has been seen and photographed.

Scottish family ghosts include the Airlie Drummer, the Hamilton family White Lady, the Carnegie's Green Lady and the Burnetts of Crathes who also have or had a Green Lady attached to Crathes Castle, seen on one occasion by Queen Victoria; then there is the Lyon family at Glamis Castle, the Gordons of Fyvie Castle, and many more. Other, non-Scottish, family ghosts include the White Lady of the Hohenzollerns; the Black Lady of Darmstadt who haunts the ex-Grand Ducal House of Hesse; the Bernadottes of Sweden and their phantom old woman; and the wraith or double whose appearance foretold the death of one of the Romanoffs, the Imperial Family of Russia.

HAUNTED OBJECTS

Just as some houses seem capable of attracting and holding a ghost or ghostly happening, so too, but more rarely, do some objects seem capable of attracting and retaining a ghostly influence. Some objects, it has been noticed, are especially likely to become Haunted Objects: many skulls are said to possess uncanny powers, and one immediately thinks of the skulls at Chilton Cantello, Wardley Hall, Appley Bridge, Burton Agnes Hall, Warbleton Priory, Bettiscombe Manor and many others. The skull at Bettiscombe, which Michael Pinney showed me in the company of Lord Gibson, resided in a shoe box and was almost certainly the skull of a prehistoric girl who died some three or four thousand years ago. Michael Pinney told me: 'It is said to scream and cause agricultural disaster if taken out of the house, and also to cause the death, within a year, of the person who commits the deed. A photographer once carried it as far as the open doorway to take pictures of it, but my wife snatched it back indoors again without anything untoward occurring.' There are scores of ghost ships, one vouched for by King George V when he was a cadet; ghost cars and ghost furniture such as the famous Busby Stoop or tall chair preserved at the Busby Stoop Inn, north Yorkshire. This is supposed to have belonged to the disreputable Busby, who was known to be a thief and a receiver of stolen goods, and was eventually sentenced to death for murder. The story goes that as he was dragged from his home cursing, out of his favourite chair, he swore that anyone who sat in his 'stoop' would die violently and suddenly – as he himself was about to die. There have been many stories of sudden death soon after visitors have sat in Busby's stoop, including an RAF pilot, a motorist, a motorcyclist, a hitchhiker, and a foolhardy local man. Most could be categorised as being unlikely to live to a ripe old age anyway but with the odds so high against all of them dying within two days of sitting in Busby's stoop, the haunted chair was moved out of harm's way. Other odd inanimate objects that seem to be haunted or figure in unexplained happenings include the strange cylindrical object seen by a responsible witness and his wife at the Tower of London and the mysterious faces that appeared in the floor of a Spanish kitchen in 1971 and again in 1982.

FRAUDULENT HAUNTINGS

Sooner or later every ghost hunter encounters the fraudulent in his search for the genuine ghost or haunting. Most frequently it will be found that what has been taken to be a ghost has a perfectly rational and normal explanation. Such mundane things as loose water pipes, an air lock, and ill-fitting floorboards should always be examined, and also cracks in walls, badly-fitting doors and a dip in the roof which suggest that the house may be moving on its foundations, causing all sorts of noises and 'strange' happenings such as 'mysterious' openings and closings of doors. Nearby water is always suspect, as a high water level in a river caused by abnormal rainfall can invade old and leaking sewers, causing the ground beneath a house to become waterlogged and unstable, which can again cause noises and happenings that can easily be regarded as 'inexplicable'.

At Netherfield in Sussex 'strange noises' caused a house to be regarded as 'haunted'. These occurred for several years until it was discovered that the spring of an alarm clock unwound itself in jerks, making faint tapping sounds, but when the clock was placed on a chair in the bedroom (as it usually was) the vibration of the tapping passed down the chair legs, through the floor and joists, and then the plaster ceiling below amplified the vibrations so that they sounded quite loud in the room underneath.

Occasionally one comes across cases of conscious fraud. I am reminded of the gadgets enthusiast who had wired his house in such a way that he could produce music in any of the rooms from an armchair downstairs; and the old man who pretended the house was haunted – having decided that his family did not want him, he drove them out of the house! I have come across many cases of young people 'helping out' so-called poltergeist activity; of branches tapping a window when the wind is in a certain direction that is taken for ghostly activity; of imagination playing its part in causing clothing in a dim light to take on the shape of a person; and of reflected light playing tricks on people who are not fully awake. In every case that is investigated it should always be a firm rule to look most thoroughly for a natural explanation for the reported activity before considering the possibility of a superphysical one – and even then still keep looking for a rational explanation; if my experience is anything to go by you will frequently find one. Of course what this often means is that you are investigating the person rather than what they claim to have seen or experienced, and because they sincerely believe that something outside the natural course of things has taken place they are very unwilling to accept a perfectly logical explanation. I have long felt that it is no exaggeration to say that 98 per cent of reported 'ghostly' happenings have a natural explanation. It is the task and duty of the ghost hunter to discover and reveal such an explanation if it exists.

SURVIVAL AFTER DEATH

This could be the most logical answer to a number of ghostly appearances; indeed in some instances it seems to be the only explanation possible. Survival of some part of the intelligence of some people seems likely in view of the available evidence, especially for a limited period; and this survival, be it temporary or permanent, would of course explain some of the well-attested instances of evidence of life after death that is to be found by the true searcher after truth among the records of spiritualism and its adherents. As far as ghost hunting is concerned, the ghosts that suggest survival after death are best investigated with the co-operation of committed but open-minded spiritualists who are aware of the many pitfalls that await the unwary in seeking proof of life after death and do not unquestionably accept any evidence that may be forthcoming.

OTHER EXPLANATIONS

Other possible explanations for some ghosts and haunting phenomena include *Time-Slips* where, for a second or a moment or longer, a past scene is replayed in the present time; *Psychic Echoes* where the *sound* of some past event recurs without any visual aspect; and *Animal Ghosts* which, if we are of the opinion that ghosts of human beings are spirit forms or in any way reflect a life after death, must force us into taking a totally different look at some apparitions. There is good evidence for ghostly horses and dogs, stories of which are especially common in the United States, Europe and many parts of Africa as well as Britain, but there are also, it seems, ghost cats, cattle, sheep and wild creatures too – birds, squirrels, bears, deer – the list is endless. The Society for Psychical Research once had no hesitation in making exhaustive enquiries into a ghost pig that was repeatedly reported near Newbury in Berkshire.

Aerial Phenomena is a comparatively recent category of ghostly activity. There are scores of reportedly haunted airfields (where some extraordinary recordings have been obtained), and dozens of reported appearances of dead airmen, and obsolete aircraft (aural and visual), and other psychic activity that defies logical explanation, such as ghost voices heard by fliers; including record-breaking Sheila Scott who has herself told me of the ghost voices that saved her life.

This is not a complete list of the different kinds of ghosts that ghost hunters may encounter, but most reported ghosts will fall into one of these categories. There are certainly other possible explanations, not forgetting the possibility that they are all mind phenomena and do not exist outside the minds of those who see them – it *is* possible, but only just in the light of the available evidence on the subject. Nor should it be forgotten that these are merely guidelines, not hard-and-fast categories, and there are many instances of *Mixed Hauntings* and cases where there is overlapping and inter-weaving of one type and another. Nothing is yet definite and clear-cut in this field, least of all the types of ghosts that may or may not exist with or alongside or outside this world of ours; what is certain is that there is something out there and sometimes the veil between our world and the ghost world is barely sufficient to hide one from the other.

2 · Ghost Hunting Equipment and Its Uses

Before looking at the essential items in any self-respecting ghost hunter's bag, it might be profitable to remind ourselves of the commoner types of haunting that the ghost hunter today is likely to encounter, for it must always be remembered that there do appear to be many different kinds of ghosts; and we can then consider some methods of investigating the different varieties.

Types of ghosts and ghostly phenomena have been discussed in some detail in Chapter 1; suffice it to say here that, putting completely aside for a moment the ghost of the seance room, the commonest reported spontaneous ghosts today are poltergeists, remnants of traditional or historical ghosts, death-bed visions, atmospheric photograph ghosts, crisis apparitions and ghosts of the living. By far the majority of so-called ghost sightings, however, are not ghosts at all but the result of mal-observation, natural causes and conscious fraud, hallucinatory or telepathic in origin, or the result of a disordered brain.

In the investigation of any of these types of ghosts we must decide what if any apparatus and equipment the serious ghost hunter will take with him, but first we will consider the items that the ghost hunter should have already collected. These items are not in any particular order, but they are all important, and most can be purchased very reasonably.

The first necessity is a bag, case or box in which to store the ghost hunting kit, and this can either be a capacious bag or stout suitcase which is quite adequate and easily transportable (for many years I used a type of leather carpet bag); or, if a car or other transport is available, a stout box (with catches and a lock) is probably the best receptacle since it can be partitioned and labelled inside and so organised that there is somewhere for each piece of equipment. I will detail all useful components for the ghost hunter's bag or box, but of course this list can be modified to suit the cash that is available or increased to suit individual requirements.

Notebooks, sheets of plain paper and graph paper, pens and

pencils are all obviously necessary for taking notes from witnesses and recording particulars of the place and people concerned. Rough plans and sketches are often of great value for later assessment of the case, and here the loose paper and pencils come into use; coloured pens or crayons are handy for indicating various differences and white and coloured chalks are useful for marking walls and furniture and have the advantage of being easily removable. Artists' willow charcoal is a worthwhile addition since it is less obvious than white chalkmarkings.

Reels of black thread and black cotton will be needed, and also white material tape, transparent adhesive tape (good quality in various widths), opaque black and coloured adhesive tapes, surgical adhesive tape (normal, waterproof and elastic), rolls of bandages, a ball of black wool, white wool, green gardening twine, thin and thick nylon twine, thin and thick string and a few cards of fuse wire and hanks of flex. In addition lead seals and a sealing tool can be useful, as can a stick of sealing wax, matches, gummed labels in various sizes, gummed red and gold stars and a few tie-on luggage labels. These will enable the ghost hunter to seal most rooms, passages, doorways and windows in such a way that he can be sure they are not opened or used without his knowledge.

Several battery torches (and spare batteries and bulbs) of varying sizes will be needed; the very small fountain-pen, keyhole or handbag type are always useful, and so is a fair-sized and solid torch. Both the rubbercased variety and those with a magnetic attachment have their advantages, while the motorist's self-standing type with a flexible head and automatic 'on and off' red warning light is often useful, as is the floating torch and the torch with an adjustable spotlight. A hurricane lamp has its uses in some instances, and the inclusion of half-a-dozen palmitine self-fitting candles and a couple of boxes of matches should adequately cover the ghost hunter's lighting requirements.

The camera or cameras that the ghost hunter takes with him must be dictated by personal preference or financial considerations, but at least one, and as good a one as possible, should be included, and a tripod. A simple and inexpensive camera is all that is really necessary and the fewer the controls the more chance the ghost hunter, or his companion, has of obtaining a print of something in the event of a sudden movement or appearance, although of course a better result will be obtained with more sophisticated equipment, and instamatic polaroid cameras have many advantages. The fully automatic cameras that are now available have many advantages too. The use of a cine camera is distinctly beneficial in some circumstances, such as poltergeist cases. At all events spare black-and-white (fast) and colour films should be included and spare batteries and flash-bulbs where applicable. The camera enthusiast will also include infra-red films, filters, various automatic attachments and other refinements.

Steel and tape measures should be included and a ruler (the type used by paper makers and publishers for measuring paper bulk is particularly useful, as is a metal ruler); impact adhesive, an assortment of small screws, nails, tintacks, screw-eyes, a small hammer and screwdriver and bradawl, wire-clippers, a pair of small pliers, a plumbline, an assortment of adhesives, luminous paint and luminous card and paper, a pen-knife, several magnifying glasses (including a large quality specimen and a watchmaker's loupe), a pair of plimsolls or overshoes, a spring-balance (for measuring the weight of any article moved by apparently paranormal means) and a strain gauge (for measuring the force necessary to close or open a door or drawer). All these articles will be found useful by the serious investigator, but he can prune the list to suit his pocket and add things that he feels he would like to have with him. The ghost hunter and each of his companions must carry a watch, preferably with luminous or illuminated dials, and they should of course synchronise watches at the commencement of any ghost hunt; in addition a stopwatch can be very useful on occasions. Various transparent envelopes and containers for the preservation of questionable and dubious matter are useful accessories.

Simple gadgets can often be arranged at the scene of the haunting, and for this purpose such items as dry batteries, switches, small electric bells, bulbs and bulb-holders, together with plenty of appropriate wire, including a coil of thin and fragile cotton-covered wire, will be required. In addition a coil of heavy-duty electric cable and an assortment of electric plugs and adaptors should be added to the collection – and if possible a voltmeter for checking electrical power faults. A portable camping stove, kettle, unbreakable mugs, thermos flask, etc, can be welcome additions to the fast-growing ghost hunter's kit.

Thermometers are always necessary, both the simple instruments, suitable for indoor and outdoor use, which need to be checked at regular intervals (the eighteen-inch or greenhouse models are especially useful for registering sudden fluctuations in temperature), and maximum-and-minimum thermometers. Such refinements as the self-registering thermograph are a great help, as are portable sound recorders, apparatus for measuring atmospheric pressure, the force of the wind and the humidity, and such instruments as metal-detectors, walkie-talkie sets, sound-scanners, magnetometers, and electric field measuring devices; but although such additions may add value to the scientific record of a haunting they also add considerable weight to the ghost hunter's kit. Even more expensive equipment for ghost hunting would include sophisticated alarm and detection equipment, closed circuit television, video cameras, capacity change recorders, infra-red telescopes and voltmeters. One ghost hunter I knew used to take with him over five tons of equipment yet, perhaps surprisingly, his reports were of no more interest to the scientist or anyone else than those prepared meticulously by an amateur with the simplest ghost hunting apparatus.

Every ghost hunter worthy of the name will, however, invent simple gadgets for himself: the bowl of mercury that detects tremors; the spirit level mounted on wood or board that can be used to establish or disprove the apparent slight movement of, say, a stair tread; the sealed tin full of fine sand with a tiny hole in the base that leaves an almost invisible trail of silver sand if it is moved; the balanced rod connected to a bell or buzzer or bulb that reveals the movement of an object placed on one end of the rod; the flour-covered sheet of newspaper that reveals footsteps or other disturbances, or spread sugar that quickly reveals the presence of someone and possibly some 'thing' by the unmistakable crunch, both substances often exposing (since they both cling) a ghost's earthly 'agent'! The list is endless and the setting-up of such simple yet ingenious ghost-catching gadgets helps to pass the long and quiet hours that form the main 'activity' of the ghost hunter. I will be most interested to hear from any reader who has succeeded in producing simple but practical and effective ghost hunting gadgets. A small paintbrush will enable you to arrange the flour or sugar or sand just where you want it and will also be useful to heighten any finger or palm prints for identification. No ghost hunting kit is complete without a large-scale map of the area to be visited, a compass, preferably a Lensatic compass, and a Milograph map measure. The Ordnance Survey, Southampton, will supply a copy of their large-scale catalogue and details of 1:1250 and 1:2500 scale maps they stock (not countrywide), and the 1:10 000 scale maps which do cover the whole of Great Britain. Personally, during the course of investigating poltergeist cases and sometimes cases of contemporary haunting, I have found it useful to have with me a pack or two of Zener cards (see p. 87) to test the possible ESP of the nexus of the poltergeist and other occupants of the house. I have also found routine and specially-written Intelligence and Word-Association Tests very interesting and often revealing. One or two small mirrors, both static and adjustable, placed in strategic positions in an occupied haunted house, have sometimes told me a great deal. I use a car wing-mirror that swivels in all directions.

It is always wise for the ghost hunter to have among his apparatus a few evocative articles: a small bell, perhaps, a paper-knife or dagger, a bible, a crucifix, a small toy, a photograph; for often the presence of such miscellanea will seem to promote apparent phenomena and in any case – as with Zener cards and the Word-Association Tests – they provide interest for everyone present, help to keep sleep at bay and also help to retain the all-important sense of relaxation and lack of the tension that can prohibit phenomena.

It will soon be acknowledged that ghost hunts in genuine haunted houses often follow a very similar pattern. After the initial enthusiasm and feeling of something approaching excitement, there follows a feeling of tension and watchfulness, especially if anything has happened that is not completely explained (the creaking of a floorboard, the hoot of an owl, the squeak of a mouse, the wind in an air-brick perhaps); this is often followed by a period of something approaching fear and a creeping coldness, exhaustion and finally the overwhelming need for sleep. It is necessary for the amateur ghost hunter to know what to expect on an all-night visit to a haunted house and to make plans accordingly.

28

Poltergeist activity is at one and the same time the most exciting and the most frustrating type of spontaneous phenomenon that the amateur ghost hunter is likely to encounter. He, or she, will probably be regaled with many accounts of startling happenings; particularly noises, movement of objects, inexplicable fires and irritating and often pointless little disturbances such as the switching on and off of electric lights, the turning on and off of taps, the opening and closing of doors.

In conducting an investigation into poltergeist activity, as indeed in any haunted house inquiry, I have always found it to be a good idea to ask the principal person concerned to relate the story at length, and then to hear the story independently from each of the other people involved. By taking copious notes (an able assistant is invaluable at this stage) it is possible to obtain almost immediately a rounded picture of the case from several viewpoints, and by careful and discreet inquiry it is fairly easy to decide whether or not genuine paranormal activity has occurred. At this stage I do not advocate the use of a tape recorder, and even the note-taking should be done as unobtrusively as possible; initially many people do not like to have their conversations recorded.

Poltergeist phenomena are almost invariably associated with an adolescent child, more often a girl than a boy, and it is obvious that any investigation of a poltergeist case will centre on this individual. On all subsequent visits, and on the initial one if the nexus of the poltergeist is apparent, one member of the investigating team should be allocated to keep the young person under close but not obvious surveillance at all times. The purpose is not to 'catch out' the girl or boy who may be 'helping out' the phenomena (although this is not unknown) but rather to detect at once any apparent phenomena that occur in the child's presence and so seek to establish any pattern to the poltergeist activity. The luminous paint, card and paper can be used to mark people; both those suspected of 'helping' with the disturbances and those investigating the phenomena (using different colours). Luminous card or paper can also be attached to people's clothing, and the paint can be used to mark small items so that they can be seen and possibly photographed in flight. Sometimes one particular room is found to be more frequently affected than other parts of a house; some poltergeists only 'perform' when the young person who is the centre of the disturbances is at rest, either sitting quietly or lying down; other poltergeists appear to be affected by the presence of certain objects, notably watches and clocks; still others most often manifest at certain times of the day, often early morning and late afternoon; and so on. The earlier that any such characteristics are noticed and established in any poltergeist case the sooner plans for investigation can be formulated that take these factors into account. Of course some poltergeist cases possess no such characteristics that are readily observable.

The investigation of poltergeist cases, which are so often haphazard and spasmodic, can involve most of the apparatus that the ghost hunter will expect to use in any haunted house: notebooks; graph paper (for making plans); tape recorder; thermometers – for recording the temperature in the locality of apparent phenomena and in the vicinity of the nexus of the poltergeist (perhaps the nexus herself or himself) in comparison with the temperature elsewhere, in the vicinity of other occupants of the house and visitors, and in the affected room when phenomena were not occurring; chalk and willow charcoal for marking and surrounding movable objects; camera; measuring apparatus; a magnifying glass; transparent envelopes and other containers; Zener cards; hand-mirrors and so forth. A second associate, during initial interviews, can often compile word-association tests which contain key words applicable to that particular case amid a number of innocuous and irrelevant words; such a 'test' often produces interesting results and provides ideas for further investigation. The inclusion of one or two gadgets creates interest and relaxation and sometimes promotes 'phenomena'.

The investigation of a traditional or historical haunting can be a fascinating business. Initially the investigator will have learned what he can about the alleged haunting: the locale, duration, season, time, position of witnesses and so on. He will then have read what he can of the history of the house and the historical character, if such the ghost is reported to be. He might then pay a quiet visit to the house and spend some time in the area reputed to be haunted, noting any impression the area may have on other visitors; he will make a point of talking to the guides and casually bring up the subject of ghosts. The guides of historic houses are usually mines of information on the subject of the house they serve and the characters who lived there, and often too they have heard reports of ghost sightings that have never been recorded or published. Of course there are historic house guides, just as there are people in other walks of life, who find it difficult to accept the possibility of ghosts and ridicule the subject.

Having obtained as much information as possible about the house, the people who lived there, and reported sightings, the investigator will retire to digest all this material and plan his investigation. A thoughtful approach to the director or owner of the property is then necessary to obtain the required permission to carry out an investigation. Often such requests are rejected out of hand, but where they are entertained the authority concerned will sometimes require an insurance cover, the installation of any equipment to be under their supervision, and they may insist on the presence of one or more of their staff during the whole of the investigation, be it day or night. When conducting all-night ghost hunts there is always the likelihood of a member of the investigating party being seen prowling about or acting rather strangely in a lit or darkened room, or indeed being abroad at an unusual hour, carrying suspicious-looking bags or apparatus, so it may be advisable to inform the local police of your plans.

Such an investigation will call for the usual note-taking materials, cameras, tape-recorders, thermometers, measuring apparatus, chalks, reels of thread, cotton, tape, wool and wire, and sealing materials for 'controlling' passages, doorways, staircases, cupboards and so forth (to limit the area under investigation); torches for each member of the party and a free-standing one for the hub of operations; soft shoes and extra clothing if it is winter time or outdoor vigilance is anticipated; and a magnifying glass and such gadgets as seem applicable and appropriate. It is wise to formulate a fairly rigid programme of events and stick to it as far as possible so that strategic places are under constant surveillance by more than one person from different viewpoints; that regular checks are made for temperature readings and so forth.

Death-bed visions, crisis apparitions and ghosts of the living do not usually offer much scope for practical investigation but all instances of such reported happenings should be carefully and fully recorded as soon as possible after the event, pre-

ferably first-hand and with additional witnesses wherever possible. Good evidence of these phenomena is always welcomed
by such organisations as The Ghost Club, the Society for
Psychical Research and The College of Psychic Studies. The
records of any of these organisations may well possess a similar
or associated case that is relevant, and the addition of another
case may shed some light on the *modus operandi* of these
strange but indisputable happenings.

Atmospheric photograph ghosts can usually be recognised
by the fact that as a rule they are always seen in one particular
place doing one particular thing, and when witnesses, seeing
these illusions which they take to be real people, approach
them to enquire what they want or to offer help, thereby
altering the angle necessary to observe them, the illusionary
forms disappear. These are the nun-like figures that always
glide along a certain path; the 'monks' who are glimpsed time
and time again in one part of a cathedral or in the doorway of
an ancient ruined monastery; the headless horseman always
seen near a particular field or farmyard gate; the indistinct but
human form that scores of motorists report seeing at a certain
spot – a sight that causes them to brake violently, but then they
see nothing to account for what startled them; the child seen at
the bottom of a garden where once such a child amused itself
for hours; the dog that its owner says he often sees walking
up the garden path; perhaps too the sounds of sighing, or
weeping, or laughing, the smell of violets or tobacco smoke,
the rustle of silk, the footstep on the stair, the squeal of a car
braking: they may be some kind of atmospheric echo, a suggestion that occasionally actions, sounds, odours and experiences may in some unknown way become impressed upon the
atmosphere, to reappear under certain conditions and perhaps
only in the presence of certain people. What is interesting of
course is the fact that there are instances of visitors to a
particular place, who have no knowledge of a ghost being seen
there, witnessing a particular ghost that has been seen by other
people at that particular place.

The ghost hunter who comes across an atmospheric photograph ghost should, after obtaining the fullest details of the
sighting, arrange to be present when, as far as possible, the
circumstances are duplicated. This will involve careful attention to time, date, atmospheric conditions, the presence of wit-

nesses in their exact positions and clothed exactly as previously and many other particulars. Then the ghost hunter should seek to recreate any particular emotional atmosphere that prevailed at the time of the original sighting and position himself close to the witness with camera ready and see what happens. He should take a few photographs even if neither he nor the witness can see anything, for there have been instances of 'something' appearing on a photograph when nothing has been visible to the human eye. The ghost hunter should also have additional witnesses (as always) and they should mostly be scattered at various viewpoints, but at least one should be immediately on the other side of the witness; sound-recording apparatus should be running, if available, and in the event of a human or animal form having been observed moving in one particular direction, all sorts of other paraphernalia can be employed in an effort to obtain some kind of record of the appearance should it return.

More than one visitor to a haunted house has come away with the conviction that it is not the 'ghost' that he feared, but the 'ghost's' earthly agent! And it has to be said that the investigator has to be continually on his toes to ensure that he is not misled. It may be that in a sense of fun someone does something, and if it is accepted as a genuine phenomenon the perpetrator is trapped: either he admits he did it and looks silly, or he keeps quiet, and he usually adopts the latter course. Then he again has two choices: he either takes no further part in the matter or he repeats the trick; either way he is not helping the investigator. Sometimes the 'happenings' may be consciously performed by someone in the house for his or her own good reasons, and it is up to the investigator to find this person and quietly have a word with him or (which is the course I usually adopt in these circumstances) ensure that he is eliminated from the possibility of doing anything further. This can be done, for example, by ensuring that he is not present at the scene at all (although he is under surveillance) or having him under constant surveillance in a separate room. Then when nothing further happens it is possible to suggest, in the kindest possible way, that the absent person may have been responsible, either consciously or unconsciously. It all points to the great care and experience that is needed in choosing fellow investigators on whom one is going to rely.

The psychic investigator should always bear in mind the possibility, nay the probability, of *any* reported happening having a completely natural explanation, and he must thoroughly explore every possible rational explanation before he begins to explore the possibility of a paranormal explanation. In short he should adopt the attitude and the methods of an open-minded private investigator, but one whose knowledge and experience of human beings and haunted houses lead him to question everything and everyone until no other explanation will fit the facts. Only then will he bring to bear on the matter his expert knowledge and his equipment in an effort to establish scientifically the reality of the psychic happenings reported.

To simplify the question of equipment: the barest of essentials that should comprise a ghost hunter's bag would be a notebook and pencils, chalk, measuring tape, sealing apparatus for doors and windows (this need be no more elaborate than coloured tape, wire, fine string, drawing pins, cotton and 'plutowax' or something similar), torch, flour, sugar, thermometer, camera and a small mirror.

Finally, here are a couple of examples that emphasise the effectiveness of both simple and sophisticated equipment. I once investigated a case of apparent poltergeist activity where most of the alleged phenomena took place in the vicinity of a young girl. Having heard the whole story I discovered, after careful examination of the property, which included measuring various distances and carefully exploring the time involved, that it *would have been possible* for the girl to have been consciously responsible for everything that had happened. I really had no option but to make an experiment that would eliminate her from my investigations.

As with many poltergeist infestations there were several items that seemed to attract the attention of the 'geist', including a potted plant that stood in the girl's bedroom on a saucer. Time after time this plant, in its plant pot, but minus the saucer, 'made its way' to various parts of the house, including the girl's father's study which she was forbidden to enter, and indeed the door of the room was kept locked.

Without anyone in the house knowing what I was doing I removed the plant from its flowerpot and inserted at the base a small tin filled with silver sand with a hole in the bottom of the tin that corresponded with the hole in the bottom of the flower pot. Replacing the plant in the pot and the whole plant and pot on its saucer I made sure, as far as I could, that no one would notice that it had been touched. That night after the girl had finally retired to bed for the night I secured a small piece of thin black cotton across her bedroom door so that the door could not be opened without the cotton breaking; I also placed a little petroleum jelly mixed with a purple dye on the underside of the doorhandle on the outside of the door, and finally I sprinkled a little flour, mixed with soot, immediately outside the door.

A couple of hours later, during a routine check of the downstairs rooms, accompanied by the girl's father and a fellow investigator, we discovered the potted plant standing on a shelf in the locked study. I then explained that my researches so far had suggested that the girl may be responsible for some of the activity, and I revealed the measures I had taken to test my theory. It was pointed out to me that the potted plant had 'appeared' inside a locked room and the girl's father showed me the only key which he kept in his pocket.

We carefully lifted up the potted plant and a tiny trickle of silver sand ran from it. We looked around and found trickles of the sand across the room towards the open window. We went outside and our torches picked up the trail and we followed it round the house, into the back door, through the kitchen, into the hall, up the stairs and to where it disappeared into the young girl's room. The cotton seal was broken. The mother and father went into their daughter's room and found her awake. We all trooped in and I asked to see her hands. On both there were traces of the purple dye. I asked to see her feet and on both there were traces of flour and soot.

At the other extreme there is the experience of Professor John Taylor in the haunted church at Borley in Essex. In 1976 I was invited to take part in a BBC hour-long feature on Ghosts. I had several conversations with script-writer John Pickford and suggested that the Borley haunting ought to be included. I introduced the producer to several possible contributors and, in the event, John Pickford went to Borley with John Taylor, Professor of Mathematics at London University, who was interested in scientifically recording paranormal activity. Accompanied by a technical assistant, they endeavoured to conduct a number of experiments with some sophisticated equipment, both inside and outside the allegedly haunted church, to see whether they could obtain evidence of anything comparable to any of the strange sounds that had been recorded there over the years. Their equipment included a magnetometer for measuring ordinary magnetic fields and electric field measuring devices that would indicate television type waves and those of long wave radio.

During the course of examination of the interior of the church, at nine o'clock in the evening, John Taylor felt 'some slightly strange sensation' in one particular part of the church. After spending half an hour quietly in the somewhat melancholy churchyard, they again went into the church. There they positioned themselves a few yards in front of the altar, ready to measure any changes in electrical magnetic fields and to see whether these changes, if they occurred, were related to any sounds they might hear or sights they might see. After about thirty minutes they left the church and discussed their conclusions so far in the quiet and still churchyard.

John Taylor was satisfied that his equipment was performing perfectly, but nothing unusual had been heard or seen and therefore there was nothing to work on. They decided to have another session inside the church. John Pickford, just before they left the church on this occasion, began to feel very cold and he experienced a feeling of unease that seemed to be coming from the tower end of the church, the area farthest away from the equipment they had set up in the church.

After a further two hours in the church John Taylor was asked to report on his feelings and opinions so far. He said he thought there seemed to be some slight movements in the area of the font (at the tower end of the church) which he thought may have been due to movement of the church foundations but when the three experimenters tried to duplicate these movements by stamping on the floor and banging on the font, they found that only reasonably strong attacks would actually cause the same level of movement. Otherwise, apart from one or two blips in the electric field, they only heard a number of sounds that were rather odd. However, they did establish that there was at least one bat inside the church, although it was impossible to tell whether it was bats that were responsible for the noises, or moths, also seen in the church, for they could make a noise that would register when they banged against windows or other parts of the church structure.

So I think it might fairly be argued that simple equipment is just as effective in the investigation of ghostly phenomena as the most sophisticated apparatus, for there are drawbacks to the latter. The value of any report is really only as good as the investigator concerned and it is not really dependent upon the equipment used. But in a computer age it is appropriate that my friends Dr Alan Gauld and Tony Cornell have just devised a 'spectre detector' that is in fact a computer-controlled ghost hunting kit in which interference with any one of various sensors (temperature, infra-red, ultra-sonic, etc) triggers cameras, video-cameras and tape-recorders, and is followed by a detailed print-out of the readings on all instruments.

3 · The Investigation of Hauntings

Ghost hunting has become something of a popular pastime in recent years and I receive a great many letters from people who want to know how they should set about investigating a haunting, usually with a minimum of equipment but boundless enthusiasm. Since I have been seriously interested in spontaneous psychic phenomena for most of my life and have been investigating hauntings for over forty years, studying the subject for over fifty years, and organising the investigation of all types of hauntings for The Ghost Club for over twenty-five years, I hope this chapter will be of help to the field worker and of interest to the armchair ghost hunter.

Methods and modes of investigation must of necessity vary according to the circumstances of the case, and each haunting will have, in my experience, its own peculiarities and significant aspects which the ghost hunter must discover, and he will then arrange his investigation accordingly. What I propose to do here therefore is to set down the basic and essential lines to follow if the investigation is to have any value as a scientific exercise; in addition I will refer to ideas for other and additional investigations which can be followed if the case lends itself to such undertakings.

The principal purpose of any investigation into a haunting is to establish the objectivity of reported paranormal activity. To do so it is necessary to eliminate all other possible explanations for what has been experienced, so the serious ghost hunter will endeavour to find out all he possibly can about: the house itself and its occupants; the ground it stands on and the surrounding area; any relevant history of either; and in fact get as full, complete and rounded a picture as possible of the environment in which the reported happenings are taking place. Only then will he attempt a scientific investigation of the house and the reported phenomena.

It is necessary to bear in mind that different people will investigate any given haunting in different ways, and however much we try to be impartial and non-partisan our natural outlook, attitude, beliefs, experience and approach to the subject will affect not only our methods of investigation but also colour our reports and affect the value of our judgement in reporting any allegedly experienced phenomena.

To illustrate this fact it is only necessary to look at two extremes, investigation by a psychical research body and by a spiritualist society. The former, equipped with all manner of elaborate and often specially-designed apparatus, will seek to establish the reality and objectivity of the haunting on a 'scientific' basis, using: sound-recording instruments; still and cine cameras loaded with infra-red and normal film; an infrared telescope (for seeing in the dark); electrical gadgets for automatically photographing and recording the presence of any 'ghost' by trip-wires or by the breaking of an electrical circuit; thermographs and other apparatus for measuring and automatically recording atmospheric conditions; frequency change detectors, vibration registers, voltmeters and other equipment for checking electrical power and locating faults. John Cutten, a former Hon. Secretary of the Society for Psychical Research, has demonstrated for me a most ingenious piece of apparatus that he invented and built, which when set up in suitable conditions told the investigator a great deal in the event of anything happening, while leaving the investigator himself free to concentrate on other matters or even continue his rest! John Cutten's ghost-detecting unit (which I describe in detail in my book *The Ghost Hunters*) comprised a camera linked to a tape-recorder connected to a series of photoelectric cells, joined to a delicate sound, vibration and temperature detector consisting of an electric light bulb wired to a circuit and a buzzer. In the event of any noise or a significant drop in temperature sufficient to operate the apparatus, which could be left unattended in a sealed and unlit room, the unit would be set off and not only record the noise and alteration of temperature but also indicate with flashing light and buzzer that something was happening, and take a photograph at the same time.

Such sophisticated equipment is not necessarily beyond the ingenuity of any practical person, although as a general rule it is a good idea to keep investigating apparatus to a minimum. Just as convincing and worthwhile results can be obtained with very simple equipment as with the most complicated – and there is less likelihood of technical faults or interference.

The spiritualist, on the other hand and perhaps at the other extreme, when carrying out the investigation of a haunted house, will take with him one or two mediums (persons known to be endowed with psychic awareness); they will hold seances, pray for the 'earthbound spirit', hold a 'rescue circle' and generally endeavour to reach and placate the haunting entity on a spiritual basis.

The unbiased ghost hunter will probably wish to carry out his investigations somewhere midway between these methods of dealing with hauntings. He should endeavour therefore to have available essential practical items and at the same time keep an open mind as to the causation of the disturbances; bearing equally in mind the possibility of the phenomena being manifestations of an after-life and open to a practical and scientific explanation.

In all haunted house investigations it is advisable to be accompanied by several reliable and sensible friends, and if they are adept in any particular fields – sound-recording, photography, note-taking, interviewing – or sensitive in a psychic sense, so much the better. It is important to eliminate anyone of a nervous disposition, for hours in any empty house, especially at night, can play all kinds of tricks with the imagination, and nervousness is catching. An early exercise, in fact as soon as possible after arrival, is to make a thorough examination of the whole house, and this should be done as a combined effort with everyone present.

First of course a careful list of all occupants of the house will be compiled, with approximate ages and such other details as may be forthcoming (occupation, hobbies, condition of health, principal witness, sceptic, believer, etc); also note any pets and their usual place or places of habitation (e.g. a cat may live in the kitchen but sleep on its mistress's bed at night; or there may be a cat-door giving access not only to the pet of the house but also to its friends). During the course of this tour of the property care should be taken to locate and note exactly the position of the mains switches, fuse boxes, power plugs and light switches. This is also the time, in the event of old and rambling houses, to ask about possible secret rooms, hidden cupboards, priests' hiding places, sliding panels and any other little-known aspect of the property.

A large-scale Ordnance Survey Map or one of John Bartholomew's excellent 1:100000 National series will tell you a good deal before you even visit the area; a 1:25000 Ordnance Survey Map will be even more useful, and from such a map you will be able to glean a great deal of information. Not only will such obviously helpful information as the proximity of rivers and streams, footpaths, railway lines, roads, tracks, rights of way, and lakes, be evident, but also the shape of buildings, their exact position in relation to farms and other buildings and the height of ground in the area, and in addition such helpful knowledge as the position of wells, ancient sites and monuments, woods, slopes, pipe lines, refuse tips and a host of natural features. The exact position of the house you are interested in will of course be shown, which will be important in taking into account the prevailing winds, the rising and setting of the sun and so on.

Maps that expressly indicate geological information should also be studied to acquaint the investigator with the natural strata of the subsoil in the immediate and surrounding area. There is no doubt that occasionally, and perhaps more frequently than is usually realised, movement of objects and 'groans' in a house can be the result of natural but unrealised geological factors such as earth tremors and pressure of underground water.

Guy Lambert, BA, CB, President of the Society for Psychical Research 1955–8, studied this geophysical theory for poltergeist phenomena and other disturbances in haunted houses and he came to the conclusion that such incidents were frequently reported within three miles of tidal water and not only in reportedly haunted properties in England, Scotland and Wales but also in France and other European countries and in the Americas.

Lambert maintained that noises of various kinds, from raps, taps and footsteps to heavy crashing noises and sounds that could be taken for furniture being moved, might well be accounted for by such natural events; as might the 'movement' of objects which could be shaken off shelves inside the house or cause loose stones or slates or tiles to fall off walls and roofs outside. He also believed that such movement could account for doors opening and closing by themselves.

At a meeting of The Ghost Club, Lambert forcefully

explained his well-researched theories adding that such happenings might well frighten the occupants to the extent of their having hallucinations of sight, hearing, smell and temperature and of misinterpreting natural phenomena for supernormal activity; clouds of drifting mist, for example, being 'seen' as moving white figures. Lambert also drew attention to luminous appearances – which seem very strange and frightening in certain circumstances – but could be the result of phosphorescent gases given off by decaying matter, possibly from cracked or broken drains.

Pressure of underground water rushing along ancient sewers or pipes after heavy rain or during exceptionally high tides could well account for earth tremors, especially if there was some geological fault in a rock formation; and Lambert made the observation that many 'hauntings' seemed to be active at certain times of the year which coincided with such natural activity as spring tides. Careful study of large-scale maps coupled with information about the geology of the area may help the investigator to view the information he subsequently obtains in a different light.

In the case of ancient houses and properties, careful enquiries in the locality and at the local council offices, and especially the reference department of the local library, will often elicit something of the history of the place, its inhabitants and its reputation, and not infrequently it is possible to discover someone familiar with the house, such as a retired servant or elderly relative of the previous occupants or owners, who is only too eager to talk about old days and odd happenings.

The initial tour of the haunted house should include the fullest examination of every part of the house, and occasional extra visits to various parts of the house (presuming that none of it has been sealed and controlled) is an excellent idea. There must be no locked rooms that are unexamined, or locked cupboards; loose floorboards are always suspect, and I once discovered a loudspeaker extension between joists that relayed 'paranormal' sounds from next door; I have also seen a cupboard that afforded entry from the house next door. While most of the occupants of reputedly haunted houses are genuine and respectable people, there are also those who, for purposes of their own or for 'fun', produce 'phenomena' fraudulently. It is therefore of paramount importance always, in every single instance, to explore every possible (and seemingly impossible) natural cause, before even considering a supernormal explanation.

Always remember that such natural things as rats and mice behind floor skirting, under floorboards, or in the loft, can produce very odd noises; as can a bird in the loft or in a chimney. Faulty electrical wiring and plumbing can result in all kinds of odd happenings and noises; reflections or shadows of street lamps, passing cars, the moon, can all too often explain 'moving shadows'; and it is always wise to walk all round the house in daylight and again at night time to be thoroughly familiar with the immediate environment and near surroundings. A railway line in the vicinity can produce vibration (and so can an underground line), and it can also produce odd sounds, lights and the familiar 'moving shadow'. Even passing traffic, the wind in a tree, an ill-fitting door or window and the measured tread of a patrolling policeman have proved to be the prosaic explanations for 'inexplicable phenomena' before now.

While ghost hunting can be exciting and is always interesting, it has to be admitted that poltergeists and other ghosts do not seem to like observers who know how to observe, and there seems to be some truth in the old adage that when the ghost hunter enters through the door the ghost flies out of the window!

The great difficulty for most ghost hunters is to find haunted houses – genuine haunted houses, that is. It is a problem for every investigator, but once his serious interest in the subject is known to friends and relatives, often someone knows someone who knows of a case ... and after a lot of enquiries and false leads, occasionally one does find something interesting. In addition, of course, one case soon leads to another. In this way one is likely to stumble across a case that has not been publicised and where the people concerned are prepared to co-operate to a reasonable extent. One ghost hunter advocates the close study of newspapers and magazines, and even subscribing to a press-cutting agency, but newspaper and magazine reports of ghosts and hauntings are not to be relied upon and almost invariably distort facts out of all proportion to what actually happened. Furthermore this distortion and inaccuracy frequently annoys the people concerned to such an extent that they either pile falsehood upon falsehood to see just how much will be believed or, more often, they do not want any further investigations from anyone. There is also the very real danger that, in beginning an investigation based on false or exaggerated reports, the substance of the inaccurate statements is likely to be retained in the memory of the ghost hunter and, quite unconsciously, colour his findings and influence any report he may prepare. Chapter 13 is devoted to cyclic hauntings and could provide endless material for the dedicated ghost hunter.

Finally, on the subject of spontaneous ghost hunting, as opposed to seeking ghosts in the darkness of the seance room, it might be well to advise the ghost hunter and his companions as to what their reaction should be if they are fortunate enough to see a ghost – and are aware that it is a ghost at the time, which is comparatively rare.

The important thing to remember is to keep calm and keep still. There is nothing to fear. Try to be as observant as possible, but *don't*, as one 'investigator' did, throw a stone at a figure he saw to see whether it was real! Note as many details concerning the apparition as possible: the exact spot it seemed to appear from; exactly where it stands or moves; its overall appearance; its degree of transparency (if any); its facial expression; its mode of gait and whether its feet appear to touch the ground; its method of disappearance; details of dress and height (compare with nearby physical objects); and whether the figure appears to walk through any objects. Do not approach the figure; try not to move at all, but to observe everything about the figure; if it moves and turns a corner or otherwise disappears from view, follow as quietly as possible (one of the reasons for soft-soled shoes) until it disappears completely – or turns out to be a human being! It is a good idea to press one eyeball slightly; if the object seen remains as before it has no objective reality; if you see double, there is something there – outside your head.

As soon as possible afterwards note down everything you can recall about the experience. Take your time, do the job thoroughly and talk to no one about the matter until you have completed the report to your entire satisfaction. See that anyone else who has seen the figure does the same, but do not compare notes or discuss what you have seen or heard until all such reports are completed, dated, timed, signed, and witnessed. Then ask yourself and any other witnesses the following questions.

1) Could the figure (assuming that it disappeared in some mysterious way) still have been a real person; did the build, the features, the bearing, resemble anyone you know; could it possibly have been a shadow or reflection or a trick of the light that misrepresented a natural object; a tree stump, a clump of bushes, a dress hanging on a line or coat-hanger, a curious formation of smoke or mist, a dog or a cow or some other animal – and are you certain beyond any doubt whatever that it was not someone playing a joke?

2) If apparently inexplicable sounds accompanied the sighting (or indeed if sounds only were heard and nothing was seen) is there any possibility of the noises having a natural explanation: a creaking branch, the wind whistling through a hole, down a chimney, or round a corner; a bird or some other creature caught in a chimney or in a trap or by another creature and being responsible; could it have been a creature moving among dead leaves or cooing or nesting somewhere, or an owl or cat hunting; could the footsteps (if footsteps were heard) have been real footsteps made by someone out of sight; could they have been made by cat or dog – sounds carry at night; are you sure the sounds came from where you thought they came from and that the sounds were not a hoax?

3) If the place where you saw or heard something you cannot explain was known to you to be haunted, you must, to a certain extent, have been expecting to see a ghost; how can you be quite sure that what you saw or heard was not the product of your own imagination?

4) Is it possible to prove that you were not dreaming?

5) Has anyone else, before or since, seen or heard the same thing, without previously knowing about the other's experience?

6) If no one else present saw or heard what you saw or heard, how do you explain this; and if anyone else did see or hear anything at that time, was anything said or done

by either or any of you that could have given the other a clue as to what appeared to be happening?

7) Have you previously had any similar experience and if so was a normal explanation ever discovered?

Only when each and every one of these questions is answered with complete honesty to your entire satisfaction and to the satisfaction of everyone else present, are you entitled to think that you may have been privileged to see a ghost, and even then the odds that it was a ghost are heavily against.

This is the only book devoted solely to ghost hunting that I can recommend, but my own volumes on ghosts and hauntings, including the first comprehensive guides to the haunted places of the British Isles, *A Gazetteer of British Ghosts* and *A Gazetteer of Scottish and Irish Ghosts* (first published in Britain in 1971 and 1973 and re-published in America in one volume in 1985), provide a useful starting-point for the adventurous ghost hunter, and for specific areas I cannot do better than suggest consultation of my volumes on Ghosts and Hauntings in Cornwall, Devon, Somerset, Kent, Hampshire, North-West England and the West Country. They all contain cases that cry out for further investigation.

The Society for Psychical Research booklet *Notes for Investigators of Spontaneous Cases* contains so much useful information and insight into the correct scientific procedure for investigating spontaneous phenomena that I cannot do better than reproduce it here, and I acknowledge my indebtedness to that Society (which I first joined forty years ago) for allowing me to reproduce the entire publication, omitting only references to the Society and its publications which might confuse the present reader.

SOCIETY FOR PSYCHICAL RESEARCH NOTES FOR INVESTIGATORS OF SPONTANEOUS CASES

Introduction

In the field of psychical research spontaneous cases include hauntings, poltergeists, apparitions, and dreams and dream-like experiences believed to have a paranormal content, whether telepathic, retrocognitive, or precognitive. In this class also come cases in which individuals who do not profess to be mediums claim to have power to obtain information, or even to move inanimate objects by paranormal means. In all the above kinds of case an investigation is necessary to establish the facts, and the following notes have been prepared to assist Members of the Society in the task of collecting evidence, whenever the opportunity occurs to do so.

The Conduct of an Investigation

The investigation of spontaneous cases involves difficulties not ordinarily met with in scientific research, and calls for tact and sympathy, as well as for the ability to collect and weight evidence. A Member invited to investigate a case, or undertaking an investigation on his own initiative, is asked to bear in mind the following considerations.

Although the Society does not hold or express corporate views, it is to be expected that the methods of investigation adopted by its Members will be taken to reflect the policy of the Society. Before starting an investigation involving inquiries into the private affairs of an individual or family, whether by visit or correspondence, the investigator should inform the parties concerned that:
1) any information given to him will, if required, be treated as confidential, and will be disclosed only to Officers of the Society competent to deal with it;
2) if publication is contemplated, names of persons and places will not be given without the consent of those concerned; pseudonyms can be used if necessary.

It is of the utmost importance to win and retain the confidence of the informant, who is usually a stranger, and great care must be taken by the investigator to observe promises given under the above heads. Careless disclosures may estrange individuals from one another, or result in a house getting the reputation of being haunted, with consequent depreciation of its value.

An investigator should avoid giving advice, even if sought, about matters regarding which the persons concerned ought to consult a minister of religion, a doctor, or a lawyer. His task is to collect information for a scientific purpose, not to solve domestic problems. Advice to the investigator as to the course he should take, if the case turns out to be one of self-delusion or fraud, is given below.

If two or more witnesses are available for questioning, it is desirable to see them separately, if this can be tactfully arranged. As a rule, one witness should not be told when he is contradicted by another.

The average informant, especially one who has not previously had an experience of the kind in question, has no knowledge of the standards of documentation and corroboration one would like to find observed, and his story may leave much to be desired in those respects. Overt criticism of any shortcomings should be avoided, and the informant should be treated on the assumption that he is acting in good faith, even if it is clear to the investigator that he is mistaken. The critical appraisement of evidence should be kept until after an interview is over.

Method of Investigation

The following notes are written from the strictly practical point of view. They imply no particular theory, and start from the standpoint of the investigator at the outset of his inquiry.

Each phenomenon is an effect of which it is desired to ascertain the cause, and the expression 'effects' is used to mean happenings as described by the reporters of them, even though the description may turn out to be wrong. A 'haunted house' means a house reported to be haunted, whether or not evidence of any paranormal agency is discovered. Effects are of various kinds, and for practical purposes may be divided into the five classes mentioned below. This classification is not scientific, as it purposely follows the specious appearance of phenomena, as presented to the investigator.

E1. Unaccountable movement of objects.
E2. Unaccountable noises (including voices and music) and smells.
E3. Apparitions, mysterious lights and shadows.
E4. Unaccountable touches, pushes and feelings of heat and cold.
E5. Feelings of fear, horror, disgust, etc, and of unseen 'presences'.

These five kinds of effect should be memorized, and a convenient way to remember them is by the sequence MNOP (M for movements, N for noises, O for optical effects, and P for pushes and presences). When the investigator is faced with a variety of effects in one case, he is recommended to examine them by classes in the above order, bearing in mind that all of them may not be due to one cause.

Causes

Causes fall into two main classes, mechanical and personal. By *mechanical causes* are meant those which are impersonal and unintentional, e.g. machinery giving rise to vibration, leading to movements of objects and raps, or car headlights causing mysterious lights in the rooms of a house some distance from the road. By *personal causes* are meant those which originate in persons, even when they issue in effects which are physical, e.g. surreptitious stone-throwing by a frustrated adolescent. Apparitions and other sensory hallucinations are classed as 'personal', whether they are veridical or not.

A veridical experience is one which conveys to the percipient information which had not been obtained by him by ordinary means, and is afterwards verified, in the sense of being found to correspond with facts which were outside the range of his knowledge and sense perception at the time of the experience. Such an experience is held to be evidence of the working of a paranormal cause, sometimes referred to as 'psi' in order to emphasize our present ignorance of its nature. In order to establish such a case satisfactorily it is necessary to obtain:

(i) accurate details of the experience;
(ii) accurate details of the facts or happenings to which it appears to relate;
(iii) accurate information as to the amount of relevant knowledge previously possessed by the subject;
(iv) an accurate inference from a comparison of (i) and (ii).

The average untested ghost story usually contains inaccuracies under all four heads, all tending to 'prove' the conclusion of it. It is the task of the investigator to eliminate these inaccuracies, and he should not be daunted by the difficulties. After this brief glance forward, a return must be made to the position of the investigator at stage (i), trying to classify an assortment of effects of which he does not yet know the causes.

Significant Patterns

The problem is to assign the various effects to their proper causes, and the key to the answer lies in the fact that different kinds of cause give rise to different kinds of patterns in their effects. The investigator, confronted with a story containing a miscellaneous assortment of effects, is faced with the task of discovering one or more 'significant patterns' among them.

49

The search for such patterns may have to go beyond the effects themselves. There may be a pattern in the social composition of the household, or in the surroundings of a haunted house.

The investigator is usually furnished in the first instance with a written report, describing the phenomena observed. If the information is received orally, it should be reduced to note form as soon as possible, every effort being made to record detail, however irrelevant or absurd it may at first sight appear to be. If there is an opportunity to visit the subject or house, it should of course be taken, but if circumstances do not permit a visit, the investigation should not for that reason be refused or abandoned. Preferably the visit should be paid *after* the preliminary report has been thoroughly examined. On a purely statistical basis the chances are that a given report will disclose no evidence of the paranormal, because genuine paranormal cases are much rarer than supposed ones. In view of this consideration, and having regard to the high cost of travelling, it may turn out to be possible to clear up the whole case by correspondence, a resort which should not be neglected. An informant seldom writes a deliberately misleading report, though that has been known to happen. In a fraudulent case it is usually the informant who is being misled by someone else, and a pattern characteristic of fraud comes out in the evidence. Assuming, then, that the report has been written in good faith, the effects in the report should be sorted out on paper into the five classes E1–5 mentioned above, every incident being reckoned as one effect.

Primary and Secondary Effects

In all cases of multiple effects take special note of the first ones to occur, especially if the phenomena have been going on for some time. If the early ones are all in classes 1 and 2 (either or both), they may have started the impression that there are uncanny occurrences taking place and those effects should be noted as being, at first sight, 'primary effects'. It may well be that these have suggested to the informant that 'almost anything may happen', and suggestion may have set up a series of secondary effects, some in classes 3, 4 and 5, among which one is unlikely to find evidence of the paranormal. These 'secondary effects' are of various kinds, and are dealt with separately below. They must be recognized as soon as possible for what they are, and their patterns must accordingly be studied. In this first sorting of effects into primary and secondary, which is of crucial importance, the working rules should be:

1) Concentrate first on the earliest, and, if necessary, strip them of obvious later inferences. If, for example, an informant says he heard 'footsteps' and then the 'rustling of a silk dress', but saw no one, it is clear that he heard a series of sounds *like* footsteps, and another sound *like* the frou-frou of a silk dress.

2) Look early to the matter of corroboration. If, for example, someone else, who was present, heard the same sounds, but, unlike the informant, did not feel 'a cold wind' or 'a sense of intense misery' as 'the unseen presence walked by', there is strong reason to suppose that the noises were primary effects, and that the feelings were secondary. On your list of earliest effects try to draw a line at the point at which secondary effects appear to be colouring the picture. If the original informant very soon after the start called in a lot of people to help in probing the mystery, secondary effects may have developed very rapidly, and the line may have to be drawn after a matter of hours rather than days. Then go back to the effects which are above the line, and look for 'patterns'. Do not, at this stage, try to frame in your own mind a theory that is going to be wide enough to cover not only them but also the more astounding 'facts' which come later in the story. If, for example, movements of objects are above the line, consider them as purely mechanical events. Usually they start in a modest way. Crockery falls off the kitchen dresser. Bells ring and doors open of their own accord, and so on. People seldom see the movements actually start. Did any observer do so in this case? Instances of objects moving in irregular paths and sailing round corners usually come 'below the line'.

Noises above the line are usually inarticulate ones such as bangs, raps, swishing sounds, and so on. Sounds described as groans, sighs, shrieks, footsteps, knocks on the door, snoring, heavy breathing, and scornful laughter may all be due to mechanical causes. Raps may sound

51

like 'morse code', or attempts at 'communication', but the investigator should be on his guard against premature inferences. Any alleged 'signs of intelligence' in the noises are probably illusory or fraudulent, and inquiry should be made as to when such signs were first discovered. They are usually secondary effects. Some noises may be caused by animals, whose presence is quite unsuspected. There is not only the rat. The breathing of an owl outside a window at night can give rise to the impression of a 'ghostly presence'.

When attempting to trace noises to their points of origin, bear in mind that the ear, by itself, is not at all a safe guide. The noise may originate at a point some distance from the place where the informant says it comes from. Treat with great caution any suggestion made to you that the noises come from, or are worst near, any particular person's bed, or that they follow so-and-so round the house. Such impressions are usually deceptive, and may be very unfair to the person indicated (see below).

Loud sounds and voices only heard by the informant and no one else within earshot, if they convey no accurate information previously unknown to the hearer, are probably of pathological origin. The hearing of voices is a common symptom of psychosis. Sounds and voices, including music and singing, especially if heard by two or more persons collectively, and appearing to be hallucinatory, may turn out to be veridical. But such experiences are of little evidential value unless they are recorded on paper very quickly, and enough is remembered by the percipient to furnish details for research. Smells are occasionally reported, but it is very difficult to establish them as hallucinations. They can be caused surreptitiously with great ease and little fear of detection. It is accordingly dangerous to assess them as primary effects.

E3 Apparitions

If an informant reports having seen quite recently an apparition not accompanied by other phenomena, i.e. as a primary effect, and believes it to have been the apparition of someone living or dead, the case should be pursued at once by correspondence, if a visit is not practicable. In any case, the informant should be asked to give as detailed an account of the experience as possible, under the following heads:

A) *Circumstances of percipient*: exact time and place, whether awake or asleep or semi-conscious, and conditions of light or darkness.

B) *Appearance of apparition:* a) colour and style of clothing; b) facial appearance; c) apparent age; d) movements if any; e) utterance, if any; f) mode of appearance and disappearance.

Information should also be sought under the following further heads:

1) Names of persons, if any, who were present when the apparition was seen.

2) Name(s) of person(s) who were told of the incident very soon after it had occurred.

3) In the case of a haunted house, was the house reputed to be haunted, and if so was that known to the percipient before his experience?

4) Details of previous appearances, etc, and information as to whether more than one person has seen the apparition on one occasion.

5) Details about the percipient, such as age, occupation, general state of health, previous psychic experiences, attitude towards ghosts, relationship to others in the household, how long he has been in the house, whether he intends to move, and so on. Most of this information can be gathered without the appearance of being too inquisitive, and it would all be relevant if there were any hint that the percipient was being imposed upon by someone else.

A veridical apparition often leaves in the memory of the percipient a vivid and lasting image which can be described in considerable detail. But as recollection of the event is liable to become distorted by lapse of time, the sooner it is down on paper the better. If the percipient has already been trying to identify the apparition by consulting books, pictures and photograph albums, some distortion of the image may have already occurred. If the apparition is described in good detail, but has not been identified, so much the better. Any question of identification is best dealt with by someone other than the percipient, in order to avoid the particular kind of distortion mentioned above. It is a task which can safely be left to be pursued at leisure.

If, on the other hand, the apparition was a vague and shadowy figure, lacking identifying detail, it is possibly nothing more than an externalisation of some anxiety in the mind of the percipient.

If the percipient claims to be 'psychic', and there is some likelihood that he will see the apparition again, he should be asked to report at once, with full detail, any further appearance, and to refrain from trying to identify any feature of it.

If, in conjunction with the apparition any other effects are reported, especially under heads 2, 4 and 5, the exact sequence should be established, if possible, in relation to the appearance of the figure.

It is important to discover whether the apparition is the primary effect, and the noises secondary, or whether the noises are primary, in which case the apparition may well be a secondary effect induced by the noises.

In the first of these two cases, the apparition may have frightened the percipient, with the result that he has afterwards attributed to paranormal causes noises which ordinarily would not have struck him as uncanny.

In the second case the apparition may be a purely subjective image, representing visually the supposed cause of the noises. In some poltergeist cases, where sounds were undoubtedly the primary effect, hallucinatory persons or animals, obviously secondary effects of the noises, have been also seen. These usually reflect childish beliefs, and may take the form of witch-like figures with staring eyes, or queer animals of indeterminate breed. Afterwards the person who saw such a figure is seldom able to give a very clear description of it.

In connection with apparitions and other visual hallucinations there is information on certain points which is required to further the study of the subject. An informant who appears to be a good witness should be asked to take note, the next time he sees an apparition, of whether or not he continues to see it if he shuts his eyes. What evidence there is on this point is conflicting. In the case of apparitions seen out of doors, it is interesting to know what the atmospheric conditions were at the time (i.e. whether clear or misty). There is a certain amount of evidence which suggests that misty conditions favour the onset of visual hallucinations, by preventing the eyes from coming to a sharp focus on ordinary objects. In the search for evidence that an apparition is veridical, the optical aspect of the matter should not be overlooked.

Mysterious lights and shadows, when nothing else apparently paranormal is seen, are usually due to some undetected physical cause. The exact places where they were seen should be noted, with a sketch map or plan, if possible, and considered in relation to the positions of nearby windows, buildings, and roads, in case the effects may be due to lights (including car headlamps) showing intermittently from a distance.

On the other hand, when a life-like apparition is seen in a pitch dark room, the effect of light is clearly not a physical phenomenon. Information as to the background and edges of the 'visual' field should be sought, and carefully noted.

E4 Touches, Pushes, etc

Effects in this class, if they occur very early in a story of rather vague haunting, may be real tactile experiences which are misinterpreted. For instance, an informant may say that he was 'pushed aside' when entering a doorway, or that when he tried to open the door someone pushed it against him, and in neither case was anyone there.

Such feelings usually occur in conjuction with unaccountable noises, and perhaps movements of objects in the house. They should be grouped with such effects for pattern-finding purposes.

E5 Feelings of Fear, Horror, etc

These are deeper-seated feelings than those of class 4, and are less likely to be misinterpreted tactile effects. If the percipient cannot explain them in terms of his own knowledge or experience, it does not follow that they are of paranormal origin, though they may be. By themselves they are very difficult to evaluate, and their significance can usually only be judged in relation to other kinds of effect.

Stories obtained from persons on the spot, e.g. that a crime was once committed in the room where the percipient had the experience, themselves require corroboration before they can be accepted as support for a paranormal interpretation of it.

Most effects of classes E4 and 5 are secondary, especially if they occur late in the story, and are consequently of doubtful value as evidence.

Secondary Effects

These are all personal, in the sense that they reflect the reactions of persons to primary effects. They are of two kinds: 1) unintentional effects due to suggestion, faults of memory, unconscious exaggeration, and so forth; 2) fraudulent acts and lying statements, with a discreditable object in view. Unintentional effects usually reflect personal beliefs and wishes, and these should be elicited by tactful questioning.

As regards the second class, one has to be on the look-out for cases in which there are no primary effects at all, and the whole affair is fraudulent from start to finish. The motive in a haunted house case is often to frighten some person(s) out of the house, in order to relieve overcrowding, or to facilitate a love affair, or to provide a distraction to cover up thefts.

Occasionally, however, when primary effects have induced in one person, usually the informant, a state of abject credulity, someone else takes advantage of the situation, for a selfish purpose of his own, and starts deceiving the former by faking effects, which go one better than the earlier ones. In such a case, a significant pattern can usually be found in the relations between different members of the household. If a person is either too little interested in the 'haunt', or is over-zealous in trying to 'lead' the investigator in hunting 'it' down, he or she should be carefully watched. As soon as an investigator is satisfied in his own mind that a case is wholly fraudulent, he would be well advised to withdraw without expressing any opinion. He is not a detective, and should avoid being involved in a family scandal. The finding or suspicion of fraud should, of course, be mentioned in the report to the Society (see below).

Where, in a case of prolonged haunting of a 'poltergeist' description, the cause has remained obscure, it is not un-common for the baffled observers to fasten the responsibility for the phenomena upon some person in the household – it used usually to be a young servant girl – who is considered to be 'an unconscious medium', through whom a 'spirit' produces the effects. The massive pressure of suggestion from all around her may actually cause such a person to fake effects. An investigator should be very cautious about accepting any identification of a particular person as an unconscious medium, as he or she may be the victim and not the cause of the phenomena under investigation.

In some cases an informant claims to have remarkable powers of telepathy, clairvoyance, or the like, or to be able to move objects by will-power. Such a person is seldom wilfully fraudulent, *if he himself invites investigation*, but may well be self-deluded, and not open to reason. His main object is to obtain from the investigator an opinion that he has genuine paranormal powers. As evidence of such is usually sadly lacking, the investigator would be well advised to express no opinion at all.

General

There is no reliable evidence as to the manner in which paranormal causes bring about their effects, and the case for believing that any particular effects are due to a paranormal cause can only be established by the process of excluding all normal causes, even if it gives the impression that the investigator is bent on 'explaining things away'. If an investigation ends up with the discovery that all the effects are patently due to quite ordinary and mundane causes, the informant's reaction to the situation should be noted. It may fit into a pattern relating to his psychological make-up, which had been only very tentatively figured out before that point.

Sometimes during an investigation an opportunity occurs to take a medium to a haunted house. In the event of such an arrangement being made, the greatest care must be taken that no information about the case is given away beforehand to the medium. Unless the medium is an automatic writer, it is difficult to get full value out of the arrangement without a note-taker or sound-recorder. It is better, if possible, to use the services of a medium who will work at home from an object brought from the house. In any case, the result may well be a story which has nothing to do with the effects already reported, and creates a new problem calling for separate and perhaps lengthy study. It is advisable, therefore, to carry the investigation as far as possible before resorting to a medium, and only to call one in when progress by other means has been brought to a standstill. Preferably only persons experienced in work with mediums should employ them on tasks of this nature.

Dreams

Dreams believed to have a paranormal content are usually very difficult to evaluate. The important points to establish are:
1) whether the dream was related to anyone else before the 'verification' of it; if by letter, whether the letter and envelope are available:
2) whether the subject is in the habit of having remembered dreams, and, if so, their frequency and character;
3) the actual happenings, in the past, present or future at the time of the dream, to which it is believed to relate.

In the case of a person who dreams frequently, there is a tendency to remember dreams which apparently 'come true' and to forget others which do not. The 'fulfilment' of a dream of a vaguely premonitory kind is often purely accidental, and a very striking correspondence between dream and event is necessary to establish a paranormal nexus between them.

Reports to the Society

Reports should contain as many exact dates and clock times of incidents as the investigator can obtain. Sometimes, before any definite finding can be recorded, an investigation is brought to a dead stop by some obstacle on the side of the informant. In such a case a report should be sent in, nevertheless, with information as to the cause of the stoppage. The data obtained may well fit into some already established pattern, when the case is examined in the light of others of a similar kind.

If fraud is encountered or suspected, or if any person involved appears to be the victim of ignorance or malice, a delicate situation is likely to arise if the investigator tries to intervene. The matter should be dealt with in the report, which will be regarded as confidential, and it should be left to the Officers of the Society to decide what action, if any, should be taken. It is of the utmost importance that investigators making enquiries for the Society should maintain an attitude of strict impartiality.

Relations with the Press

It has been found desirable not to discuss current investigations with newspaper representatives. Publicity can embarrass or distress the household concerned, and may discourage others from reporting cases to the Society. It can also hamper the investigator in his work. Newspaper representatives rarely have a detailed knowledge of the subject and, although writing in good faith, can give a misleading impression of the work in hand and of the Society, if its name is mentioned. Such misconception may be aggravated by the almost inevitable cutting and sub-editing which is done in newspaper offices. An investigator, whether he is acting in response to an invitation from the Society or on his own account, is accordingly advised to exercise extreme discretion, if relations with the Press should arise.

*　　　*　　　*

SEANCES

The ghost of the seance room calls for a very different line of investigation. Seances are (usually) private meetings of spiritualists who seek, with the aid of mediums (people who are endowed with highly-developed psychic powers) to converse with the dead. Certain mediums, known as physical mediums, are alleged to produce materialisations or ghosts of dead people, composed of ectoplasm, a sticky muslin-like substance that is exuded from the orifices of the medium and builds up into a human form.

Spiritualism is a religion and those who practise spiritualism are (usually) devout, sincere and genuine people who find in their religion comfort, strength and a way of life that takes away the fear of death. Understandably they do not welcome the sensation-seeking ghost hunter and many have no interest in proving to anyone else that the materialisations are genuine, for past experience has proved to them that such manifestations are possible and they feel under no obligation to prove their convictions to anyone. The only honest way therefore for a ghost hunter to investigate the induced ghosts of the seance room is to be invited to take part in a materialisation seance, faithfully and wholeheartedly to adhere to any conditions laid down by the circle members, to observe quietly and graciously, and always to remember that he is a guest.

Observing such conditions and quietly and unobtrusively

watching as well as I could all that has happened I have been privileged to witness some astonishing, bewildering and quite inexplicable happenings, but not, I hasten to emphasise, under scientific or even controlled conditions. Occasionally it may be possible to persuade a medium to submit to test conditions but in those fortunate circumstances it is to be hoped that the amateur ghost hunter would seek the help and advice of someone with experience in the investigation of mediumship, for the manifestation of an independent entity under truly scientific conditions would be a breakthrough in psychical investigation.

Spontaneous ghosts offer the easiest and most rewarding possibility for the amateur ghost hunter: hundreds of ghosts are reportedly seen every year in Britain alone and it is by no means beyond the bounds of possibility – even likelihood – that with patience, commonsense, the right companions and a lot of luck, you will see a ghost. I hope very much that you will let me know if you do.

4 · The Photography of Ghosts

Cameras may vary in their complexity, dexterity, sensitivity and automatic action but, whether it be one of the most sophisticated and expensive pieces of apparatus available or the simplest and least expensive on the market, a camera is an indispensable part of the ghost hunter's equipment.

Those who have studied and investigated psychic activity have always been interested in the possibility of obtaining concrete evidence of an after-life or, at any rate, of some demonstration of the genuine psychic phenomena they believe they have witnessed. In their anxiety to obtain such evidence and/or records they have become willing victims for charlatans and in fact anyone with a little knowledge of conjuring and the scientific process of photography.

'Spirit' photography was an early claim by fraudulent spiritualists. In 1837 extensive 'communications' were received at Mount Lebanon in America predicting that spiritualistic phenomena would soon spread all over the world – which they did. Andrew Jackson Davis (1826–1910), the so-called Pough-keepsie Seer, made a similar prediction in 1847. In March 1848 the Fox sisters (Kate, 1841–92, and Margaret, 1838–93) were disturbed by continual rappings, and they are regarded as the pioneers of modern spiritualism with its purported ghostly manifestations, levitated trumpets, apports, slate-writing, raps, messages, perfumes, lights, movement of objects, etc. William Mumler of Boston, Massachusetts, is regarded as the first 'spirit' photographer; in 1862 he began to produce portraits in which ghostly, semi-transparent 'extras' appeared beside his sitters.

Mumler was the head engraver of the jewellery firm Bigelow, Kennard and Company, and one day, so runs the story, he tried to take a photograph of himself in a friend's studio by focusing the camera on an empty chair and then rushing to position himself in the chair after uncapping the lens. When the plate was developed an extraneous figure was discovered: a young, transparent girl seemed to be sitting in the chair, her lower parts fading away into a mist. Mumler said he recognised his cousin who had died twelve years previously. Repeating the experiment time and time again Mumler became satisfied that the extra faces he obtained on his photographic plates were of supernormal origin.

News of his discovery and his conclusions quickly spread and he found himself besieged with requests for sittings from people anxious to obtain 'spirit' photographs of their dead loved ones and Mumler soon gave up his position with the jewellery firm and became a professional spirit photographer.

Mumler's work in this field soon attracted the attention of the aforementioned Andrew Jackson Davis, at that time editor of the *Herald of Progress* in New York and he sent a professional photographer to test Mumler. When he received a favourable report he decided to conduct an investigation himself. He too came away convinced that the new psychic manifestation was genuine, for it seemed that it did not matter whether Mumler carried out his work in his own studio or at other studios, nor whether he used his own chemicals or not.

Numerous photographers, professional and amateur, now visited Mumler and one searching enquiry followed another but always the verdict was favourable. The inventor of the nitrate of silver bath, a man named Black from Boston, offered Mumler £50 for a genuine spirit photograph and after Horace Weston, an experienced photographer, returned to Black with a favourable report Black went to Mumler himself, made the most scrupulous examination of the studio and the photographer himself, developed the plate personally and to his utter astonishment found another form on the photograph beside his own, a man leaning on his shoulder.

Mumler's credibility seemed to be established, he found himself in popular favour, and for a time he did tremendous business, but then scandal began to ruin his reputation for from time to time it was discovered that the 'spirit' portraits he obtained were of people who were very much alive. He asserted they must be doubles of the living but even devout spiritualists did not accept this and began to accuse him of trickery. The outcry showed no sign of abating, indeed it became steadily worse, and in 1868 Mumler left Boston and set up his headquarters in New York.

There he prospered for a time until he was accused of fraud

by a newspaperman, and he was arrested on the orders of the Mayor of New York. At the trial, however, a number of professional photographers testified on his behalf and he was acquitted. His later life was full of ups and downs and he eventually died in poverty in 1884. The story of his successes, accusations, disappearance and disgrace was to be repeated many times by later 'spirit' photographers.

Frederick A. Hudson, the first English 'spirit' photographer, experimented with Mrs Samuel Guppy, the famous apport and transportation medium discovered by Dr Alfred Russel Wallace (1823–1913), the distinguished naturalist, and eventually Hudson obtained a white patch, resembling the outline of a draped figure, behind a portrait of Mrs Guppy. The experiments were repeated with increasing success, Dr Wallace obtaining two different portraits of his dead mother, unlike any photographs taken during her life. The editor of the *British Journal of Photography* investigated Hudson, using his own collodion and new plates and still found abnormal appearances on the resulting pictures. William Howitt (1792–1879) the author and pioneer spiritualist, obtained the photographs of two deceased sons, the existence of one of whom even the friend accompaning Howitt was ignorant; but accusations of imposture soon arose and Hudson was exposed by William Stainton Moses (1839–92), the English medium and religious teacher, for whom Hudson had produced many 'spirit' photographs that agreed with Moses' clairvoyant visions. Hudson, it was found, sometimes played the part of the ghost by dressing up, and then John Beattie, a noted professional photographer, demonstrated conclusively that on occasions Hudson's 'spirits' were faked by simple double exposure.

One of the most skilful and artistic 'spirit' photographers was the Frenchman Edouard Buguet who, in an alleged partial trance, produced many remarkable likenesses of high artistic quality representing deceased relations of his sitters; while many of them were well-known people it was said that other photographs of comparatively obscure people suggested evidence of genuine 'spirit' presence. For a time his reputation was high and he was acclaimed for apparently photographing the double of Stainton Moses in Paris while the sitters were in London. However in August 1875 he was arrested for fraud and sentenced, on his own confession, to imprisonment for one year and a fine of 500 francs.

In his confessions, in which he admitted that all his pictures were faked, he stated that at first he dressed up his assistants to play the part of the ghost and used double exposure to produce the required result; but later he constructed a doll which, variously draped, served for the figure of the ghost, and this figure, together with a stock of various heads, masks and other trimmings, was found by the police at his studio. Buguet also used assistants to obtain information about his sitters, particularly concerning the appearance of departed relatives. On his release from prison Buguet retracted his confession and declared that he had been tricked by a promise that he would be acquitted if he confessed.

Richard Boursnell (1832–1909), an English 'spirit' photographer, obtained 'psychic markings' on his plates as early as 1851. After being accused by his partner, however, he stopped taking 'spirit' photographs for forty years, when he returned to the art. He was successful for a time, before being repeatedly denounced. Many of his pictures were exact duplicates, apart from the sitter, and tracings taken from one would perfectly register over another.

One of the most famous, or notorious, of all 'spirit' photographers was William Hope (1863–1933), a carpenter at Crewe, whose psychic power, it was said, was discovered accidentally in 1905. He and a friend photographed each other one Saturday afternoon and the plate which Hope exposed showed an extra figure, a transparent woman, behind whom the brick wall was visible. Furthermore the figure was recognised as the sister of Hope's companion, dead for many years. A circle of friends was formed to sit for 'spirit' photography, and the famous 'Crewe circle' produced scores of photographs depicting 'extras' on them. But controversy arose when Archdeacon Thomas Colley, an ardent psychical investigator for forty years (he exposed the medium William Eglinton in 1876), accepted a 'spirit' photograph as that of his dead mother, but Hope thought it was someone else; and indeed a Mrs Spencer of Nantwich recognised the photograph as that of her grandmother. Hope informed Archdeacon Colley of his mistake, but Colley said it was madness to think a man did not know his own mother and he advertised for people who remembered his mother to meet him at the rectory. There eighteen persons selected the photograph from several others and testified in writing that the picture was a portrait of the late Mrs Colley who had never been photographed.

In 1922 a second and more damning controversy surrounded Hope when he was accused of imposture by Mr Harry Price (later Chairman of The Ghost Club) in a report published in the *Proceedings* of the Society for Psychical Research. Price maintained that he caught Hope in the act of substituting plates and that Hope handed him two negatives (one of which contained a psychic extra) that did not bear the secret mark which the Imperial Dry Plate Company had specially impressed on it. Subsequent investigation revealed the possibility of a conspiracy, for the wrapper was found and it bore marks of having been tampered with, and one of the original marked plates (which showed an image on being developed) lay about for four weeks in the offices of the Society for Psychical Research, open to tampering and substitution. Hope immediately offered new sittings under stringent control, but the offer was refused. Hope never commercialised his psychic activities and there have always been those who believe he was a genuine medium; but shortly before his death in 1933 he was again accused of fraud in the *Proceedings* of the Society for Psychical Research by two photographic experts, Fred Barlow and Major W. Rampling Rose, who not only built up a formidable case for fraud but also illustrated the method that had been used.

One of the biggest fakes in the history of 'spirit' photography was the series of Armistice Day pictures produced by Mrs Ada Emma Deane, an elderly former charwoman whose psychic career was the subject of much criticism and suspicion owing to her strange habit of keeping the photographic plates close to herself for 'magnetising'. The photograph of the Cenotaph ceremonies showing 'spirit faces' floating round overhead was found to include copies of press photographs of well-known footballers and other living sportsmen!

Nor surprisingly Mrs Deane – although championed by people like Dr Hereward Carrington and Sir Arthur Conan Doyle – was denounced by such organisations as the Occult Committee of the Magic Circle and people like Fred Barlow writing in the *Proceedings* of the Society for Psychical Research.

In recent years John Myers (who once visited Mrs Deane and was allegedly detected in fraud by Lord Donegall and Cyril Wilkinson of The Ghost Club) has collaborated with American parapsychologist Hans Holzer and worked as a psychic healer as well as a 'spirit' photographer. Some of his photographs are included in Holzer's *Psychic Photography* (1969).

The apparent photography of 'thought forms' has come to the notice of people like Professor Jule Eisenbud following the results obtained through Chicago 'photographic medium' Ted Serios. There exist many puzzling photographs which appear to be the result of thought forms originating from Serios registering on photographic film or other light-sensitive surfaces. Over the years Dr Eisenbud and other scientists have subjected Serios to just about every conceivable test and still he gets results.

Most of the early 'spirit' photographs were produced by means of double exposure, the 'spirits' being photographed, usually from paper reproductions surrounded by cotton wool, before the sitters. Under-exposure enabled the 'spirit' to be given a suitably transparent or ethereal appearance. Another common method, as revealed by at least one 'spirit' photographer, was for a suitably made-up accomplice to show himself through an opening in the background, where of course he would be unseen by the sitter. Careful choice of lens aperture would successfully put the 'spirit' face out of focus and give it the required 'unearthly' quality. Yet another method was to sketch the extra onto a plain background with quinine sulphite which was invisible to the eye but was recorded clearly by the photographic emulsion. On occasions William Hope used a small flashlamp with which he flashed the plate, either under the cover of the focusing cloth or in the darkroom. A similar effect was sometimes produced chemically by the use of a suitably-coated rubber stamp.

There are a great number of photographs that are alleged to depict ghosts, but very few are convincing in themselves or have a convincing provenance. In fact fraud and malobservation have long been so prevalent in the field of so-called psychic photography that serious attention has been diverted from those rare examples that may well be genuine photographs of spontaneous ghosts.

I have examined many photographs that appear at first sight

to depict an unexplained figure, but which on careful enlargement are seen to be the result of an unusual combination of light and shade. There is one frequently published photograph that appears to depict a figure in the window of a house which is almost certainly nothing more nor less than the result of reflection. An outstanding example of a photograph that has never been satisfactorily explained, however, is that taken of the staircase at Raynham Hall, Norfolk, seat of the Townshend family. I have before me, as I write, a copy of the December 26, 1936, issue of *Country Life* containing the first publication of this remarkable photograph. In September 1936 *Country Life* arranged for two professional photographers to visit Raynham Hall for the purpose of taking a series of photographs of the interior of the mansion. Captain H. C. Provand and his assistant arrived at the 300-year-old property during the afternoon of 19 September and proceeded to set up their equipment in the hall. Captain Provand took a flashlight picture of the staircase and was preparing to take another when his assistant remarked that he thought he could see a shadowy form on the stairs. As the form glided down the stairs towards the photographers another exposure was made and the figure vanished, but when the second photograph was developed the shadowy form of a hooded female in a flowing dress was clearly discernible.

I believe the original photograph is still preserved in the *Country Life* photographic library (it was a few years ago) and experts who have examined it and the plate are satisfied that there was no trickery involved in producing it. The photograph presumably depicts the famous Brown Lady of Raynham Hall, possibly the ghost of Dorothy Walpole, a direct blood relative of the Townshends, who suffered mental depression and spent the last years of her life confined to an upstairs room. Her ghost has been seen by a number of houseguests over the years including Captain Marryat, the novelist, in addition to members of the Townshend family, including the late Marchioness of Townshend who told my Ghost Club friend Dennis Bardens that she had seen the Brown Lady on several occasions. In judging allegedly paranormal manifestations caught by the camera it is not only necessary to examine with an expert and critical eye the photograph itself, but also to be satisfied as to the source and origin and circumstances surrounding the taking of the photograph. On all these counts the Raynham Hall photograph seems to have an impeccable derivation.

So too it seems has the equally remarkable and puzzling photograph taken at the Queen's House at Greenwich. While visiting the National Maritime Museum at Greenwich on Saturday, 19 June 1966, during the course of a holiday in England, the Reverend and Mrs R. W. Hardy from White Rock, British Columbia, photographed the Tulip Staircase in the Queen's House; and when the photograph was developed, after their return to Canada, a shrouded figure appeared to be clutching the stairway rail! A cousin of a member of The Ghost Club was shown the transparency and, with the approval of the Rev. and Mrs Hardy, the facts of the case were placed in the hands of The Ghost Club, who organised an investigation of the story and of the transparency, and subsequently arranged an all-night vigil at the museum.

The Tulip Staircase was designed and constructed by Inigo Jones in 1629 at the command of King Charles I. Rubens, the Flemish painter, was a frequent visitor to the Queen's House, originally started for Queen Anne of Denmark (King James I's queen), but her death caused a general lack of interest in the project. It was not until Charles was about to marry Henrietta Maria that his thoughts turned to the incomplete Queen's House at Greenwich, and he commissioned the completion of the work, with a free hand regarding costs. Today the Queen's House and the graceful Tulip Staircase are in a perfect state of preservation, and, although the staircase is not accessible to the public, the house is open to visitors. The perfect symmetry of the staircase is particularly evident from the foot, which is the spot from which the curious photograph was taken. Optically the photograph is somewhat confusing, due to the spirality of the staircase, and one has to realise that the vast expanse of staircase that appears on the left of the picture is the underside of the spiral staircase as it lifts overhead.

Lengthy correspondence on the subject between The Ghost Club and a long-standing member, the late Mr Hector MacQueen, his cousin, Mrs Joyce Fraser of North Vancouver, British Columbia, and the Rev. and Mrs Hardy, was followed by a personal interview between the then Hon. Secretary of The Ghost Club and the Rev. and Mrs Hardy when they were again in London in 1967. It was then established that the day on which the photograph was taken had been fine but cloudy (and this was subsequently verified by the Meteorological Office of the London Weather Centre), and that the camera used was a Zeiss Ikon Contina – Prontor S V S Zavar Anastigmat lens: 1:3.5f = 45 mm, with 'skylight' auxiliary haze-filter – and the film was a Kodachrome X, daylight, 35 mm colour film with speed 64. The light used was that which was available: daylight with the electric candelabra which appear in the picture; no floodlight or flash. The Hardys are now unable to state the aperture with certainty but suggest that it was probably about f4; the time is also now uncertain but probably about 4–6 seconds. What is certain is that the photograph was taken at about 5 p.m. during normal opening time of the museum and, to quote, 'there is no possibility of a double exposure on this camera; besides which, each picture on the roll is accounted for by number.' The picture immediately prior to the 'ghost picture' is of the colonnade outside the Queen's House and the one immediately following is a figurehead; needless to say, neither remotely resemble either the shrouded figure or the staircase.

The Ghost Club next contacted Commander W.E. May, then Deputy Director of the National Maritime Museum, who told us that he knew of no previous ghostly association connected with the building (although we later learned of one or two vague stories which will be recounted later), with a view to having some members of the club spend a night in the Queen's House in the vicinity of the Tulip Staircase. We found Commander May and his staff most helpful and co-operative. We obtained the necessary permission from the Ministry of Public Buildings and Works, which involved agreeing to a number of conditions. These included the following: taking out an insurance policy in the sum of £5,000 to cover loss or damage to the permanent collection of paintings housed there; the understanding that after admission in the evening we would be locked in and not allowed to leave until a set time the following morning; smoking, alcohol, and the use of naked lights would not be permitted; all our equipment was to be inspected and installed by their engineers; two 'warders' were to be present with us at all times; and the payment of a not inconsiderable fee. It was eventually arranged that a small party of Ghost Club members, under the leadership of two council members, should spend the night of Saturday/Sunday, 24/25 June 1967, at the Queen's House.

On first examination the picture appears to show a single figure, with an exceptionally long right hand reaching ahead of it, but closer scrutiny establishes that both the hands on the stair rail are *left* hands and that they both wear a ring on the marriage finger. The 'top' figure is oddly convincing since the shadow falls directly across the light rays emitted by the electric candelabra. It is possible to see the shrouded figure leaning forward, apparently in pursuit of the 'shadowy' figure as they ascend the stairs; viewed in this light there is a distinctly malevolent air about the pursuer. A plausible explanation would be that both left hands are both those of the same person who is photographed twice mounting the stairs, but listen to Mrs Hardy: 'My husband actually took the picture as his stronger and steadier hands were better than mine in holding the camera steady ... thus I was free to watch for any possible intrusion of anything visible during the exposure time. Actually, a group of people who noticed our preparation apologised and stepped back, although I explained that my husband was not quite ready. I mention all this to indicate that no person or visible object could have intervened without my noticing it. Also, we had previously tried to ascend the staircase but were blocked by a "No Admittance" sign and a rope barrier at the foot of the stairs.' The Rev. Hardy, incidentally, is a retired United Church Minister and neither he nor his wife have previously taken any interest in psychical research, and in fact have always been somewhat sceptical of apparitions.

The party of Ghost Club members who spent the night at the Queen's House included Dr Peter Hilton-Rowe, Mr Hector MacQueen, Mrs MacQueen, Richard Howard and myself. During the course of the night still and cine-photography was employed with special filters and infra-red film; sound-recording apparatus was running continuously; thermometers were repeatedly checked for any possible abnormal temperature reading (easily detected at the Queen's House where the temperature is kept constant to protect the valuable paintings); some dozen doorways were sealed off with cotton to aid control of the rest of the building; the portion of the staircase-rail which appeared on the photograph was smeared with diluted petroleum jelly and at the end of the investigation this area was checked for fingerprints; instruments were employed to detect draughts, vibration, and other variations in the atmosphere; objects were distributed over the staircase at set points (and ringed) to detect movement; and during the night attempts were made to tempt any unseen entities to communicate by various kinds of seances and methods of communication.

We did not succeed in scientifically proving that a ghost exists at the Queen's House but a number of curious sounds were never satisfactorily explained, and several members of the party had distinct and inexplicable impressions during the night. The Senior Museum Photographer, Mr Brian Tremain, FRPS, joined the party and took a number of photographs during the night. Mr Tremain told us that he had used yards of film trying, unsuccessfully, to reproduce the effects in the Hardys' picture. During the night we spent in the Queen's House we heard, in particular, footsteps on more than one occasion, which did not seem to emanate from any member of the investigating team; these were heard during periods of otherwise complete silence in total darkness (a strategy we employed periodically) when members of the party were stationed at intervals up and down the Tulip Staircase.

As regards the photograph itself: examination and investigation by Kodak and other photographic experts resulted in the unanimous conclusion that there was no trickery or manipulation as far as the transparency itself was concerned: the only logical explanation from the photographic point of view was that there must have been someone on the stairs, and against this we have the evidence of the Rev. and Mrs Hardy, quoted above; and the fact that the staircase is not open to the public and the museum warders are very strict and would certainly not countenance any dressing-up or playing about in the Queen's House.

One of the questions I asked our secretary to put to the Rev. and Mrs Hardy was: why had the photograph been taken at all? The Queen's House and in particular the beautifully proportioned hall on the ground floor – a perfect cube – with its fine mosaic floor and balcony seemed to me to be very photogenic, while the Tulip Staircase, leading off from a doorway in the hall, would not, I felt, be the feature most likely to attract an amateur photographer. The Hardys' answer I found typically straightforward and acceptable: Mrs Hardy had seen a photograph of the staircase in a book before their visit to England and she liked it so much that she wanted a photograph of it for herself. She discovered that it was impossible for her to obtain a photograph at the angle from which the picture she had seen had been taken, and she had to content herself with a shot of a small section of the stairway. In order to do this to best advantage it was necessary to crouch down at the side of the doorway and tilt the camera upwards, and this is what had been done.

We made efforts to identify the ring which the figure in the picture is wearing and particularly to establish whether it could have been associated with the unpopular and unhappy Henrietta Maria, Queen of England and daughter of Henry IV of France. She had close ties with the Queen's House and must have known the Tulip Staircase, but these investigations, which included consultations with the National Portrait Gallery and the Victoria and Albert Museum, were abortive.

Among the unsubstantiated stories of possibly paranormal activity in the vicinity of the Queen's House there is the evidence of a former museum attendant who found the doorway to the staircase (where the Hardys had taken their picture) uncomfortable and disturbing. Time and time again he found his attention being drawn in that direction when he was on duty and although he never saw anything unusual he always felt that there was something malevolent about the Tulip Staircase. This attendant claimed to have seen an unexplained figure in the tunnel which runs underneath the colonnade immediately outside the Queen's House; and he and other museum warders have heard footsteps, which they have been unable to account for, while on duty in the Queen's House. There is also an old and unsubstantiated story that many years ago a married couple, servants, living in rooms in the Queen's House, had a baby and, at a time when there was a domestic brawl of some kind, the infant was dashed to its death from the balcony to the mosaic tiled floor below. But the facts of this story, if it has a basis in fact, like so many other stories about the famous, and haunted, houses of London, are now lost in the mists of time and seem unlikely to be connected with any sinister phantom apparently creeping up the Tulip Staircase.

I consider the Hardys' photograph to be the most remarkable and interesting one I have seen in half a century of ghost hunting. Certainly, for me, it is far clearer and more convincing than the Raynham Hall photograph, and, although the night spent at the Queen's House by members of The Ghost Club produced no real evidence of a haunting, that is not to say that no ghost haunts that historic house. It is to be hoped that other visitors will take photographs of the spiral staircase at the spot where it leads into the main hall on the ground floor, in case they too get a surprise when the photograph is developed, for remember that this remarkable photograph was taken in daylight during normal museum opening hours. Needless to say I would be most interested to hear of any such photograph, whatever the result. If there *is* something haunting the Tulip Staircase at the Queen's House at Greenwich, it is possible that they, or it, can be photographed again.

Less well known but equally puzzling photographs in the possession of The Ghost Club include a kneeling monk or priest in the church of St Mary the Virgin, Woodford, Northants, taken when the church was empty, and a photograph taken at the church of St Botolph's in Bishopsgate, London, by a professional photographer and a Ghost Club member who arrived early for a wedding. He obtained permission to see inside the church before any guests arrived and decided to take a couple of photographs. He and his wife are adamant that the church was completely empty, but one of the photographs shows a tall female figure on the balcony. As with many such photographs there was no thought of ghosts at the time the photograph was taken and there appears to be no logical explanation.

There is also the curious photograph taken by Sherrard Cowper-Coles who co-operated with Admiral Moore, an early Ghost Club member, in a deliberate attempt to photograph ghosts. In daylight in the sitting-room of Rossel House, Sunbury-on-Thames, a photograph was taken of a vacant armchair by a window. After developing the photograph was seen to depict a transparent form, a man, seated in the armchair, resting his head on the back of the chair, the striped chintz covering clearly visible through the figure. There seems no doubt that the chair was vacant when the photograph was taken and that no one was in the room at the time, other than Sherrard Cowper-Coles and Admiral Moore – neither of whom remotely resembled the figure appearing in the photograph.

Then there is the curious photograph taken by the Rev.

R.S. Blance at Corroboree Rock, 100 miles from Alice Springs in Australia. The site is known as a place where Aborigines carried out gruelling initiation rites and ceremonies in the past but there was, we are told, no human activity of any kind anywhere in the area at the time that a ghostly figure appeared on this photograph.

An old house near Bristol was reputed to have been haunted for many years when Mr A.S. Palmer and an Army Officer undertook to spend a night in the house. All was quiet until 2.45 a.m. when a curious light seemed to appear in the room; Palmer took a photograph and the disembodied head of an evil-looking monk appeared on the resulting photograph.

Another well known ghost photograph is known as the Combermere Ghost. A lady friend of the family had taken Combermere Abbey for the summer and, being struck by the fine panelling in the library, she decided to take a photograph of it. When the photograph was developed there was the figure of a man sitting in the armchair on the left of the photograph: a figure that was recognised as that of Lord Combermere who had been in the habit of sitting in that particular chair but whose body was being buried some four miles away at the very time the photograph was taken. It will be noticed that the figure appears to have no legs.

Photographs, however, are not as persuasive as the best eye-witnessed accounts and in common with sound recordings are easily faked, sometimes very convincingly. Yet it would be an arrogant investigator who stated categorically that no ghost photograph is genuine; the difficulty is in deciding which are genuine and which are faked or the result of natural circumstances (unusually marked background, etc) in common in fact with so much evidence facing the psychical researcher. Whatever the chances of catching a ghost on film and whatever the likely explanations for such photographs as have been obtained, there is always the possibility of obtaining such photographs at haunted places, so it is always worthwhile for ghost hunters to have their cameras ready at all times and in any case to take a few photographs throughout the course of their investigations.

5 · Useful Forms of Questionnaires, Word-Association Tests and Instruction Leaflets for Ghost Hunters

There is a great deal that prospective ghost hunters can and should do before they even put a foot inside a haunted house. They must have some knowledge of the enormous amount of recorded evidence pertaining to ghosts and haunted houses that has accumulated and been carefully collected over the years; they must accept that parapsychology is a serious subject with enormous implications; a lot can be learnt from published works (see Recommended Books) and also by joining an organisation such as the Society for Psychical Research for The Ghost Club – but I have to stress that membership of the latter is normally by invitation only. If they undertake ghost hunting seriously (and only a foolish person would conduct such investigations in any other way) it is going to occupy a lot of time and perhaps money for, in all probability, very few satisfactory results and certainly little financial reward.

It is also important for the potential ghost hunter to be as sure as they can be that they are mentally suitable for the purposes of psychical investigation. They may have religious convictions or dogmatic views that make them unsuitable for the task. If, for example, they believe that all ghosts are 'spirits of the dead' or that there are no such things as ghosts for 'it is all in the mind', then it would be quite wrong and completely valueless for them to undertake ghost hunting.

Those who aspire to the former viewpoint rarely accept the possibility of any other explanation for ghosts (although the concept of a 'spirit' has no place in science), while those who hold the latter viewpoint are seemingly unshaken by overwhelming evidence from every part of the world, from all sorts of people, in every condition imaginable, since the beginning of recorded history. The one essential feature of a good ghost hunter is that he or she has an open mind, is prepared to listen, adjudge, sift, search and question everyone and everything. Preconceived ideas must give way to rational observation and investigation; the idea that there are ghosts may be difficult to accept but all the available mass of evidence overwhelmingly suggests that people who are healthy in mind and body do sometimes see ghosts. Ghosts cannot harm a person, but the unknown can be unnerving, so be prepared. Try to assess calmly all events and activities, always seeking a balanced and responsible attitude, and carefully and rationally noting everything that happens: the event, the time, the date, climatic conditions, the temperature, other people present and their positions, etc. To help in the recording and evaluation of people and possible psychic activity, there are a number of forms and schedules that have been found to be useful in ghost hunting.

Initially it is helpful to have in writing as much information as possible about a person who claims to have seen a ghost or has had a psychic experience. For this purpose I have devised a Form on the following lines; it can be altered and adjusted to suit individual requirements but something like this is extremely helpful in assessing a person and a case, both before and after an investigation.

QUESTIONNAIRE U1

Confidential   N.B.   This information will not be published or used in any way without previous permission.

Name: (capital letters please)   Age:

Address:

Telephone number: Occupation:

Please use a separate sheet of paper if there is insufficient room for any reply.

Describe what you saw and/or felt:

When did you (last) see the ghost? (Date and time)

Were you alone at the time? (Give names and addresses of anyone else present)

Where exactly did you see the ghost? (As exact as possible, please; e.g. 'in the front bedroom, on the left-hand side of the window, at 111 Rose Lane, Hatfield, Herts')

How far away from you was the figure?

Had you heard of a ghost being seen there before your experience? (If so, give names and addresses of anyone who told you about the ghost)

Do you know anyone who claims to have seen the ghost on a different occasion? (If so, give names and addresses and other details)

Did you feel anything or have a sensation of being touched? If 'yes', describe as fully as you can:

Were you asleep or nearly asleep just before the experience? If so, what woke you up?

How long did the ghost remain?

What was the lighting at the time?

Was there a mirror anywhere near and where was the nearest window?

Did the form you saw seem to be aware of your presence?

Did you have an animal with you at the time? If so, did it show any reaction?

Did you recognize the ghost? If so, was that person much in your thoughts lately?

Did the form appear gradually or suddenly?

Do you have good eyesight?

Had you been drinking?

Did you have a headache or were you feeling unwell?

Did any sound accompany the sighting?

Did the figure appear to be solid or transparent?

Was the appearance in colour or black-and-white?

Did the figure appear and act naturally? (e.g. through an open door) Or did it appear suddenly and inexplicably?

Can you describe the figure? (e.g. a tall man wearing a cape)

For how long did you see the figure?

How did it disappear?

Did you attempt to speak to the figure?

Did the figure speak to you or appear to try to do so?

If it did speak, what did it say?

What clothing was the figure wearing?

What was your immediate reaction when you saw the figure?

How did you feel when you saw the figure? (e.g. frightened, sad, unmoved, etc)

Did you notice any variation in the temperature:
  a) before you saw the figure?
  b) when the figure was present?
  c) after the figure had disappeared?

Had you had a long journey or were you very fatigued just before the experience?

Did you notice anything else unusual at the time? (e.g. any sound, a breeze, unusual quiet, etc)

Is the building or place where this happened reputed to be haunted?

To whom did you first report your experience?

How soon after the event?

What was his or her reaction?

Have you had any previous experiences of this kind? If so, when and where?

Do you know anyone who has had a similar experience anywhere?

Have you had any kind of psychic experience before?

If you were awake when you first saw the figure can you describe your state of mind immediately before the experience? (e.g. relaxed, apprehensive, happy, frightened, tense, sad, etc)

How did you feel immediately after the experience?

Did you feel a difference in the atmosphere afterwards? (e.g. warmer, lighter, darker, colder, etc)

Would you like to have the same experience again?

Please add any other information that you think may be revelant:

Date: Signature:

                               Witness: (name)
                                                           (address)

Thank you very much for your co-operation.

Such a Questionnaire can be modified or extended according to the circumstances and, since there are people to whom forms are anathema, it is wise to send a preliminary enquiry to ensure that they are willing to fill in and return such a Questionnaire. If they are not prepared to do so a personal visit may result in obtaining answers to some, if not all, of the questions. Afterwards the person concerned should be shown the filled-in form and asked whether they agree with the answers and whether they have anything to add. They should then be requested to sign the form, adding that the investigator will act as witness. Some of the questions are purposely very similar.

Word-Association Tests can also be very useful in certain cases. Nearly ten years ago now I had a message from an estate agent who told me that there were 'disturbances' at his home; objects were being moved all the time – would I like to come along and see for myself?

Within a couple of hours I was at his home, accompanied by my wife and two Ghost Club members. It is *always* advisable to take at least one reliable person with you on any investigation, preferably two extra people and, even more desirable, three, and include if possible a person of the opposite sex to your own. Single, uncorroborated testimony is worthless; when there is one corroborative witness that is something, but two are better and three better still.

When we arrived at the house we found so many people were present and living in the house that we found it a little confusing, but eventually we sorted everything out. There were Mr and Mrs White, the owners, who had lived in the house for nine years without any previous untoward incident; Mrs White's nephew, who was in Spain on holiday; and Abdul, a Arabian friend who suffered with his nerves and was under professional treatment which included depressive and sleeping tablets. These were the only permanent occupants of the house but also present during our initial visit were Mr and Mrs Evans (Mrs White's brother and sister-in-law) and their three children, Olive (twelve years old), Daphne (nine years) and William (three-and-a-half years). Also present were Mr and Mrs Jackson (the Whites' nineteen-year-old daughter and her husband) and their son Miles (twenty-four months). The Jacksons had arrived just over a week before from New York where they lived. The Evans family had arrived about four weeks previously on a six-month holiday. (I have altered the names of the people involved but all the other details are exactly as they occurred.)

The first unexplained incident had taken place two weeks before our visit. Abdul found his door locked and the key missing and he was unable to get into his room until Mrs White used her master key. Abdul was in the habit of keeping his room locked as this was thought best in view of the young children and the various pills and tablets he had in his room. On the same day two windows were found open which Mrs White kept closed: the bedroom window and one in the attic; the children Olive and Daphne were in the attic but said they had not opened the window. On that particular day the Whites had had the builders in so they decided that they must have left the windows open by mistake, although the builders denied this. In the case of the attic window, this was opened but the blind was drawn down. Next day, when the builders returned to clear up and take their things away, they discovered Abdul's bedroom key in the garden.

The same day the Whites' bedroom door was found locked and the key missing. Eventually they had to break down the door and purchase a new lock and keys. Two days later the door of the washroom downstairs, a small room containing the boiler, an ironing board, etc, was found locked from the inside when no one was inside to lock it! One of the children had to be helped through a small window to unlock it. Later the same day, when Mrs White was inside, the door 'locked itself' again. Four days later Mrs White was again in the washroom alone when the door became locked. She heard no click as when the door is locked normally and in fact one of the puzzling features of the case was that no noise of any kind was heard connected with any of the disturbances; another was that most of the happenings occurred in the afternoon, usually from 4 p.m. onwards; rarely in the evenings and never at night.

The following day Abdul's room was disturbed. He was studying engineering and seemed to be a quiet, very pleasant and meticuously tidy individual. This particular day he had to spend at the hospital, and while he was away Mrs White had occasion to take a parcel of books into his room. She was astonished to find the room in a state of confusion; the bedclothes were unmade, the radio set was on the floor, his pipe and ashtray were not in their accustomed places, his dressing-gown and a pair of trousers (usually hanging on a hook behind the door) were thrown on the floor and his prayer mat (he was a deeply religious Moslem) was screwed up on the floor. Mrs White tidied the room, taking perhaps five minutes, and then returned downstairs; thirty minutes later she took something up to Abdul's room and found it exactly as it was previously – everything in a mess! Again Mrs White tidied the room and returned downstairs, very puzzled. Her brother then arrived from Jamaica and Mrs White lost no time in telling him and her sister-in-law about the peculiar happenings; and together they saw that the room was perfectly in order. Fifteen minutes after Mrs White and her brother and sister-in-law had seen the room in good order, Abdul returned from the hospital and found the room yet again in disorder! In addition this time some of his books had been pulled out of the bookcase. They all left the room as it was and went downstairs. Three minutes later they returned and the books had been put back into the bookcase, other things had been hurriedly moved, seemingly to their correct places; the prayer mat, for example, was back in its proper place but askew; the bedclothes, however, were still ruffled. Mrs White felt that someone or something had tried to tidy the room, hurriedly. Abdul swore nothing like this had ever happened before.

Next day (a Friday) the room above Abdul's was found locked and the key was missing. The closet in the hall was also found locked and the key missing; later this lock was removed so that the door could be opened, and the useless old lock was placed on a shelf nearby. Several times subsequently this lock was found placed back in position on the closet door and the three screws partially screwed in, as it would be possible to do with one's fingers. Once the lock was found with old and rusty hair-pins in the screw-holes. After that Mrs Jackson kept all the keys. The same night the three wardrobe doors in Mr and Mrs Whites' room were found locked and the keys missing, when they went to bed. They had to force the locks. That night Mrs White, not knowing what to do, telephoned her doctor who suggested she contact the College of Psychic Studies, which she tried to do next day but could obtain no reply. The following day she did get through and they gave her my name.

That same Friday Olive, the twelve-year-old, said she was on the second step from the top of the first flight of stairs and facing Abdul's room where the door was open and she saw a book float out of the bookcase, float upwards some six inches and then slowly and silently drop to the floor in front of the bookcase. Abdul was annoyed and disturbed by this happening and said whatever force had removed the book would have to put it back again. He prayed and concentrated in his room but the book remained on the floor all night and next morning it was still there. After breakfast Mrs White went up to his room and returned asking Abdul whether anything had happened to the book. He said, 'No, it is still on the floor, leave it there.' But Mrs White had found it replaced in position in the bookcase. Abdul was very pleased and felt it had been replaced in answer to his prayers.

The following day, a Saturday, the disturbances took a more serious turn and Mrs White found the thermostat on the boiler turned up to 180°F. This happened again after it had been corrected, and then the whole family went out to a christening party. When they returned nothing had been moved or interfered with. Next day, a Sunday, Mr White thought he would make a determined search for the missing keys, and eventually he found some of them right at the bottom of the linen basket, and others tucked away among clothes in a chest on the landing. The same day some of the clothes in this chest were found taken out and placed on the floor or on top of the chest, and this too happened several times. The Whites had guests next day and they were present when the clothes were found out of the chest. We were told all the children were in the garden at the time. The same day the thermostat was again turned up and the electric boiler switch turned off. Also, the drawers in the dressing-table of Mr and Mrs Jackson were found removed and on their sides in front of the dressing-table, and five minutes after Mr White had passed the chest on the landing it was found with some clothes hanging out of it. This was also five minutes after the dressing-table drawers were found removed. Half-an-hour later some clothes were found taken entirely out of the chest, which was in fact emptied.

The following day, a Monday, Mr and Mrs White decided to tempt the poltergeist, and taking the closet lock, which had again been moved, they tied it to the dinner gong in such a way that if it was touched the gong would sound. Soon afterwards all four electric burners on the oven were found turned full on and were red-hot. When Mrs White went upstairs to tell the rest of the family Olive came in from the garden and found two kitchen chairs overturned; when she came downstairs again Mrs White found three chairs upturned in the television room. The same day a long net curtain on the second flight of stairs was found draped across the stairs; on this occasion little $3\frac{1}{2}$-year-old William went to his aunt and asked her why she had her curtains like that! Also the closet cupboards were again locked and these keys were never found. Once the cat brought in a dead bird and, when the children went to bury it in the garden, they found a missing key.

On our first visit, after an examination of the entire property, I arranged for everyone to be downstairs and I sat so that I could see the stairs. It was agreed that no one would leave the room but, after about half-an-hour, as we sat quietly talking, I noticed Mrs Jackson take her little son upstairs to change him and Olive trailed along behind her. Since the 'control', such as it was, had been broken, I closed the door and discontinued my watch on the stairway. A few moments later I was called upstairs and shown some clothes hanging half-way out of the chest. Daphne had gone upstairs before me and said she did not notice whether or not the clothes were hanging out, but both Mrs Jackson and Olive said they saw them when they emerged from the bedroom.

With all this information I said we would like to think about the case and arranged to return in three days' time. This we did, and by then I felt that Olive was, consciously or unconsciously, responsible for most of the happenings. Certainly she *could* have been responsible for most of them and I thought it likely that she had become bored with playing with much younger children and *might* be doing all this to attract attention. In view of the possibility that she might be the nexus of the poltergeist I decided to test her ESP and we ran through two series of tests with Zener cards. Chance expectation would be ten and she scored thirteen each time; Daphne and Mrs White and Mrs Jackson all scored no more than might be expected by chance, and little William was also high – although of course many, many runs through the cards are required before any real idea of a subject's ESP can be established. I also gave Olive a simple Word-Association Test which I had compiled. This comprised a list of simple words which I read out, one at a time, and asked her to give me the first response that came into her mind. I inserted some key words such as 'Arab', 'lock', 'book', 'keys' and 'baby' among a wealth of irrelevant words such as 'ball', 'yellow', 'Italy', 'desk', 'pencil' and some fifty other words. Her responses to the key words left me in no doubt that she was, unconsciously, jealous of the baby and had almost certainly been responsible for the movement of objects reported to me, perhaps in a state of disassociation. In fact the Word-Association Test provided few surprises and I told *all* the occupants that I had discovered a great deal about what had been happening, but I believed that the disturbances had reached their zenith just before our first visit and I thought that little further would happen. A few days later I was pleased to hear that nothing had occurred since our visits. I left it that the Whites would contact me if anything further took place, but I had no further word from them. It was an interesting little episode in ghost hunting although perhaps more psychological than paranormal.

There is also an Intuitive Word-Association Test which I have found useful in helping to decide whether or not a subject may be intuitive, likely to rely on mental perception without

84

reasoning and may possibly be psychic. Against each of the twelve key words there are four possibly associated words and the subject is asked to choose the one of the four in each case which is their immediate reaction to the key word. The twelve key words at the end are those which are accepted as indicating an individual with intuitive perception. The higher the 'score' of correct answers the more intuitive, and possibly psychic, the subject is likely to be; any other answers are irrelevant.

INTUITIVE WORD-ASSOCIATION TEST

Key words	Four possible associated words
1) White	*a*) sunlight *b*) snow *c*) angel *d*) black
2) Two	*a*) both *b*) one *c*) none *d*) astral
3) Star	*a*) snake *b*) comet *c*) pentagram *d*) shine
4) Wood	*a*) longevity *b*) tree *c*) fire *d*) plank
5) Milk	*a*) honey *b*) baby *c*) cup *d*) friendship
6) Coins	*a*) earth *b*) treasure *c*) enmity *d*) purse

7) Anchor	*a*) restriction
	b) security
	c) home
	d) love

8) Violets	*a*) grave
	b) perfume
	c) blue
	d) success

9) Sword	*a*) war
	b) cut
	c) air
	d) metal

10) Giant	*a*) monster
	b) legend
	c) bible
	d) warrior

11) Peacock	*a*) feather
	b) pride
	c) envy
	d) beautiful children

12) Devil	*a*) ritual
	b) destroy
	c) sacrifice
	d) creator

The correct intuitive words are said to be: 1(d) black; 2(b) one; 3(a) snake; 4(a) longevity; 5(d) friendship; 6(a) earth; 7(b) security; 8(d) success; 9(c) air; 10(c) bible; 11(d) beautiful children; 12(d) creator. These words are supposed to be psychically associated with the key words, through either supposed dream significance, positive and negative relationships or magical associations. Any other choice is said to indicate an earthly level of relationship.

Telepathic tests are also useful in coming to some sort of decision as to the psychic awareness of a subject or inhabitant of a haunted house. Spontaneous telepathy is now generally accepted, and it seems likely that telepathic powers play a part in some so-called hauntings. Packets of 25 Zener Cards containing five cards depicting a circle, a square, a star, a cross, and wavy lines, are obtainable from the Society for Psychical Research, and so are pre-printed ESP scoresheets. Distance makes no difference in tests for telepathy, although if the sender (or 'agent') and the receiver are in the same room precautions will naturally be taken to ensure that the target card is not reflected or is visible in any way to the receiver or percipient. If the percipient is in another room an assistant should be in the same room to ensure that the test is strictly controlled. The cards are shuffled (or 'randomized') and, while the investigator or his assistant (the 'agent') turns the cards face upwards one at a time, the person being tested (the 'percipient') records his or her guesses while screened or otherwise separated from the agent and the cards. In assessing the possible presence of extra-sensory perception present in the percipient it is, of course, necessary to take into account chance expectation. In addition to being of some interest and assistance to an investigator in a haunted house investigation the use of such tests act as a diversion and tension-reducer, and usually all the occupants of a house can be persuaded to take part. Although a hint of extra-sensory powers may be suggested after only a few runs it will be appreciated that many dozens of runs are necessary before any real conclusions can be reached. Obviously anyone showing a persistently high score will be investigated further and, especially in poltergeist cases, the young persons in the household should be given the opportunity of several runs through the Zener cards, which, incidentally, were specially designed by Dr J.B. Rhine, the American parapsychologist, based on an idea suggested by a psychologist, Dr Zener.

Another example of the use of forms in ghost hunting is exemplified by the Questionnaire I compiled in connection with the Paranormal Phenomena Award which carried a prize of £25,000. The phenomena had to be produced under test conditions to the satisfaction of The Ghost Club Adjudicating Panel whose members included the Rev. Canon John Pearce-Higgins, vice-Provost of Southwark; John Rogers, CBE, MP; Dr Paul Tabori and Sir George Joy, KBE, CMG, former Governor of St Helena, in addition to myself. This is a verbatim copy of that particular Questionnaire. I should perhaps add that the award is no longer outstanding and sadly no demonstrable physical phenomena were produced to the satisfaction of the Adjudicating Panel.

PARANORMAL PHENOMENA AWARD

Questionnaire to applicants

Please answer all the questions below and return this form before September 1st 1970 to: The Ghost Club, c/o National Provincial Bank, Mayfair Branch, South Audley Street, London W1.

1) Which of the following types of paranormal (psychic) phenomena do you believe has occurred to you:
   a) The following forms of extra-sensory perception: clairvoyance; clairaudience; telepathy; precognition or allied effects.
   b) Psychometry (ability to describe owners of objects shown to you).
   c) The following forms of physical phenomena: materialisation; telekinesis (movement of objects at a distance); levitation; psychic photography; poltergeists or allied effects.
   d) Travelling clairvoyance (verifiable observation during out-of-the-body experiences).
2) How often, approximately, have these experiences occurred?
3) When was the most recent of these experiences?
4) Do you believe that the phenomenon you have described could occur in a place chosen by the Adjudicating Panel?
5) If so, are you willing to come to London on a specified date?
6) If this is not possible, what location or kind of location would be necessary?
7) Can the phenomenon be demonstrated, by you alone, to the Adjudicating Panel under simple controlled conditions specified by the Panel?
8) If not, what conditions would be required?
9) Have you taken part in previous controlled tests? If so, please give details.

10) Please give a brief summary of your paranormal experiences. (Note: continue on back of sheet or write on seperate sheet if space is inadequate.)

Name (in full): Permanent Address:
Telephone Number: Age: Sex: Occupation:
Marital status (single, married, widow, widower):

Declaration: I hereby accept the rules governing The Ghost Club Paranormal Award. I understand that the award may be made in a single sum, or divided, according to the decision of the Adjudicating Panel. I agree to pay all my own expenses involved in my demonstration, including travel. I agree to abide by the criteria established by the Adjudicating Panel for my demonstration. I accept that all literary, film and television rights to the story of my demonstration and award belong exclusively to The Ghost Club and I accept that the decisions of the Adjudicating Panel are final.

Signed: Date:

During the course of his investigations at Borley Rectory, long known as 'the most haunted house in England', Mr Harry Price, one-time Chairman of The Ghost Club, devised a 'Haunted House Declaration Form' which I have never found bettered.

'HAUNTED HOUSE' DECLARATION FORM

I, the Undersigned, in consideration of having had my services accepted as an Official Observer, make the following Declaration:

1) I will fulfil all conditions and instructions, verbal and written, which are given to me.
2) I will pay my own expenses connected with the investigation.
3) I am not connected with the Press in any way.
4) I will not convey to any person the name or location of the alleged Haunted House.
5) I will not write, or cause to be written, any account of my

visit/s to the Haunted House, and will not lecture on my experiences.

6) I will not photograph or sketch any part of the Haunted House or grounds without written permission.

7) I will not allow any person to accompany me on my Investigation who has not signed the Declaration Form.

8) I will fulfil my obligations as regards Observational Periods, at the times and on the dates as arranged.

9) I will furnish a Report after each Observational Period.

10) I will not use the Telephone installed in the House except for the purpose of reporting phenomena to the person or persons whose names have been given to me, or for requesting assistance from those persons.

11) I will lock all doors and fasten all windows on my leaving the House, and will deposit key/s to person as directed.

Date: Signed:

During the course of the Borley investigation Harry Price also produced a Blue Book of Instructions for his Observers, and this too I reproduce since the booklet has become excessively rare and it contains much sound advice, although it is obviously intended to apply only to the investigations at Borley.

THE BLUE BOOK: INSTRUCTIONS FOR OBSERVERS (PRIVATE AND CONFIDENTIAL)

1) Attend carefully to all written and verbal instructions, and carry out to the letter.

2) Each Observer should provide himself with the following articles, in addition to night clothes, etc; note-book, pencils, good watch with second hand, candle and matches, pocket torch, brandy flask, sandwiches, etc. If he possesses a camera, this can be used. Rubber or felt-soled shoes should be worn.

3) When going on duty, search the house thoroughly, close and fasten all doors and windows. If thought necessary, these can be sealed.

4) Visit all rooms, etc, at intervals of about one hour, unless circumstances call for your presence in any particular part

of the house or grounds. Before going on duty at each period, inspect grounds.

5) Occasionally extinguish all lights, wait in complete darkness (varying your observation post), and remain perfectly quiet.

6) Make a point of taking meals at same times each day or night. Depart from this rule if circumstances warrant.

7) Make the fullest notes of the slightest unusual sound or occurrence.

8) Take exact times of all sounds or happenings; also make notes of your own movements, with exact times. Record weather conditions.

9) Frequently examine grounds, and, occasionally, watch windows of house from exterior of building.

10) If with companion, both he and you should act in unison (in order to have a witness), unless circumstances determine otherwise. If several Observers present, party can be divided between house and grounds.

11) For one half-hour before, and half-hour after dusk, take up position in Summer-house. Remain perfectly quiet, and watch the 'Nun's Walk' on far side of lawn. It is this path that a black, draped figure is said to frequent.

12) If phenomena appear strong, or if experiencing a succession of unusual events, immediately communicate with one of the persons whose telephone numbers have been handed to you. Detail exact happenings. Expert assistance, or further instructions, will be sent to you.

13) Establish your base in one room, and keep all your equipment, etc, at this post. This will prevent your hunting for an article when wanted in an emergency.

14) Keep the torch *in your pocket always*, whether in or out of the house. Be careful with all lights, matches, cigarette ends, etc.

15) Should strangers call, be courteous to them. Do not permit them to enter the house; do not encourage them to remain; *on no account give them information or opinions* of any sort. This applies to villagers, hotel staff, etc, equally.

16) Regarding meals: you should come provided each day with sandwiches, etc, and hot drinks in a vacuum flask. A rest can be obtained on the camp bed provided, but excellent meals and beds can be procured at 'The Bull', Long

Melford (2½ miles), or at Sudbury (2¼ miles). It should be possible to obtain sufficient rest during the 24 hours, but, if two are on duty, take turns at resting, and wake your companion if anything unusual occurs. Leave your car in the appointed place, screened from the road.

17) When asked to take charge of instruments, examine them regularly with torch, and record readings and times in note-book. Carefully note anything which may appear unusual. Change charts when necessary, marking on each the time it was changed, and date.

18) Spend at least a portion of the day and night (in complete darkness) in the Blue Room.

19) No Observer is permitted to take a friend to the house, unless permission has been given, and the necessary Declaration Form signed.

20) Your report and notes should be posted to the Honorary Secretary, University of London Council for Psychical Investigation, 19 Berkeley Street, Mayfair, W1, as soon as possible after you have completed your 'watch'.

Possible phenomena which may be experienced. There is some evidence for all of these alleged manifestations during the past forty years.

BELL-RINGING. If a bell rings, immediately ascertain which bell, and from what room or place the 'pull' was operated. Note if bell-pull is in motion, and record duration of ringing and exact time.

MOVEMENT OF OBJECTS. When going on duty, see that objects are on chalked outlines and check frequently. When an object is heard to fall, immediately ascertain in which room object has fallen, and draw rough plan of room, showing the direction of flight. Estimate approximate force expended, and, if object *seen* in flight, note speed, course, force, and trajectory. Examine object and restore to chalked outline.

FOOTSTEPS. If footsteps are heard, try to judge direction, note duration, and record type (heavy, soft, pattering, shuffling, etc), and at what time they were heard.

FORMS OR APPARITIONS. If seen, *do not move and on no account approach the figure*. Note exact method of appearance. Observe figure carefully, watch all movements, rate and manner of progression, etc. Note duration of appearance, colour, form, size, how dressed, and whether solid or transparent. If carrying camera with film ready for exposing, quietly 'snap' the figure, but make no sound and do not move. If figure speaks, *do not approach*, but ascertain name, age, sex, origin, cause of visit, if in trouble, and possible alleviation. Inquire if it is a spirit. Ask figure to return, suggesting exact time and place. Do not move until figure disappears. Note exact method of vanishing. If through an open door, quietly follow. If through solid object (such as wall) ascertain if still visible on other side. Make the very fullest notes of the incident. The 'nun' is alleged to walk regularly along the 'Nun's Walk' in grounds. (See Instruction No. 11.)

RAPS OR KNOCKS. Ascertain exact location and intensity, and whether soft or percussive. Imitate knocks with knuckles or foot, and note whether your signals are duplicated. If so, say aloud that you would like a number of questions answered, and that the 'entity' can reply by giving one rap for 'yes', two for 'no, and three for 'doubtful or unknown'. Endeavour by these means to ascertain name, age, sex, condition, etc. Ask 'entity' to knock at a letter while you call over the alphabet. Information can thus be conveyed, and intelligent sentences formed. Ask 'entity' to return, making definite appointment. It is alleged that knocks can frequently be heard in the Blue Room. (See Instruction No. 18.)

PERFUMES. If air becomes scented, try to identify perfume, and ascertain whether it is general or localized. Look for any dampness.

LIGHTS. If lights are seen, note mode of appearance, judge exact position in room or grounds, size, shape, height from ground, duration, colour, and whether lambent or percussive. If travelling, direction and trajectory, and method of disappearance. Note whether odour accompanies lights.

APPORTS (objects abnormally brought or precipitated into house). Note exact time of arrival, if possible, and endeavour to ascertain their origin. Carefully preserve and continue inquiries.

DISAPPEARANCES. Note under what conditions the object disappeared, exact time of disappearance, and if accompanied by sounds of any sort. Search for object and note if, how, and when it makes its reappearance.

THERMAL VARIATIONS. Transmitting thermographs are used for recording changes of temperature. These should be read frequently. (See Instruction No. 17.)

EXTERIOR OF HOUSE

The above suggestions apply equally in the case of phenomena occurring *outside* the house. But poltergeist phenomena (such as stone-throwing) outside the house may be observed from within the building. The fullest particulars concerning such phenomena should be recorded.

IMPORTANT NOTE

Although some – or all – of the above phenomena may be observed, it is very important that the greatest effort should be made to ascertain whether such manifestations are due to normal causes, such as rats, small boys, the villagers, the wind, wood shrinking, the Death Watch beetle, farm animals nosing the doors, etc, trees brushing against the windows, birds in the chimney-stack or between double walls, etc.

A high percentage of ghost hunting time is spent simply watching and waiting and attending to routine matters concerning the investigation; there is also a lot of preparatory work, and this includes the preparation of relevant Questionnaires, pertinent Leaflets of Instructions and note-taking – all are of inestimable value when the time comes to evaluate and write-up the case.

6 · The Problem of The Poltergeist

We have already looked briefly at 'poltergeists', but the very strange happenings usually attributed to them are among the commonest 'ghostly' manifestations reported today, and we should consider them in greater depth. In common with other paranormal activity they occur in old houses, new houses, large houses, small houses, among rich people and poor people, intelligent people and ignorant people, old people and young people, although there is often an adolescent girl or boy associated with the case, and when this young person reaches full adulthood the 'poltergeistic' disturbances completely cease. There seem to be very good grounds for regarding poltergeist activity as some form of excess energy that is occasionally created in some way which we do not yet understand, in the presence of a young person (usually). This energy 'explodes' resulting in all sorts of meaningless, annoying and irritating happenings. There does not seem to be much evidence to suggest that poltergeists have anything to do with dead persons.

So-called poltergeists make their presence known by mysterious bangs and crashes, unpleasant smells, movement of heavy furniture and (usually) light objects, coldness, inexplicable fires and the appearance of water, the appearance and disappearance of objects, the levitation (occasionally) and touching (frequently) of people, sometimes inexplicable and undecipherable voices and stone-throwing. All or any of these and other disturbances are known as poltergeist phenomena or, to the parapsychologist, 'recurrent spontaneous psychokinesis' (RSPK).

The outbreak of poltergeist disturbances usually starts suddenly, continues for a few hours, a few days, sometimes a few weeks, and then ceases as mysteriously as it began. Since there is often an adolescent in the affected household, not infrequently a subnormal or disabled person, it has long been thought the happenings are the result of some kind of excess adolescent energy, for the adolescent is invariably the centre or nexus of the happenings; but recent cases have occurred in premises only occupied by elderly people, and it is now thought that frustration, loneliness and a feeling of isolation are some of the ingredients contributing to poltergeist activity.

What is certain is that poltergeists are a reality, they have occurred throughout history and have been copiously studied and reported from the beginning of recorded history. In the twelfth century and for years afterwards they were regarded as an evil force created by the Devil. Numerous exorcisms were carried out, and are still sometimes conducted today, but they rarely, if ever, have any lasting effect. It is likely that the impressive and solemn service has the effect of impressing the human occupants of the premises, for a time, and then the disturbances usually continue for their alloted span, whatever that may be. But why does it cease? Perhaps, as Ghost Clubber Dr A.R.G. Owen has suggested, the activity eventually ceases because it is not a disease, but the cure.

Beds and bedrooms seem to have a fascination for poltergeists and it may be that the relaxed environment of the sleeping epicentre or focus of the disturbances contributes to whatever is necessary to produce the energy required, and of course energy is involved; energy must be used to move objects. In all the poltergeist cases I have personally investigated objects that had moved 'by themselves' ended up at a lower level than that at which they started, thereby using the minimum of energy. Nevertheless some energy is involved and sometimes the strength and force that is at work is quite considerable.

In the Enfield case (1977–8) part of a gas fire was wrenched out of the fireplace, a heavy chest of drawers was moved and also a double bed. Interestingly enough, poltergeist-projected objects have been seen moving, but they never seem to be seen beginning to move. Objects have been seen in flight many times – indeed they have been photographed in flight – but it is almost as if the human eye is a deterrent, for frequently when an object is seen in flight it drops to the floor and is still. Often such objects are warm to the touch. There is no really good evidence of a poltergeist-projected object seen to begin movement.

The big question about poltergeists is where do they store the energy required to move objects? They may obtain it, in

ove left: Fox Tower, Farnham Castle, long said to be haunted by the ghost of Bishop Morley (died 1684) who lived · years in a small cell-like room here. (Photo: Edward Griffiths.)

ove right: Bourne Mill, one of many haunted properties at Farnham, Surrey. (Photo: Edward Griffiths.)

...amber, Sussex, a village where ghostly children run after passers-by and vanish when they are spoken to. (Photo: ...ris Underwood.)

The foyer of the old Castle Theatre, Farnham, where a suicide is said to have been committed from the curved beam and where many people have experienced curious sensations. These two photographs were taken within seconds wh the photographer thought the exposure was incorrect. No explanation has been discovered for the white markings or one of the photographs. (Photo: John Birch.)

The plaque dedicated to the ghost nun at Chicksands Priory, Clophill, Bedfordshire. (Photo: Tony Broughall.)

The 'haunted gallery' at Chicksands Priory, Clophill, Bedfordshire, where a ghost nun, Bertha Rosaca, is said to walk each 17 August. (Photo: Tony Broughall.)

The puzzling photograph taken on the stairway at Raynham Hall, Norfolk; possibly the famous 'Brown Lady'. (Photo: The Ghost Club.)

The curious photograph taken in 1959 at Corroboree Rock, Australia. No one was visible when the photograph was taken. (Photo: Keystone.)

A typical 'spirit' photograph of the 1920s. (Photo: The Ghost Club.)

The Old City Hall, Queen Street West, Toronto (photographed in about 1914), where many strange happenings have been reported over the years. (Photo: City of Toronto Archives.)

The eerie cellars of the former British Embassy at The Hague, the scene of curious happenings for over sixty years. (Photo: Department of the Environment.)

An example of the work of 'spirit' photographer William Hope (1863-1933). (Photo: The Ghost Club.)

Haunted Lake Leane, Killarney, Co. Kerry, where the ghost of Irish hero O'Donoghue is said to glide over the waters once a year. (Photo: Irish Tourist Board.)

The White House, Washington, where several ghosts have been reliably reported. (Photo: United States Travel Service.)

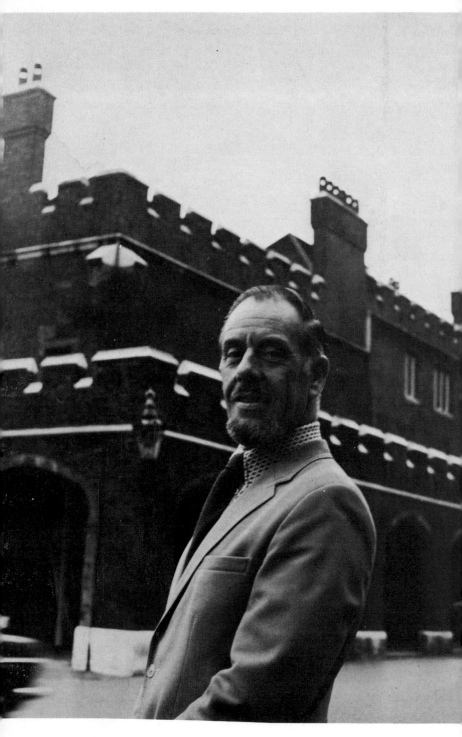

The author outside St James's Palace, where the ghost of a murdered man reportedly reappears each 13 May. (Photo Thomson Newspapers.)

some way which we do not understand, from an adolescent or elderly person, but where is it stored? Could it be that the 'cold spots' so frequently encountered in cases of poltergeist infestation provide us with a clue? A lot more work is necessary in the sympathetic investigation of poltergeist activity.

Poltergeist disturbances seem often to be a nuisance to the particular household, and so vary from case to case. During the course of a poltergeist haunting at Ham, between Richmond and Kingston in Surrey, the reported disturbances included interference with any clock or watch in the bedroom of the solitary inhabitant, so all clocks and watches were removed from the bedroom, causing considerable inconvenience to the elderly occupant. In another case I investigated, objects belonging to the child of the family – but not the adopted child – were interfered with, which caused distress to the whole family.

It seems likely that severe stress is the spark and a firm but sympathetic approach is the right one for poltergeist cases. What is certain is that poltergeist activity is too widely reported and carefully investigated to be ignored or explained away as conscious fraud.

Extensive examination of poltergeist activity by Dr George Owen has resulted in little evidence to support the idea that poltergeist activity is a completely independent entity; rather it would appear likely that the activity is an extension of the personality of the adolescent usually at the centre of the case.

The word 'poltergeist' is an obsolete German word meaning 'noise-spirit'; it is now used to differentiate 'poltergeist activity' from other kinds of spontaneous paranormal activity such as hauntings. Poltergeist activity is always of limited duration, but it is in effect a case of a haunted person as opposed to a haunted house; this has been repeatedly demonstrated by temporarily removing the 'poltergeist adolescent' or 'nexus' of the disturbances to another environment when, it has been found, the disturbances take place there and cease at the former residence of the adolescent.

Great tact and sympathetic understanding is necessary in any investigation of poltergeist activity; the young person concerned is sometimes frightened by what is happening and the adults in the household are likely to be puzzled and angry and inclined to blame the young person entirely or look for a spiritual or objective cause unconnected with their son or daughter. Interesting as poltergeist phenomena may be to the investigator, he or she must always remember that a child is not a showpiece or an experimental animal, rather it is a case of a human being who is ill or in trouble.

Poltergeist activity is often limited to the production of noises (tappings, knocks, bumps, dragging and rustling noises) and movement of objects. Frequently these occur in the immediate vicinity of the poltergeist subject. For example, if the young person is in bed, the noises seem to originate from the bed itself and the raps and knockings may cause the bed to vibrate; similarly the bedclothes, pillows and articles near to the bed are likely to move without anyone being near them. While any noise or movement of an object can take place at any time in a poltergeist infestation, there are likely to be periods of quiet followed by little bursts of activity, almost as though the requisite energy is building up.

During any investigation of alleged poltergeist activity, as with all other types of spontaneous psychic phenomena, it is important to look for a natural or physical explanation before considering the possibility of a supernormal cause for the activity. Apart from deliberate fraud, hallucination and un-reliable observation and exaggeration, it should be borne in mind that some curious noises can be caused by such mundane matters as underground water and central heating systems. Doors often open by themselves if they are not carefully closed, others close by themselves due to the way they have been hung or the weight of the door itself or certain draughts. Vibration from road or rail traffic or aircraft can, in certain cases, cause the movement of objects; for example a plate may be moved minutely by vibration and gradually edge off a shelf; rodents and other nocturnal creatures can make some very strange noises. I remember one 'haunting' I investigated where the occupants reported a breathing or wheezing noise that was often, but not always, heard in the front room of the house, especially during the evening. I discovered that an owl had taken a liking to their front porch and frequently perched there, waiting for some unsuspecting prey, and his heavy breathing could only be heard in the front room of the house.

There is often an element of aggression in poltergeist cases and it is known that anxiety promotes aggression. It is advisable to find out as much as possible about the people occupying a house plagued by a poltergeist, and not infrequently a sympathetic personal interest in the poltergeist activity will hasten the ending of the trouble. Publicising the matter and giving the impression that it affects or frightens the investigator or anyone else frequently seems to cause an increase in the strength and frequency of the curious incidents.

The religious beliefs and outlooks of the inhabitants can often help the investigator to help the occupants. Where a certain religious ritual is acceptable to the subconscious mind of the poltergeist subject, it will often be found that once definite action is taken – such as calling in a priest, a vicar, a medium, a psychologist, or a doctor – the disturbances completely cease. On the other hand there is often a lack of respect for objects of sanctity and in many instances attempts at exorcism, intercession, prayers, rites and the employment of sacred objects have seemed to provoke the poltergeist to anger and renewed activity. There is little doubt that there is usually a psychological element in poltergeist activity, but let us look at some of the curious poltergeist hauntings from several parts of the world.

Cesare Lombroso, the founder of criminology, investigated a poltergeist disturbance at Turin in 1900, having heard that strange happenings had been reported from the cellar of a wine shop in the Via Brava. Lombroso lit six candles and placed them in various parts of the cellar. He then saw numerous bottles move from the shelves on which they were standing and end up on the ground, landing lightly, 'as if they had been carried'. Always it seems he saw the bottles as they were about to land, not as they began to move from the shelves. Having carefully examined all the bottles and ascertained that there was no thread or wire attached that might have accounted for the movement, Professor Lombroso came to the conclusion that the poltergeist phenomena were genuine and occurred through a pot boy employed by the wine shop. Another employee, an accountant, told Lombroso that he had seen both full and empty wine bottles crack and break in front of his eyes, and then the fragments continued to crumble. This could hardly be a description of bottles of wine exploding due to fermentation, although this possibility too was explored.

A very full account of poltergeist activity, and in particular spontaneous and violent rappings on the walls and floors of a country villa in the south of Sweden, has been written up by Hjalmar Wijk of Gothenburg in conjunction with Dr Paul Bjerre. The disturbances only took place in the vicinity of Karin, a bright and happy young lady.

The affair was found to date from attacks of fainting and shaking spells that Karin suddenly suffered several times a day, and she was confined to her bed. After some weeks the attacks became less frequent but they were followed by periods of intense anxiety and tremors that began in the arms and extended to the rest of her body. After some months these attacks became weaker and finally ceased. Karin now moved to a villa that had a bad reputation; it was said that unexplained lights and strange noises had long been associated with the place. Soon after they moved in Karin and two other people heard knockings; and knocks and rappings for which no natural explanation was ever discovered continued to be heard intermittently for the next few months. Sometimes Karin had the feeling of an invisible presence in the room and a pattering noise, something like a shoe or boot sliding over the floor, was heard by Karin and another occupant.

During a visit by two investigators strong and loud knocking sounds were heard, both men being satisfied that the knocks were paranormal in origin. Under hypnosis Karin was requested to arrange for three raps at a certain times and the knocks were duly heard by four witnesses. This experiment was repeated on several occasions. After many sessions of hypnosis the experimenters asked for four raps and then for all disturbances to cease. Eventually the rappings became weaker and, after returning in strength for a short period, they did completely cease.

A poltergeist case in Poona, India, has become something of a classic, and the reported phenomena included levitation and considerable movement of objects. One witness, Dr J.D. Jenkins, reported: '... it was broad daylight ... a small table, apparently untouched by anyone, came hobbling across the room ... imprisoning the Major in his chair. That evening ... the salt cellar began to dance before our eyes. The whole contents of the table were cleared by unseen hands.'

Another witness, Miss Kohn, commented on the fact that

Damodar Bapat, a boy of eight, seemed to be the focus of the disturbances. One evening, as the boy was undressing for bed, a small glass jar which stood among other jars in a closed cupboard in the dining room was suddenly hurled from the room into Miss Kohn's bedroom. In order to land where it did, the jar must have turned a corner. On landing it broke into many pieces.

On another occasion when Miss Kohn and a friend were having tea in the dining room, Damodar went into Miss Kohn's bedroom; at the same moment a small screw-top jar containing ink was hurled from her brother-in-law's study at the front of the house, across the dining room in which the two ladies were taking tea and into the bedroom where Damodar stood. This jar also broke on landing, spilling the ink.

Other bottles were thrown by 'invisible hands'; a heavy padlock was opened; a basket was thrown 'from a great height'; dozens of household articles disappeared or were moved: once 41 eggs completely disappeared. Sometimes a breakable article would land gently without breaking. Once a tin of shoe polish was missing, but appeared out of mid-air and landed without rolling at the feet of the person looking for it. Next day when the same person found the shoe polish was again missing, she called out, 'Shoe polish, please,' whereupon the tin of polish appeared and came to rest gently at her feet!

Several times coins fell from the air in broad daylight. Sometimes the coins were only seen when they fell but at other times Miss Kohn and others actually saw the money appear in the air, before it fell. The disturbances continued for some months and then ceased as mysteriously and inexplicably as they began.

Unexplained fires have been reported in many poltergeist cases. In the case concerning the Dagg family of Clarendon in the Province of Quebec, articles were moved, milk pans emptied, windows smashed, water appeared from nowhere, a little girl had her hair pulled, a gruff voice threatened the occupants, stones were thrown and fires broke out spontaneously – as many as eight occurring in one day, six being inside the house, burning the curtains, and two outside. This happened in daylight when the family and friends were present.

Among the many poltergeist cases I have personally investigated, one included unexplained outbreaks of fire. The Stringer family lived in Trafalgar Avenue, Peckham, London, and consisted of Graham and Vera and their three-year-old son Steven. Before she was married Vera lived at New Cross with her sister, and there unexplained movement of objects included the displacement of the lids from two large china ornaments that stood on the mantelpiece. Time and time again these deep-lipped lids were discovered removed from the vases and placed in the centre of the mantelpiece. Each sister thought the other had moved the lids until they both found that in fact neither had touched the vases. And still the lids were moved, scores of times in a matter of weeks, I was told.

Vera and her sister decided to try to find out what was happening, and they sat up throughout one night, determined to watch the vases the whole time, but of course they dozed off; when they opened their eyes the pot lids were once again in the middle of the mantelpiece! This time when Vera tried to replace them she discovered that she was unable to do so, even using both hands. Something seemed to be pushing up out of the vases to prevent the lids from being put back on. After about five minutes she tried again and then found no difficulty in replacing the lids.

At their Trafalgar Avenue home, at eleven o'clock one night, some toys belonging to their little boy were found alight on a chair by the window in the living room. After they had all retired to bed Vera suddenly said she could smell smoke, and the toys were found, blazing fiercely.

A year later, at Eastertime, Graham's mother bought some woollies for Steven and some stockings for Vera. They were left on the table in the dining room. Next morning, before any fire had been lit and before anyone had entered the dining room, Vera and Steven were out buying some hot cross buns, when the woollies were found alight. They were burned right through the middle down to the bottom, although the stockings, underneath the woollies, were unharmed.

Other fires were more serious, and one, in the main bedroom, had to be extinguished by the fire brigade who were unable to ascertain the cause of the fire. Another time Vera and Steven were in the garden when they chanced to look up at their little boy's bedroom window and saw the curtains alight; again the fire brigade had to be called and again they were unable to suggest how the curtains came to be alight. The police were equally baffled, and when I visited their home the Stringers told me they were not insured for fire because they could not find a company who would insure them. I examined several articles severely damaged by fire and although I deduced that it would have been theoretically possible for one of the family to have been responsible for most of the incidents, this did not apply to every event, and there were reported incidents that I could not conceive as being manufactured by any human hand. The disturbances became less and less frequent and eventually ceased. As with so many cases of reported poltergeist activity, it had run its course and then stopped.

On the continent Professor Hans Bender, of the University of Freiburg in West Germany has long been a leading investigator of poltergeist activity, and one of his outstanding investigations, the Rosenheim case of 1967–8, deserves special mention because of the interference with electrical equipment, manifestations that were investigated by experts and engineers well equipped to locate normal faults and defects. Neon lighting on a high ceiling repeatedly malfunctioned; electric light bulbs and strip lighting exploded; electric fuses blew without apparent cause; telephones acted curiously and at times almost impossibly, as when enormous numbers of calls were registered as having been made to the 'speaking clock', far more per minute than could actually be dialled and it seemed that mysterious bursts of energy were tripping the relays; electrical apparatus (tested and in perfect order) failed to function in the affected premises; a $1\frac{1}{2}$-volt battery registered 3 volts; and these happenings frequently occurred in the vicinity of a new employee, a nineteen-year-old girl. When she walked along the corridors electric lights, far above her head, began to swing, and this phenomenon was recorded on film. Frequently, when bulbs exploded for no apparent reason, the pieces flew towards the girl and the phenomena decreased in frequency as she passed.

Professor Bender tells me that towards the end of the case there seemed to be an intensification of the events, with paintings swinging and turning, drawers moving by themselves, documents being displaced, and a heavy cabinet twice moved from its position against a wall. The girl nexus of the disturbances grew more and more nervous until she finally displayed hysterical contractions in her arms and legs. When she was sent away from the premises, all was quiet, and when she finally left and moved away no further happenings occurred – although similar but less violent disturbances took place for a time in her new place of employment. The case is remarkable and important since it was fully investigated by parapsychologists and physicists in addition to telephone and electric supply engineers, and video recordings were obtained of some of the disturbances.

Guy Playfair, an investigator who explored and wrote up the curious Enfield poltergeist, has suggested that the evidence leads one to suppose that poltergeists do not seem to be a part of our dimension but to exist in a separate, unidentified area, and such a theory might explain the numerous reports of poltergeistic 'interpenetration of matter' as at Borley when bottles and other articles apparently passed through closed doors; the well-attested Ringcroft case where pot-hooks and other articles seemingly 'moved' through several walls; eggs that emptied themselves from a box while it was being sat upon in the Black Monk of Pontefract case; and there are many other instances. This 'teleportation' is only one weapon in the armament of the poltergeist, and personally I think an answer to poltergeist phenomena will be found without resorting to the fourth dimension – but I could be wrong!

Sometimes poltergeist activity is encountered in an otherwise routine haunting and I have come across several cases where there appears to be, for a brief period, an element of the poltergeist. Occasionally, as at Borley, there is reportedly a wealth of poltergeist-like activity taking place in a traditionally haunted house and the fascinating thing about Borley is that strange happenings are still being experienced there!

Borley Rectory, on the Essex-Suffolk border, was built by the Rev. H.D.E. Bull in 1863 (on the site of a previous rectory) and he added to the rambling building as his family increased. He was succeeded in 1892 by his son the Rev. Henry Foyster Bull (known as 'Harry'), who was succeeded in 1928 by the Rev. G. Eric Smith who was in turn succeeded by the Rev. Lionel A. Foyster in 1930 who left in 1935. In 1938 the property was destroyed by fire whereupon the entities seemed to transfer their activities to the rectory cottage and the church just across the road. Be that as it may, everyone who occupied Borley Rectory – the Bulls (two generations), the Smiths, the Foysters, Harry Price and his investigators, and the Gregsons (during whose ownership the fire occurred) – all reported hearing and seeing things they could not explain, and all the occupants during those 76 years considered the property to be a very haunted house.

The full story of the Borley haunting has already been told in four full-length books; it has been the subject of long chapters in a score of books; and it has been the source of several radio and television programmes and literally hundreds of lectures and articles in magazines throughout the world. Suffice it to say here that amid the wealth of extraordinary happenings at Borley (the ghost nun and six other ghostly figures; a phantom coach; audible phenomena that included voices, music, bell-ringing, footsteps and crashing sounds; visual phenomena that included the writing of messages on walls and scraps of paper; windows that mysteriously lit up; movement of objects and such miscellaneous phenomena as odours, coldness, touchings, and many other unexplained happenings) there was also reported to have been a lot of poltergeist activity: mysterious fires, matter-through-matter, objects disappearing and reappearing, displaced and projected articles, and unexplained sounds of practically every description.

Hardly a week goes by when I do not receive a letter asking me something about Borley or telling me something about this strange case, for there is no doubt that some people who visit the area to this day experience things which they are totally unable to explain. As I said at the end of a chapter devoted to the case in my book, *Hauntings* (1977), 'What is the answer to the mysteries of Borley? Some of the hundreds of reports of curious happenings can certainly be dismissed; perhaps some of the recorded noises have perfectly normal explanations; perhaps some of the sightings of the nun are the result of inaccurate observation, imagination or wishful thinking. But it does seem to me that of all the celebrated cases of haunting ... this remarkable and lengthy story has so many unanswerable problems, innumerable puzzles and strange incidents reported by responsible, independent, unbiased, sane and sensible witnesses that it stands alone in the annals of psychical research as a continuing problem for the materialist and an exciting challenge for the psychical researcher.'

Can we explain the poltergeist? No, we cannot, but we are beginning to understand the circumstances in which poltergeist activity is likely to be encountered. There is likely to be a young person or an elderly person who is not highly intelligent at the centre of the disturbances. There is likely to be someone in the household who is unwell or who has a poor health record or is of a neurotic disposition. There is often an air of frustration in a poltergeist-infested house and after all possible trickery and natural causes have been eliminated there is some evidence suggesting an independent entity, and rather more suggesting a kind of extension of the mind – an offshoot of adolescent intelligence perhaps – that originates entirely within the young person or the elderly person who is the poltergeist focus.

The frequency of a feeling of coldness; the preoccupation with bedrooms; the purposelessness and irrational and irritating activities; the fact that *most* poltergeist-projected objects move downwards and fall much more slowly than they would normally do under the influence of gravity alone; the apparent heating of objects moved by poltergeist force; the reason that poltergeists prefer the presence of some people and utterly refuse to 'perform' in the presence of others; the occasional cyclic element – these and many more aspects and problems will have to be solved before we can begin to explain the poltergeist. In the meantime the careful accumulation of good evidence is likely to hasten that inevitable day.

7 · Mediumship and Exorcism in Ghost Hunting

Mediums can sometimes be helpful in exploring a genuine haunting; these special people are psychically attuned to what to the rest of us is the unknown. These quiet, sensitive people who are so often right in what they feel and sense in haunted houses do have a part to play in certain cases; especially perhaps where individuals feel they are under attack from unseen forces.

Most mediums are honest and reliable people, but there are dishonest people who pose as mediums and who cheat and charge exorbitant fees. Organisations such as the College of Psychic Studies and the spiritualist periodical *Psychic News* can often advise people of a reliable medium in their particular area, as can, very often, a local spiritualist church.

If you are lucky enough to find a good medium it can be a very interesting exercise to take him or her along to a haunted house. It is perhaps necessary to keep a firm hold on one's imagination and to adopt a sympathetic but realistic approach to whatever may happen and to whatever may 'come through'. Nor should it be overlooked that not everyone can be a good 'sitter'; indeed there are those who consider 'sitting' to be an art in itself which has to be learnt, and many people fail altogether to learn it – and then wonder why they do not get any good results.

More than sixty years ago Dr Eric John Dingwall, sometime Research Officer for the Society for Psychical Research, warned that mediums 'are not always quite normal, and this is not in any derogatory sense, but simply as a fact'. Of course if they were quite normal they could hardly be mediums, but there is a more to it than that. Dr Dingwall, whom I talked with on many occasions, found mediums to be highly complex people, both emotionally and mentally, and, perhaps consequently, they are usually extremely suggestible and touchy; capable of warm friendships and strong dislikes; forgiving and without malice but with a strong sense of justice; often quick-tempered and frequently seemingly self-centred. Every medium is different but it is essential to get to know a medium, and discover as much as possible about their character, and that knowledge will help in adjudging anything that may happen pertaining to his or her mediumship.

If you choose to sit with a medium in a haunted house (as I have done on many occasions) you should do so with an open mind; preparing yourself for a serious undertaking – as indeed is the whole precept of ghost hunting – and it is important that the subject is not approached in any spirit of levity or silly curiosity; although every attempt must be made to obtain a relaxed and happy atmosphere. Do not hesitate to take what you consider to be legitimate precautions against fraudulent activity, for genuine mediums never object to tests, providing they understand what is happening and have faith in the integrity of the chief investigator.

It may well be that information coming through the medium seems to be nonsense, but this is not necessarily so; it could have something to do with the medium's mental process or it may refer to matters about which you are totally ignorant. At the same time you should not think that because you cannot understand how information comes or because it is original and previously unknown, that it must have come from beyond the grave. Always try to preserve a scientific attitude and use scientific methods; simply concentrate on collecting facts, classifying those facts and forming a theory that takes those facts into account. Never jump to conclusions on insufficient data and do cultivate the habit of making extensive notes, as soon after an event as possible.

To give the reader some idea of the kind of information that might come through a medium at a haunted house I quote verbatim the Report I received of a dated seance held in haunted Langenhoe church on the Essex marshes. The story of the Langenhoe haunt is contained in my volume *A Host of Hauntings* (1973); it is a case which I investigated over a period of several years. It had a number of unusual and interesting features, and perhaps one day I will publish the whole story including the typescripts of sittings and seances held at Bournemouth and elsewhere.

Very briefly, the haunting appeared to originate in a murder in the vicinity of the church and the hurried burial of the victim's body in the church precincts. Legend has it that many years ago an important local man became infatuated with a young girl and when she became pregnant he murdered her. During the course of an investigation that extended over twelve years I uncovered a wealth of evidence for the appearance of the apparition of a 'veiled girl' who was seen to walk from the priests' door round the side of the church and disappear into the solid wall of the church. There was also evidence that a similar form had been seen inside the church, at a spot corresponding to where the form would have been had she walked through the wall; and there were numerous accounts of strange happenings in and around the church that suggested a remarkable and in some ways unique case of haunting. I was fortunate in being involved almost from the beginning of the reported haunting, following it closely with the assistance of several helpers, and being in at the end, for eventually the haunted church was demolished.

This particular seance was carried out inside Langenhoe Church. It opened with prayers and hymn-singing at 9.30 p.m. and ended at 1.30 a.m. the following morning. Those present were Mrs Lampard, a medium from Bournemouth; Miss Cubitt; the Rev. John C. Dening and his sister; Steuart Kiernander (representing The Ghost Club); Leonard Sewell, who lived for a time on the site of Borley Rectory and was a first-class photographer; and Mrs Harris, who acted as note-taker.

Mrs Lampard (giving clairvoyance and receiving impressions from the past): 'The water nearer than at present. Boats. Priest blessed men before they went off to fight – Norman, Roman contact. More wooded land behind, water in front. Roman chief settled here with colony of people. Grew to love this part of the world. He had to leave but is drawn back here. Perhaps married (or whatever they did in those days) to a British girl. Form of a young woman behind Mr Kiernander. Frail figure in light garment, perhaps a summer dress; high drooping headgear. Now an old time clergyman. Full oval face, moustache, baldish, average height, dark, grey-streaked hair, straight nose and penetrating eyes. Girl is to do with farm. Conscious of fear. Man dressed like a knight, crusader, has been kneeling in front of the side altar. Stands up. There is a cross in the panel of his mail. He is a Wellington-type: prominent nose, crag-like.

He is probably Norman. Standing now with hand on dagger, on guard by a window. There is a struggle in the aisle. Some-one has been killed in the church. Nasty feeling. Fighting for life. When they were on earth they were fighting. A man and a woman. Feeling that another man has come in. Bad influence. Not the type to be thwarted by anything. No mercy. He has a descendant not far away. Nasty man, nasty thoughts, hateful, doesn't like what we are doing. Would like to stop us. Many years ago, long, long way back, but he is still drawn here. Revenge, selfish, cruel, passionate nature. Would like to clear us away from here. He used to read from the Bible – could he have once been a clergyman? He was a property owner, thought of himself as very important. He had rights over many, wives, children, he would take them. There is no love in his make-up. Presence very, very strong. The church is in his control. Roman Catholic element not so strong as at Borley. Sad music is playing and I get the words: "I am different from the average woman and I stay and play sadly and slowly ..."' (*Here the medium went into a trance and the voice of a girl came through, sobbing, crying and struggling ...*) '"Oh, you, you ..."' (*The girl's voice faded and that of a gruff man came through.*)

Man: 'Go. Go.'

J.C.D.: 'We've come to help you.'

Man: 'Don't say these things to me. Who are you?'

J.C.D.: 'We love you. We've come to help you.'

Man: 'Why do you love us? You are an intruder. Why come you here?'

J.C.D.: 'We live in the present; the twentieth century.'

Man: 'I am here now, now, now. It is mine. Mine. What do you here?'

J.C.D.: 'We come to tell you that you are are no longer in your body.'

Man: 'Oh fool. Fool.'

J.C.D.: 'We are in a body. We live in the world today. You have lived here a long time ago.'

Man: 'I live here now.'

J.C.D.: 'Would you be happy?'

Man: 'Let me go! Why do you hold me here? Who are you to hold me here? Let me go. I am strong. I go not for you. You are not of these parts. I don't know you. It is mine. Who are you people ? I won't go. I won't go.'

110

J.C.D.: 'I command thee in the name of God to go.'

Man: 'What priest is this? It is mine and I am happy here. What is it to you what I am or what I do? I will send my men. Come, come help me to fight these people. I will not go.'

(*Throughout the latter part of this exchange the medium, who had taken on the personality of the man who was communicating, struggled violently and the sitters sought to restrain him (her?). They struggled to retain their hold and the medium, in the personality of the communicating entity, stood up to shake them off but was forced down into the chair again. Finally, his personality was withdrawn from the medium and almost at once the girl came through again, sobbing and crying.*)

J.C.D.: 'We have come to help you. We are your friends.'

Girl: 'God help me. No! No! Where shall I go? Help me my God. God's house. I came to seek peace. It came not. No. No. No. Do not let me. He stands there. He stands there. Jesus. I am belonging to him (*i.e. the man*), he is my master. I must obey him. I cannot. I know not. You are standing here. Thou shalt see these things. And see that which he would do to his people. He is master here and I cannot flee. O God. Send light of love to him. I weep for him. He is a forlorn soul. This is not Thy will, O Lord. Surely Thy people Thou wilt save. Let him not fall into hell fire. He is Thy son. Let me pray for him, for his soul. (*Prays on her knees for a moment*) Pater noster ... dulci amor ... Oh thou, bless me in the name of God ...'

J.C.D.: 'I bless thee in the name of Christ and give thee peace, and rest, and joy.'

Girl: 'Sir Robert. No. My lord and master come unto the Father: amor patri. He must come. The light. The altar. Save him. See the light. Can you see the light, Sir Robert?

Miss Cubitt: 'You must go to the light.'

J.C.D.: 'What is your name?'

Girl: 'Mary. Oh Mother of God. Kind friends that ye are. Ye come surely in the Lord's name. It must be true. I will come. God calls me in thy Name, Christ and Lord, Christ our Saviour. I come. I come. I come.'

(*The personality of the girl was then withdrawn from the*

111

medium. The medium stood up and her guide Red Hawk spoke through her.)

Red Hawk: 'It is all right. It was a struggle. Man not fully under control. He is so anxious to retain the things of earth. Very fine clergyman present here also, been trying to help him for years. The little lady was attracted to the Roman Catholic faith, I feel she was part Roman Catholic. She will find rest. She will not be a restless, forlorn soul. She has overcome great power here this night, to be released. You are not very strong in the cosmic laws. You don't realise how it is possible for one to rise. He (*i.e. the man*) is liable to cause a little disturbance. He is still lurking and is not yet released, but you have helped him a little. The clergyman has been fighting 1–200 years for his soul. Connected with Borley Rectory. Wonderful soul. Certain amount of affinity with Kiernander. Attracted to him for some time. Name: Jack Allan, or Allin, Alleyne, or Oulan; maybe 6–700 years back. Guardian of this church is a crusader (*many priests were attached to the crusades*) named Michael. Guarding over influences until better spiritual influences come or church is disintegrated. Robert man connected with the Borley family. At one time he had a big house here. I think the house has been built upon. I feel that there is a very strong link with the person who is in the house now. The girl's name is Mary Felicia or Felicy or Phyllis. Her mother has been here for the last 200 years, trying to help.'

Red Hawk suggested that the girl may have been a maid at the manor house. The man had taken her life by stabbing her through the heart at the west end of the church. Sir Robert had wanted to make her 'not his honourable wife'; and added: 'you can find trace of the murder even now.' The body was hidden and then buried in consecrated ground but not in the church. Red Hawk was asked about the present rector's extraordinary experience at the manor (i.e. being embraced by an

112

invisible woman in a bedroom) and he replied that this would have been the same girl, probably seeking protection. The guide then went on to relate various interesting particulars about the activities of disembodied spirits in the church. There were elemental sub-human spirits present, the party were told, who were able, when sufficient power was available, to produce phenomena. The present rector had provided a considerable amount of power and if he had been present on this occasion things would have been much 'hotter!' Red Hawk also mentioned that there were other human spirits present beside the man and the girl, including mischievous ex-parishioners. He seemed to imply that these were not earthbound in the same way as the man and the girl. On the question as to whether any phenomena had been heard earlier in the sitting it transpired that everyone present had heard a metallic-sounding click or knock that appeared to come from the west end of the church. Red Hawk said this sound was produced by tapping one of the hanging lamps with a rod. The sitters were anxious to know whether it was possible for them to witness some phenomena at that time and Red Hawk was unsure as to whether it would be a good thing to let the power build up again. J.C.D. suggested that the bell might be rung but Red Hawk advised against this, saying that sounds heard in the church already that night (the hymn singing, etc) would cause local comment. He finally agreed with some reluctance to the party sitting quietly to await possible phenomena, but nothing further occurred.

In the interests of accuracy and objectivity I have to say that I keep an open mind on the value of evidence so obtained and I feel it is not unfair to state that in spite of considerable research no corroboration was ever obtained to support any of the 'facts' that came through at this seance; although there were several interesting aspects. There *was* a link with Borley: several rectors in the seventeenth and eighteenth centuries held the living of both Borley and Langenhoe and at least two of them lived at Langenhoe; there could have been 'a certain amount of affinity' between the clergyman 'connected with Borley' and Mr Kiernander, as the latter's family once held the living of Borley; there do appear to have been conflicting faiths at Langenhoe as there were at Borley, and so on. In any case, such seances and communications cannot but be of interest, especially to those taking part, who it must be emphasised were much impressed; and of course for those people who may be sympathetic to the spiritualistic hypothesis that *could* explain some hauntings. Mrs Harris, the note-taker, apparently 'caught a glimpse' of 'Mary Felicity' and later drew a sketch of the girl she had seen clairvoyantly.

The American parapsychologist Hans Holzer, whom I have met at The Ghost Club and with whom I have discussed ghosts and haunted houses, believes that only with the help of a medium, under the control of a competent investigator, can those 'ghosts' – which are in fact 'the surviving emotional memory of a person who has died in tragedy, suddenly or gradually, and who cannot free himself from the emotional entanglement that binds him to the place of his death' – be helped to escape into the 'non-physical world into which we all go when death is normal'.

Holzer, who is a ghost hunter who hates the dark, was deeply impressed when he accompanied the gifted medium Eileen Garrett to a haunted house in Rockland County owned by the Broadway columnist Denton Walker. Reported disturbances included a wide range of noises, the sound of someone in heavy boots walking downstairs, mysterious dents appearing in kitchen utensils – one had five distinct indentations that looked like the imprint of a large hand – glass doors and windows cracking for no apparent reason and sometimes the complete disappearance of objects.

During a tour of the house, Eileen Garrett, who had been told nothing about the case, quickly located the 'haunted room' and promptly described her psychic impression of the history of the house and the background to the haunting. Subsequently she entered a trance-like state and produced an alleged personality who had died in terrible circumstances in the house – and it was his spirit, it was said, that haunted the house. Much of what the medium said in trance was later verified by research, and whatever the explanation Denton Walker always maintained that the atmosphere of the house improved tremendously after the visit by Eileen Garrett and Hans Holzer, and in fact there were no more unexplained disturbances.

There is no doubt that some mediums can 'pick up' past events at certain 'psychically disturbed' houses and I remember vividly two incidents that impressed me. In the company of Tom Corbett, one of Britain's best-known clairvoyants, my wife and I visited the Crown Inn at Bildeston, Suffolk, reputed to be haunted, particularly by the ghost of an unknown man, sometimes seen in the vicinity of the bar wearing an overcoat and an old-fashioned hat.

At a time when Tom Corbett was not in the bar some people entered with a large retriever dog. They walked to the bar and then across the room to a seat in the corner; their dog followed them to the bar and the logical thing for it to have done would have been to have followed them to the seat across the centre of the room; instead, it carefully walked as far as possible from the centre of the room, hugging the wall of the bar to the corner and then the other walls of the room until it eventually reached its owners, when it thankfully slid under a seat and out of sight. When Tom Corbett came back into the bar he immediately said there was now the ghost of a man in the room, which the retriever had evidentally sensed. Tom Corbett said the ghost in the bar was that of a man who died about eight years previously; a fat and jovial man with a great sense of humour, who was addicted to snuff. The landlord described a number of odd things that had happened: potato crisps flying through the air, a tap on the shoulder, lights being switched off – all when no one could possibly be responsible; and Tom Corbett felt that this bore out what he had said: the ghost was that of a practical joker, harmless and friendly. We went all over the house and in one room Tom Corbett stopped and said that the room was haunted, in fact the most haunted room in the house, but still a friendly one. The landlady agreed, adding: 'I don't know how you know but you are quite right; sometimes I feel something cool against my forehead; it's soothing and friendly.' Having satisfied ourselves that there was no normal draught in the room, Tom Corbett said that only one thing could cause the drop in temperature which he could experience: the ghost of a woman. He felt she had looked after children in the room many years before; perhaps in the 1700s. She had been a gentle, kind woman, very fond of children; she may have been a nanny or a nurse of some kind.

Subsequently we heard that parts of the house had been much larger at one time and some two hundred years earlier Tom Corbett felt that the room he had described as the 'most haunted' had been a kind of dormitory with lots of beds containing sick people, and they had been looked after by the ghost who still haunted the room. Although the house has been an inn for many years (certainly it was an inn in the eighteenth century) it seems more than likely that the first floor room of the building had once been used as some kind of hospital.

I also vividly recall taking medium Trixi Allingham-Macquire to lunch at The Grenadier, a haunted public house in Wilton Row near Hyde Park Corner. I had told her nothing of the reputed haunting and she knew nothing whatever about the place, yet, as soon as we were in the bar, she said she didn't like the atmosphere; a serious quarrel had taken place there and a fight – and there was a ghost in the cellar.

The Grenadier was once the officers' mess for the Duke of Wellington's Regiment but in those days the inn was called The Guardsman. One of the bars was situated in what is now the cellar, and the present bar served as a dining room for officers. Not infrequently officers off duty would drink to excess and gamble beyond discretion, and this sometimes led to quarrels and brawls. In one such fight, when an officer was caught cheating, rough justice was handed out by his companions. He was flogged on the spot and afterwards he staggered down the steps to the cellar, more dead than alive. There he expired and, it is said, his ghost haunts The Grenadier to this day, especially during the month of September, the month of his death.

Such experiences with mediums, sensitive people who somehow 'tune in' to past events on occasions, cannot but be interesting, and although it is certainly possible to theorise on the reason and *modus operandi* of such incidents they are undeniably impressive. While there may well be a place for mediumistic involvement in the investigation of haunted houses, such evidence as comes through at seances can rarely be proved to be authentic, although certainly interesting clairvoyant or clairaudient phenomena; and since it is hardly scientific anyway, perhaps it is wise to concentrate on investigation that is more likely to be accepted by today's scientific establishment.

By the same token I have yet to be convinced that exorcism, in whatever form it may take, is either necessary or indeed appropriate in the vast majority of hauntings. And let me say at once that I have been present at eight exorcisms and in every case the ritual brought comfort to the human occupants of the house, but it had no lasting value as far as the haunting itself was concerned. This is not to say, of course, that exorcisms have never been successful, and I am well aware that there are convincing accounts of exorcisms apparently ridding a house completely of disturbing influences; but I have not myself been involved in such a case.

Exorcism is the act of persuading evil spirits to abandon a person, place or object by command, ritual or prayer. At one time the power to perform exorcisms was considered to be a special gift which was bestowed on a favoured person; later a special class of clergy, called exorcists, was entrusted with the practice, but today anyone may perform an exorcism ritual, although the religious type of exorcism is usually performed by an ordained priest who has previously obtained special authorisation from his bishop. There are a number of priests in the Church of England and in the Roman Catholic Church who specialise in exorcisms and indeed who frequently carry out such services; lay exorcisms are conducted by occult practitioners who are well versed in occultism and magic. The principle of exorcisms presupposes that it is possible to transfer a spirit or force from place to place by ritual acts and words, and while belief in such principles has decreased over the years the incidence of apparent or believed possession seems to have increased.

Exorcisms can be minor and entail simply adjurations: 'I rebuke thee! I rebuke thee! I rebuke thee and summon thee forth from this place ...' and such earnest requests, loudly addressed to the unseen ghost, are sometimes remarkably effective, it would seem; or exorcisms can be major and comprise ritual fumigation, the sprinkling of salt and holy water, prayers, invocations and continued visitations with bell, book and candle. There can be no doubt that such exorcisms, or 'Christian deliverances' as some clerics prefer to define them, are most impressive, but whether they are more than a complex procedure hiding a well-conceived illusion that is embedded in the superstition of another age is perhaps a question that needs answering.

Among the sincere and dedicated exorcists that I have known I count Dom Robert Petitpierre O.S.B. as one of the most down-to-earth, practical and convincing. He had a hundred tales to tell of brown-robed medieval friars appearing during modern Anglican communion services, of ancient ghosts haunting modern London mews flats, of a ghost stag followed by a pack of hounds and Tudor horsemen racing through the billiards room of a country house, of 'place imprints' and 'little devils'. Dom Robert never liked anyone unknown to the priest to be present at an exorcism, and this applied in particular to newspapermen and other media reporters – and I may say I hold the same views with regard to the serious investigation of haunted houses but for somewhat different reasons. The Earl of Lauderdale, speaking on the subject of exorcism in the House of Lords in 1975 said, 'We are bedevilled by ignorant handling of this delicate subject by the media; they do not begin to understand what they are talking about'.

Dom Robert believed there was a spiritual danger in which spectators might find themselves in the event of a 'little devil' found to exist in a haunted premises, managing to get loose; I simply prefer to have with me on an investigation only those people I can trust implicitly and who are prepared to accept without question all appropriate rules, and who will play a useful part in the investigation. Ghost hunting is not a game, it is a serious matter, and in my opinion there is no room for 'lookers-on', sensation-seekers, or the wrong kind of person.

Dom Robert always removed from a house, before conducting any form of exorcism, all animals and children, each of whom he provided with a prayer of protection and a blessing. Frequently he had present a doctor or a psychiatrist whom he knew. Usually, in an inhabited house, he would gather the adult members of the household into one room which had first been exorcised and blessed, and there they would all stay until the end of the whole operation, which might take well over two hours. Always before commanding a 'demon' to 'come out' from a person or from a place, Dom Robert would first 'bind' the demon; that is he would command it in the name of the Lord to harm no one, 'whether the patient, persons present or anyone else ...'. At one time Christian exorcism for the protection of a person ended with the 'sealing' of the nine openings of the body with holy water so that no evil influence could regain entrance.

Any Church of England bishop can appoint an Official Exorcist in his diocese but by no means all do so. Present-day clerical exorcists tend to see their encounters as a battle of cosmic forces, although the more enlightened recognise that the key may well be energy 'with a parasite force tapping energy off the host', as one bishop put it to me. A sharp drop in the temperature of a person present, he believed, may be a pointer, but on occasions, I pointed out to him, one encounters a rise of temperature! I did agree with the bishop, however, when he said that exorcism tends to be what the victims expect; so expectation seems to precede activity and this does not suggest any outside force. People who need exorcism are looking for an explanation, not a devil or devils, and instead, he added, 'people should look at reality rather than at signposts'. I couldn't agree more.

The idea of exorcism is based on the theory that God created not only man and the universe but also vast orders of angels who are intelligent, capable of independent action and not allied to matter. The chief of these was Lucifer, who rebelled against God and, together with a large company of fellow insurrectionists, was cast out of Heaven. The Church of England set up a commission on the subject in 1963 and published a report in 1972, and although not church law its recommendations have, in general, been followed ever since, especially the warning that careful medical attention be employed to avoid, for example, a paranoid schizophrenic being made worse by the ceremony. Other recommendations that are generally followed include that no exorcism be carried out without the permission of the bishop and that a trained diocesan exorcist be appointed wherever there is the demand or necessity. Holy water was permitted to be used, or the subject could be breathed on or simply held between the hands. The recommanded formula of exorcism began with the words, 'I command you, evil spirit, in the name of God, the Father Almighty, in the name of Jesus Christ His only son, and in the name of the Holy Ghost, that harming no one you depart from this creature of God and return to the place appointed you, there to remain for ever ...'.

The Catholic formula, promulgated by Pope Pius V who excommunicated Queen Elizabeth I, is somewhat more abrasive, telling the 'spirit not of this world' to be gone, and referring to 'He who ruleth the highest heavens and the lowest depths, who ruleth the winds, the sea, and the tempest, so

119

orders you ... listen and fear ...' and so on. Today the Roman Catholic church has very explicit and practical instructions for those who practise the act of exorcism, warning the practitioner to take great care to distinguish so-called 'possession' from disease; to prepare by prayer and fasting and to ensure that the priest-exorcist 'be holy, humble, and of blameless life ...'. He should avoid superstition in all its forms and leave the medical side to physicians. He should conduct the service of exorcism whenever possible inside a church, but if it must be at a private house witnesses should be present; 'this is especially important if the subject to be exorcised is a woman'. The demon or whatever may be contacted should not be 'idly questioned' and the Blessed Sacrament should not be used 'for fear of irreverence'. A crucifix, holy water and relics can be used. The exorcist must wear a surplice and violet stole when performing the ceremony.

Congregationalists are more down-to-earth, and perhaps we will let them have the last word on exorcism. 'Sometimes,' one experienced missionary who has used exorcism extensively told me, 'I just tell Satan I have spotted him and he can mind his own business. I tell him to buzz off in the name of the Lord Jesus Christ.' Exorcisms can be just as effective in one form as in another – and, perhaps unfortunately in my experience, just as ineffective.

8 · Step-by-Step Investigation of a Haunting

This chapter is intended to show the way to proceed in the investigation of a hypothetical haunted house. Although it does not represent an actual investigation, it does incorporate real aspects from many different cases, and seeks to show, in an ideal situation, the best way of proceeding. All the material presented comes from actual cases that have been investigated and the original notes come from my files and note-books. I hope it shows the excitement and thrill of ghost hunting as well as depicting the inevitable hard work and painstaking application to any case that we undertake to investigate.

At a Ghost Club meeting a member mentioned that a friend has told her of a haunted manor in Somerset, a property that had been occupied by the same family for many, many years. The member had asked her friend to put in writing as much as she knew of the haunting. Ten days later I received a letter from the member enclosing a long letter from her friend. The gist of this somewhat rambling epistle was that Cushing Manor, a mediaeval manor house, was haunted by several ghosts, all of whom had been either seen or heard by some of the present occupants and, according to documentary evidence, for more than a hundred years by previous occupants.

The reported ghosts were a Grey Lady who haunted the main staircase, a Cavalier who had most frequently been encountered in the panelled gallery, and a White Lady who had been seen on the balcony and in the vicinity of the ornamental pond in the garden. In my reply I asked the Ghost Club member to ascertain whether the occupants of the house would be co-operative to a quiet, serious and confidential investigation. Five days later I received a letter telling me that the occupants were agreeable to talking to me about their ghosts on the understanding that there would be no publicity.

I immediately wrote, giving this assurance and asking them whether they would prefer me to call and talk to them about the case or whether they would prefer me to send them some forms which they could fill in to provide me with information about the house, its occupants and the reported ghostly happenings. They were kind enough to invite my wife and me to spend a couple of days at the manor, and they suggested a date three weeks ahead when all the family would be at home but there would be no other guests.

I promptly rearranged an appointment I had previously made for the suggested dates, wrote a brief note accepting their kind invitation and saying that we would do our best to cause them as little inconvenience as possible, reassuring them that there would be no publicity and giving our estimated time of arrival.

Much of the intervening three weeks was spent researching the house, the area, the family and everything I could think of that might have some bearing on the case. My first reference, as always, was to my Confidential Files on haunted properties, a system devised by my good friend Air Commodore R.C. Jonas, OBE. This is a card index system with sections divided into English counties, Scotland, Wales, Ireland and foreign countries, with a cross-index of 28 types of manifestations: Apparitions and Materialisations, Unidentified Footprints, Temperature Changes, Tactual Phenomena, Odours, Lights, Appearance and Disappearance of Objects, Fires, Writing on Walls or Paper, Crashing or Breaking Sounds as of Crockery, Sounds of Moving Furniture, Displaced or Projected Objects, Rustling Sounds, Raps, Taps, Bumps and Knockings, Music, Horses' Hoofs, Opening and Closing of Doors, Voices, Footsteps, Scratching, Bell-Ringing, Sounds of Fighting, Animals' Reactions, Sensations of a Presence, etc.

A further word about this excellent system may be of interest. The two sections of the system are indicated by blue celluloid index tabs for the counties and countries while the various manifestations are indicated by red tabs. The cards devoted to specific properties (in the counties and countries sections) measure nine by five inches and are two-sided. One side (the front) has four boxes spread across the top: 'Location', 'Owner', 'Occupant' and 'First Recorded Date of Phenomena'. The rest of the front of the card is reserved for 'Bibliography and other Sources of Evidence' with the whole of the reverse of the card devoted to 'Brief History of Case'. A compact three miles to one inch Road Atlas of Great Britain is incorporated into the system by being ruled from the margin of the appropriate page to indicate the 'haunted' site. The manifestations cards, of the same size and ruled both sides (indicated by red tabs), list and number the relevant cases to each and every manifestation so that, at a glance, it is possible to ascertain the frequency of any reported manifestation and the location of that reported manifestation and its proximity to the case in hand.

I discovered an entry for the house, under Somerset, with a reference to 'verbal information' from a named correspondent ten years earlier and also an intriguing reference to an article in a local Historical Society publication. The volume number, issue number and date of the copy together with the address of the Historical Society were recorded and I lost no time in writing to request a copy of the relevant issue, enclosing £2.00 to cover cost and postage with the proviso that I would send the balance by return if there was more to pay. I also dug out the letter referred to from my correspondence files and I contacted my nearest Ordnance Survey Agent (the Ordnance Survey Information Branch at Romsey Road, Maybush, Southampton, will supply a list of their agents, a price list, a copy of their large-scale catalogue and a useful National Grid leaflet on request) and ordered a 1:2500 scale (25 inches to 1 mile) large-scale map (approximately £14) that covered the area of the haunted Somerset mansion. Unfortunately their 1:1250 (50 inches to 1 mile) covers only urban areas. However, I knew from past experience that the 25 inches to 1 mile scale map would be invaluable and give detailed information about the countryside and the area, showing not only roads, railways, canals, lakes, rivers, buildings and sites of antiquity but also permanent tracks, walls, fences, hedges, ponds, watercourses, and height information and administrative boundaries. I was thus able to establish the shape and position of the property in respect of other properties, prevailing winds, the sun, moonlight, proximity of trees, water and so on. I also contacted the Reference Librarian at the Public Library in the nearest large town who put me in touch with a local Historical Society official, who supplied me with a wealth of historical material on the area in general and the manor house in particular, and also pointed out further areas for research.

Meanwhile I had been in touch with a Ghost Club member who lived in the vicinity, and he had made extensive enquiries in all sorts of places, discreetly and quietly, providing a lot more material for the already growing notebook and file that I had opened on the case.

During the course of the initial visit that I made to the house in the company of my wife I was able to hear the story of the house and of the ghosts that apparently haunted the manor from the lady of the house. As soon as we had been welcomed and sat over coffee the owners asked how I would like to set about my enquiries and, since it was already clear that the lady of the house was most interested and most voluble on the subject, I said I thought it might be a good idea if I heard the whole story from her in the first instance, with no one else present. Then perhaps I might hear whatever anyone else had to say, separately and individually; and if each person would sign a report that I would prepare of what they had said that would give me a very good idea of the evidence in the case.

So it was agreed, and we learned that the Grey Lady was the most active of the reported ghosts, having been seen seven or eight times in the last ten years, always in the vicinity of the main staircase and usually in the early evening in Springtime. She had been seen by three of the present occupants, by four of the previous occupants and by several visitors and servants. Where possible I obtained the present address or latest address of all witnesses not now residing at the manor.

The Cavalier was more reticent, it seemed, although he had been reportedly seen in the panelled gallery three or four times in the past ten or twelve years. One witness, an historian who was researching a book on English panelling, had distinctly seen the solid-looking figure standing in a doorway leading off the gallery with one hand on the doorknob one April or May morning, seemingly watching the historian at his work. The historian had in fact turned back to his books and then looked again, but the form had completely disappeared. He had gone to the open door but there was no one in sight and he could find nothing to account for what he had seen. Another stranger to the house had distinctly seen the form of a Cavalier walking away from her along the gallery, on 16 May the previous year, the plumes of feathers in his hat swaying in the breeze he caused by his movements. He had seemingly disappeared through a door in the panelled wall, but when this witness reached the spot where she was certain the Cavalier had disappeared, she could find no trace of any door or opening. Both sightings had taken place in mid-morning.

Finally, the White Lady had been seen on the balcony of the house overlooking the gardens and walking beside the ornamental pond. Two children, visitors to the house, said they had seen her by the pond about eighteen months previously and seven or eight people had seen her one evening on the balcony after a dinner party. When the butler approached her, thinking it must be a servant sleep-walking, the figure suddenly disappeared. There were no other sightings of the White Lady in living memory. I was promised a list of the early summer dinner party guests, and made a careful note of the other witnesses who could be traced (if at all possible), asked to relate their experiences independently and afterwards sign the accounts as correct.

After an exhaustive tour of the house and gardens I conducted interviews with the other occupants of the house. The next day I saw all the servants, and also two local people whom the owners had asked to call as they were able to tell me about the previous occupants and their servants and the stories they had related about various odd happenings. All this information was carefully noted, signed and the signatures witnessed. Before leaving the house it had been agreed that we could bring an investigative team to the house for an all-night visit the following month (the month when most of the happenings seemed to be reported) on a date to be mutually agreed.

Back home the extensive notes and signed statements were studied by several experienced investigators and by my wife and myself, and a coherent account of all the reported disturbances was prepared together with the history of the house and all other relevant information that had been collected to date. This interim Report is always prepared with excessively wide margins in which are added notes and comments for further clarification, enquiry and study.

The date having been fixed for the all-night investigation, a team of selected Ghost Club members was chosen (the Club keeps a Register of members willing and able to participate in such exercises), and a Ghost Club Pre-Visit Procedure Notification was sent to each member of the prospective team. This read as follows (the names and locations are fictional):

THE GHOST CLUB
(Founded 1862)

CONFIDENTIAL

Investigative all-night visit to CUSHING MANOR, 3 miles south-west of Milvertown, Somerset, on Friday 10 May 1985

Owners and Occupants: Mr and Mrs James J. Knight-Jackson.
Telephone: Milvertown 218302 – *use in case of emergency only*

Tentative schedule:

May 10 7.00–7.30 pm   Assemble at Cushing Manor as discreetly as possible.

8.00 pm   Introductions and meet the Owners, hear something of the history and haunting, tour the Manor and decide on and establish Base Room where all activities will be initiated and controlled.

9.30 pm   Refreshments. Draw up sketch plans, synchronize watches and plan strategy for the night founded on what has been learned, taking into account the whereabouts of the occupants. Seal those rooms and portions of the house not subject to investigation.

10.30 pm   Place apparatus: automatic cameras, frequency change detector, vibration detector, thermographs, sound recording apparatus, etc, place and 'ring' possible 'trigger' objects, thermometers, etc, in strategic positions as shown on sketch map. Decide on rota for required number of Members to have haunted areas (the main stairs, panelled gallery, outside balcony) under constant surveillance. Tour all parts of property subject to investigation and attempt to obtain reactions from 'sensitive' Members, dowsing practitioners, etc, in various parts of the house; various Members taking turns if practicable. Periods of total darkness: no sound or movement between whistles; Members in every part of the property under investigation. All actions and responses to be logged.

11.30 pm   Check thermometers, start recording apparatus and begin rota of investigators: half-hour watches.

May 11 1.00–1.45 am   Rest and refreshment period.

2.00 am Resumption of rota and checking instruments etc. Attempts at seances and other activity in accordance with evidence and experiences.

4.00 am   Rest and refreshment period. Discussion and initiate any new ideas for investigation that may have come to light during the night. Ensure every part of property under investigation is thoroughly studied. Re-investigate any area where apparent phenomena have been reported or recorded.

5.00–6.00 am   Final period of rota, checking instruments, etc.

Further attempts at seances, dowsing, automatic writing or any other activity suggested by experiences – in different parts of the house with different Members taking part.

7.00 am   Collect and remove all investigative apparatus, remove any chalk markings, seals, etc, clean up as necessary throughout the house. Tidy Base Room and pack apparatus, etc, into cars.

8.00 am onwards   The owners are providing a snack breakfast.

NOTES for all participants:
Please contribute the agreed sum per head to be paid on or before 10 May towards Club expenses. All Members be sure to equip themselves with additional warm clothing; refreshments for themselves – food and drink (not alcoholic) for night; one or more torches; a notebook and pen or pencil; a watch, preferably with second hand; a whistle; soft shoes. As previously arranged individuals will also bring tape recorders, cameras and other equipment and also experimental equipment as agreed.

Special Note: In the event of anything unusual being seen or heard at any time stand completely still and observe as much as possible, quietly following if manifestation moves out of sight. As soon as practicable draw the attention of another Member to the apparent manifestation by flashing torch three times in quick succession or by blowing three short blasts on whistle. Immediately after event make detailed notes including time, locale, description, other witnesses, etc, report immediately to Base Room, having first detailed a substitute if you are on a scheduled rota of investigation.

Please remember at all times that you are a guest in a private house.

My wife and I will be spending the nights of 11 May and 12 May at the Riverside Hotel, Milvertown. Milvertown 12345

(signed) Peter Underwood (President)

During the course of the night a number of curious incidents were reported and these were carefully studied and filed for future reference since they were the objective observations of experienced and level-headed investigators. Perhaps the most spectacular were several photographs with distorted pictures and coloured streaks and shapes, and the recording of a swishing sound on the stairway, almost like someone passing in a long skirt, and an unidentified voice on a sound recording that no one could account for. But there were also other interesting incidents. Footsteps were heard by three members; they were at first taken to originate from a member of the investigating team (although at a time when it was agreed that no one would move) but subsequently found to have no natural explanation, every single person being accounted for at the time the footsteps were heard. On investigation the sounds ceased and no explanation was discovered. Other unexplained sounds that were heard, logged, verified and sometimes mechanically recorded included a loud rustling sound; an intermittent whistling sound; taps, as on a wooden surface, received in answer to a request; the unexplained jamming of photographic and other apparatus; and a drop in temperature (verified by each member of the team and by instruments) in one area, a rough circle with a diameter of $3\frac{1}{2}$ feet in the middle of the panelled gallery. All the night's reports were carefully studied, critically examined and verified before being compared with the recorded history of the house and the allegedly paranormal activity reported.

After a Full Report had been compiled and a copy sent to the owners of the property under investigation, the salient facts of the case were transferred to the Confidential Files on haunted properties, and finally the Full Report, original on-the-spot Reports, and a complete record of the whole investigation, including photographs, tape recordings, etc, was boxed and preserved in the permanent archives, with a covering note that read, like so many others: 'Case No.... Unsolved to date.' A resumé of the investigation would later be published in the confidential Bulletin issued only to Ghost Club Members.

9 · Britain's Most Haunted Areas

It is strange fact that more ghosts and ghostly phenomena are reported from some areas of the world than others, and more from some countries than others. Some towns are more haunted than others, some villages have more ghosts than others and one place has apparently been haunted for at least a hundred years ... in 1886 Mrs E. Byford left her employment at Borley Rectory because of 'ghostly footsteps,' and I have before me as I write a letter from a visitor to Borley in April, 1986 (exactly a century later!), describing 'ghostly footsteps' that he and a friend both heard from different vantage points during the course of their visit to haunted Borley.

Britain seems to have more reported ghosts per square mile than any other country and Britain's most haunted towns might well be Farnham, in Surrey, and York. Indeed there is, I suggest, a case for regarding Farnham, fascinating and fairest of the towns of Surrey, as the most haunted town in England. Where else could you find a haunted castle, a haunted malthouse, a haunted farm, a haunted park, a haunted church, a haunted theatre, several haunted shops, a haunted hotel, a haunted mill, a ghost train, a ghost army, haunted inns, private houses and open spaces; while innumerable ghosts haunt the surrounding countryside where many UFOs have been sighted. Small wonder that a local police constable, John Birch, quickly discovered more than twenty examples of ghostly phenomena, claimed by scores of eye-witnesses, in an independent investigation he carried out. We had several chats and I am grateful to him for telling me about several 'new' ghosts in the locality; incidentally his score of reported ghosts in Farnham soon exceeded fifty!

Farnham has many claims to fame. There is the inn where William Cobbett was born and the grave in which he sleeps; the house where Charles I stayed for a night on his way to trial in London; a specimen of Norman timber in the shape of a wooden pillow with scalloped capitals shaped by a carpenter nine hundred years ago; and a plaque to Gilbert Talbot, the inspirer of Toc H, who worshipped here before he went to France and died on the battlefield in 1915. Visitors to the episcopal palace dominating the town included: William of Wykeham, Lord High Chancellor of England, founder of Winchester College and New College, Oxford; Cardinal Beaufort, half-brother of Henry IV, son of John of Gaunt and one of those who watched the burning of Joan of Arc in the market place at Rouen; Cardinal Wolsey, builder of Hampton Court Palace, and a man whose magnificence was said to have outshone that of the king, Henry VIII, who also knew Farnham; Henry's daughter, Queen Mary I (on her way to marry Philip of Spain at Winchester); Queen Elizabeth I; King James I; George III; and Queen Victoria.

Let us start our tour of haunted Farnham at the picturesque Castle, whose history goes back to Saxon times when King Ethelbald gave some of its lands to Saint Swithun, chaplain to Egbert, King of the West Saxons, Bishop of Winchester, and the subject of the popular legend that rain on his day (15 July) foretells rain for the succeeding forty days. There were bishops living within these walls for eight hundred years, while the great Norman keep, built by King Stephen's brother, Henry of Blois, is a proud monument that is open to the public, and those who reach the highest points are rewarded with sweeping panoramic views of the surrounding countryside. To reach the ramparts we must climb the flight of steps from a gateway with the grooves of a portcullis still in the walls, and it is here that we may meet our first ghost in Farnham. He, or rather she, is an unidentified shadow, perhaps the more frightening because no one knows for sure who she was or why she haunts this part of the castle, but many people have felt rather than seen a presence here at the entrance to the keep, a 'definite something' that haunts the ruined guard room, the oldest part of the building. Other visitors have reported catching a glimpse of a stern-faced lady in a light-coloured gown with a long cord girdle, possibly twelfth or thirteenth century, and there are whispers of intrigue and dark deeds long ago – even murder – that may have left some kind of impression, reflection, reverberation or resonance upon the atmosphere here, or in the very stones, that occasionally is seen or felt by sympathetic visitors.

The present castle, now occupied by the Centre for International Briefing, was built by a grandson of William the

Conqueror. In September, 1974, I visited the castle with Mrs Elizabeth Cox and was shown over the whole building. Later, due to the understanding and kindness of the then Director, Mr W.E. Grenville-Grey, half-a-dozen members of The Ghost Club spent a night there, most of it in the Great Hall, where Kings and Queens of England have feasted many times over the centuries.

Elizabeth Cox had written to me from Hove, telling me that she had been a maid at the castle over fifty years earlier, in the days when the property had been a private residence of opulence and elegance, the walls draped with tapestries brought back by the Crusaders, furniture fashioned from the castle oak trees, and the seats of chairs made of deer-skin from animals that roamed the park, for there were always at least 365 deer, one for every day of the year.

Elizabeth Cox arrived at Farnham Castle in December 1919, when she was fourteen years of age, yet she had already been in the service of the Hon. Anne Cunliffe at Kensington for a year, one of eight maids and a butler. On arrival at Farnham Castle, huge, cold and grim but with an enormous log fire burning in the Great Hall, the new maid was shown to the top of Fox Tower, where the five housemaids were quartered. There she was ushered into a small room with stone walls and floor, a small window high overhead and the minimum of furniture. Having unpacked and changed into the black ankle-length uniform provided, she was taken to the servants' hall for high tea, where she joined the rest of the staff, sitting on long wooden forms on either side of the long white-wood table. She was told that a bell was rung in the tower for staff meals, a bell that could be heard for miles ... and in recent years various inhabitants of the castle and of the town have reported hearing, just for a moment, the distinct clang-clang of a bell from the direction of the castle tower, although of course no bell has been rung there for many years.

Christmas and holiday times at the castle were great events, and then there was plenty of life with guests, family and friends, from far and near, and enormous banquets in the Great Hall. On such occasions Elizabeth Cox and some of the other servants would steal into the gallery and peep over at the entertainment and meals being enjoyed by the family and their guests. There would be perhaps thirty people or more, seated at the long table, made from oak from the park, the walls covered with rich tapestries interspersed with portraits of present and previous owners and occupants, the whole room illuminated by candle-light flickering on silver and elaborate floral arrangements and showing up the beautiful gowns of the ladies and the uniforms and evening wear of the men. She would see the plain oak floorboards polished to perfection by the footmen, the roaring log fire in winter, the stags' heads over the huge mantelpiece and the axes and spears that had been brought back from the Crusades. It was on such an occasion, while she was in the long gallery, overlooking the Great Hall, that she saw the ghost of a priest or monk.

He appeared to be looking out of a window at the far end of the gallery, a window that overlooked the moat where a procession of phantom monks were said to walk and where a well is thought to hide several bodies. Elizabeth Cox has always thought that the monk may have been looking down on some formal ceremony that involved his brethren – but why was he not down there taking part in the procession? Or was he looking down at the well; worried about what might be uncovered one day? Elizabeth Cox never forgot the figure she saw. He was tall, dressed in a brown habit with a round cap on his head. He appeared to be solid and quite real, yet she knew at once that it was a ghost she was looking at. She remembers turning away for a moment, and when she looked again the figure had completely disappeared.

Fox Tower is reputedly haunted by the ghost of Bishop Morley (died 1684) who lived for years in a small cell-like room in this tower. He spent thousands of pounds restoring the castle after the Restoration of Charles II, but doubtless as a penance for some long forgotten misdeed he slept in a coffin for twenty years, and there he died. His ghost has been seen and heard perambulating the corridors and in particular one of the landings that he must have known well.

Other ghosts at Farnham Castle include a little dancing girl who must have displeased the castle owner for he made her dance and dance until she dropped exhausted and crawled out of the Great Hall and expired half-way up the stairway. At the spot where she died many people (without knowing the story) feel an overwhelming sadness; others hear the dying gasps; and others see the pathetic little figure.

132

Another of the ancient stairways in this ancient castle is apparently haunted, for I have first-hand evidence of a ghostly, grey-robed, monk-like figure that glides down the stairway on sunny afternoons. Again the figure is not wispy or transparent, which is the way most people think of ghosts; it appears to be solid and real, but it does move in an odd fashion, and one moment it is there and the next it has disappeared.

Unexplained footsteps have been reported from many parts of Farnham Castle over the years and one occupant told me that in 1975 she heard the sound of footsteps in the older part of the castle where other people, residents and visitors, have reported hearing similar sounds that have never been satisfactorily explained.

I have also talked with a Farnham resident who once had occasion to spend a night at the castle. She slept in the older part of the building and during the night she found herself suddenly wide awake with the awful feeling that she was not alone in the room and then she felt her bedclothes slowly being pulled off her bed. Frightened, but aware of what was happening, she took a firm hold on the top of the bedclothes and to her horror found that she had to exert considerable strength to keep sheet and blankets from being drawn away from her. She turned over to get a better hold on the bedclothes and then became aware that there was 'something' in the corner of the bedroom. It had no definite shape but seemed to be crouching, huddled in the darkness, pulsating almost and exuding a sense of evil. After what seemed a long time but in reality was probably only a few moments – even seconds – the frightened visitor became aware that the dark form was no longer there and the bedclothes were no longer being pulled down the bed. My informant tells me that the experience is something she rarely talks about if she can help it for although it happened many years ago it is still a very vivid and frightening memory – and nothing would induce her to spend another night at Farnham Castle.

Outside the castle the steep hill is reputedly haunted by the sound of heavy boots crunching on gravel, especially on cold winter nights; yet the narrow and dangerous road here has been macadamized for many years and there is no physical reason for the sound of shifting gravel, sounds that seem to emanate from the centre of the roadway. Perhaps there is some

133

connection between these sounds and the unidentified figure of a shadowy female form occasionally glimpsed in the castle gateway.

Lower down Castle Street there is a ghost of Regency days, when this beautiful street must have been a wonderful sight. A dandy of the period, it is said, alights from a phantom coach and swaggers across the wide street to disappear into a house, much altered now, where once he is said to have strangled his mistress in one of the bedrooms. The house is not far from the original Castle Theatre (once an old barn where someone was found hanged) which is, or was, also haunted.

Some years ago the Director of Productions at the time, Peter Gordon, told me that lights were frequently switched on at night, when the theatre was deserted; records on a gramophone were mysteriously changed; a loud banging noise was heard on several occasions that seemed to originate within the empty building; a clock on the stage stopped at the same time during four different performances; and the sounds of heavy footsteps were repeatedly heard from a deserted room. Mysterious movement of objects was also experienced, people reported strange experiences in the vicinity of the stairs in the foyer and Peter Gordon said he could personally vouch for the switching on of lights in the deserted theatre, that he had 'definitely switched off' (no one else having access to them), the quite inexplicable movement of one particular record, and saws and other tools that 'disappeared' were 'later found in exactly the same spot they originally were and strange footsteps ... such happenings are *not* to be explained, by carelessness or thoughtlessness'. During the run of the play *Dear Brutus* there were reports of many apparently inexplicable happenings that seemed to be associated with J.M. Barrie's chair, borrowed for the production. Years later a subsequent Director told me of footsteps that sounded in the same room, situated over the auditorium, and my wife and I spent some time in the haunted room and wandering about the rambling building on the night of the last performance there in 1974. That evening I was introduced to Sir Michael Redgrave (after whom the new theatre in Farnham was named) and he told me that he had performed in many haunted theatres but for his money the Castle Theatre beat them all.

Among the private houses in Farnham where paranormal

activity has been reported is an old house in East Street where the figure of an unidentified female has been seen in the doorway of a bedroom, dressed in an old-fashioned full-skirted dress. Perhaps it is a long forgotten family nurse or 'nanny', for a curious feature of this particular haunting lies in the fact that the figure is usually glimpsed at a time when some member of the family occupying the house is expecting a child. In April 1986 I talked with a businessman who told me that the property is now used entirely as offices, one of which he occupies; since no family now lives on the premises perhaps at least one ghost of Farnham has departed forever. Such a figure was reported at different times by the grown-up son of the last family to occupy the house, also by his mother, and twice by visitors – each time when an addition to the family was imminent. During the course of a bridge party one player was puzzled by the extra lady, dressed in an out-of-date dress, who seemed to hover in the doorway; and when she chanced to mention the matter to the lady of the house, the latter reassured the bridge player by saying, 'It was probably our ghost; my daughter is expecting a baby any day . . .'. This ghostly midwife or nanny or, more frightening, some childless former inhabitant who is jealous of the lucky mothers, sometimes apparently shows her presence by light footsteps and quiet knocks on various doors. Another private house in Farnham has two ghosts, those of a fair lady who was generous with her favours, and a dashing young man who visits her.

There is a shop in Farnham that boasts a ghostly black dog. Just why this lovely Queen Anne property in West Street should harbour such an apparition is unknown, but several occupants of the house have occasionally caught sight of such an animal in various parts of the house. Once the owner was about to walk upstairs when what appeared to be a friendly black dog bounded down the stairs towards her; when she turned to see where the animal went, she found that it had disappeared. Another time a black dog ran into the kitchen and stood quite close to an inhabitant who was just about to put something into the oven. She thought one of her own dogs had come in, but when she turned from the kitchen, no dog was to be seen and both her own pets were curled up asleep in another room with the door closed. Former occupants of the same property reported seeing the figure of an old woman standing in a mournful posture, silent and unmoving, in the bathroom. She seemed to be dressed in a nightdress; one moment she was there and the next she had disappeared. Nevertheless, the descriptions of various witnesses all correspond to a remarkable degree; always the figure is unmoving, always dressed in a long, loose and shapeless covering that could well be a nightdress, the hair is always described as 'untidy' or 'uncombed' and there is always an overall impression of sadness. A curious sound has also been reported from this house and always in the vicinity of the staircase: a sound like a roll of drums. It is difficult to suggest any tragic or violent happening that might have resulted in such ghostly manifestations: a friendly black dog, a sad old woman and a roll of drums!

Another shop where a ghost has been reported is a stone's throw away, facing Castle Street. There, before they closed in 1974, stood for many years a well-known local jewellers who held a Royal Charter. The firm was founded by a local man and it always remained a family business. When at last it was necessary to close down, it was a sad occasion for the family and for the town. It seems that the long-dead founder returned to take a last look at the prosperous business that he established and that bore his name, for when the shop and workrooms had been cleared a contractor was put in to remove the shelves and cupboards and, as he worked alone in the deserted back rooms, he became aware that he was not alone. Several times he glimpsed the figure of an elderly man wearing a jeweller's apron, standing watching him. The workman was somewhat annoyed at first, thinking that the family could not trust him to do his job without getting some old fellow to keep an eye on him; but, after the figure disappeared in circumstances that seemed mystifying, he mentioned the matter to the family, who told him that they had certainly not arranged for anyone to watch him at work. When they produced a photograph of the founder, the workman at once recognized the figure he had seen.

A ghostly old woman haunts West Street itself and several local people as well as visitors to the town have remarked upon the arresting spectacle of an old woman wearing a mob-cap hobbling with incredible speed along the pavement, keeping very close to the houses and disappearing in one of the doorways. This figure only seems to be seen on wet nights during the winter months.

The lovely eighteenth-century Ranger's House in Farnham Park, a square and solid property, has long had the reputation of being haunted by the ghost of a pretty girl, but no one knows who she was or what happened to her to cause her ghost to be seen. A few years ago the owner was intrigued by the story and kept an eye open for the ghost, but all in vain. 'Perhaps I look too hard ...' she said afterwards.

The Lion and Lamb, situated in one of the delightful cobbled passageways which abound in Farnham, has long had the reputation of being haunted. I recall taking a party of Ghost Club members there, and the manageress told us about the ghost of a lady dressed in grey who had been seen in the restaurant (as it then was) many times over the years. She was always taken to be a real person until, suddenly, she was no longer there. A former manageress told us that she suddenly found herself about to serve a quiet, gentle-looking little old lady with some tea; she turned to offer the customer some cakes, and when she turned back the person she had been about to serve had completely disappeared. As with most true experiences of ghosts, the figure appeared to be solid and quite normal in every way – until it was no longer there. Later it transpired that some other members of the staff, or some member of the public present at the time, also saw the harmless figure, while others were not aware of the presence of the lady in grey who always wore a large hat. On occasions, we were told, the figure would be seen several times in one day and then months would pass before she was seen again.

The rambling building once formed the stables of a six-teenth-century inn, and it is an interesting fact that other parts of the building, unconnected with the one-time restaurant, have also been the scene of apparently supernormal activity. In particular, heavy footsteps have sounded in deserted passages and the occupants of several self-contained flats have reported noises and the displacement of objects that they have been unable to account for. One old staircase, especially, seems to be associated with footsteps that seem to climb upwards on certain evenings, although the stairway is seen to be deserted. Outside the Lion and Lamb stands an ancient lead pump and occasionally the figure of a maid in old-fashioned dress is reported to be seen standing in what was once the yard of an inn.

The parish church of Farnham has several ghosts, some well-authenticated, including that of a little old lady (Farnham seems to have a preponderance of female ghosts!) who has been seen time after time entering the church at a time when she might be expected to go there for evensong, but she has never been seen inside the church. Once two curates followed her along the cobbled path and through the main doorway but when they were themselves inside the church there was no sign of the little old lady who, a moment before, had been only a few steps ahead of them. Other witnesses have said that a similar figure has been seen to pass through a bricked-up door at the side of the church.

Some time after I first published a brief account of this apparition in my *Gazetteer of British Ghosts* (1971) the Rev. Allan Wheeler was good enough to write to me from Hayes to say that he was one of the curates concerned. 'Believe me,' he wrote, 'I thought she was absolutely real and so did my colleague.' He went on to tell me that this ghost was still about and had been seen within the previous twelve months by a friend of his 'who described her wonderfully and said she seemed to try to speak'. Mr Wheeler also informed me that a churchwarden at Farnham told him on one occasion he had found himself talking to a phantom priest (many priests who were refuguees from the French Revolution are buried in the churchyard), and sounds like horses champing and pawing the ground have been heard from the back of the church. This is interesting because Mr Wheeler goes on to say that he understands that at one time Cromwell used the church as stables.

There are other ghosts inside Farnham Church. During the last war a fire-watcher, alone in the deserted church one night, suddenly became aware of the sound of Latin chanting, that seemed to originate from the dark nave of the church. As the deep men's voices rose and fell, he quietly walked towards the far end of the nave, and then he saw tiny points of light in the darkness; as he drew nearer he could distinguish candles being carried in procession. He stopped and watched for several minutes with no sense of fear, only a feeling of great peace. Gradually the lights disappeared and the sound of chanting died away. He spent scores of nights in the church, alone and in the company of others, but this was the only occasion on which he heard chanting and saw ghostly lights, although a police sergeant once witnessed the arresting spectacle, quite unaware that it was paranormal in origin.

In 1960 a visitor to the church, kneeling at the back, raised her eyes after praying and saw a pre-Reformation High Mass being celebrated at the altar. It seemed to her that the church was nearly half full of people, although it had been empty when she had entered a few moments earlier, but now she watched the ceremony unfold before her eyes. She saw a gold-clad celebrant accompanied by brightly-clad assistants, each playing their part amid the rising incense smoke. Some of the worshippers were motionless, she noticed, like herself, while others moved up and down the north aisle. At any moment she expected to hear music or chanting, but the whole scene was enacted in total silence. Then the church door opened; she turned to see the rector enter accompanied by a church-warden – and when she looked back towards the altar, all the people she had seen had disappeared and the church was deserted, as it had been when she entered.

For years the best-known haunted hostelry in Farnham was the Hop Bag Inn, (now called The Downing Street) on the main coach route and a stopping place when coaches were horse-drawn. Outside the present impressive Police Station opposite there is an equally impressive modern bridge over the River Wey; once this Longbridge was the final obstacle for the tired coachman and his passengers (and his horses) before a welcome stop at the inn that was then known as the Adam and Eve, and it is over Longbridge that a phantom coach and horses are said to travel, silently and swiftly, to turn again into the yard of the welcoming inn. There is a theory that some hauntings, almost like batteries, run down, and where once a phantom form was heard and seen as time passes nothing is seen but the sounds are still heard, and then, years on perhaps, nothing is seen or heard except by certain animals and people endowed with psychic awareness. At all events the sound of a coach and horses has been heard at the inn fairly recently, and I have talked with a visitor who was awakened by the sound of panting horses, the grind of heavy wheels and the clank of harness that seemed to come from the inn yard, beneath her window. Wondering what was happening at such a late hour, she slipped out of bed and looked out of the window. The bright moon lit up the deserted inn yard as though it was day; but now all was quiet and there was nothing to account for the noises that had awakened her.

An ancient story associated with the inn and the phantom coach and horses tells of such a coach pulling into the inn yard late one night where the coachman had the task of breaking sad news to a girl who had long waited in the yard for her lover. The story goes that the coach had been way-laid by highway-men, and in trying to help the coachman and his terrified passengers the young man had been brutally murdered by the highwaymen, and all the coachman could offer the heart-broken girl was his dead body.

Other haunted properties in Farnham include the Old Mitre Inn (formerly a restaurant) where there are several reported ghosts: a couple haunt the stairs, a man in the uniform of Wellington's day has been glimpsed near the entrance, and a girl in early nineteenth-century costume has been seen at the back of the premises. The ancient Bush Hotel, in the centre of the town, has a bedroom that is said to be haunted by the ghost of an old-time serving girl. Not long ago a girl occupied the room on the eve of her wedding. She found herself awake in the early hours of the morning, and became aware that the form of a young servant girl stood beside her bed. She said afterwards the ghost looked friendly and seemed almost to smile, so she was not really frightened by the experience, until the form slowly 'melted into nothingness', when she did begin to feel a little apprehensive.

Farnham can boast still more ghosts: there is a lady in a Queen Anne crinoline who has been seen on a former stairway at the very ancient building that was once a picturesque mill; a shadowy figure apparently interfered with taps and other bits and pieces at a building in Bear Lane where one caretaker's dog showed evidence of its awareness of the presence of the ghost; a phantom Roman army marches up the ancient hill south of the town (not far from where some Roman coins were once unearthed); a ghost train is reputed to have been heard running along the railway lines east of the town – the Runfold track that has long disappeared, having been taken up years ago by the railway authorities; and at a mid-Victorian cottage in Waverley Lane the figure of a woman in Victorian costume has been seen on the landing, once having apparently come out of a bedroom occupied by children. The parents made no mention of the figure that had been seen, but shortly afterwards the eldest boy told his mother that one night he had found himself awake and saw a woman sitting on his bed, an indistinct figure that vanished when he looked harder to try to identify her. There is a farm on the outskirts of Farnham where yet another female phantom has been seen; the former occupants told me that the figure was supposed to be connected with some tragedy in the past, but details have long since disappeared. Then there is the old malthouse by the river where the ghost is that of a head maltmaster who was drowned in a vat.

The Public Library is housed in Vernon House, a beautiful old property where Charles I stayed on his way to trial in London, and it is the room that he occupied (now used for office purposes) that is said to have a 'heavy psychic atmosphere'. Certainly when soldiers were billeted there during the last war a number of strange and apparently paranormal happenings were reported.

Turning to York, it seems that the enormous interest in the ghosts of York began with a visit I paid to that city in 1974 when I presided at the original Ghost Weekend there. Certainly in the ensuing thirteen years or so thousands of visitors have been attending similar weekends laid on for tourists; there have been nation-wide television and radio programmes, magazine articles and booklets about the ghosts of York, and some of York's ghost stories have been included in several books devoted to ghosts and haunted houses.

The best-known ghost story from York is probably the Roman soldiers, marching in formation in some cellars.... Harry Martindale was a young apprentice, working on the installation of pipes in one of the cellars of the Treasurer's House in the early 1950s, and he has himself told me the story of that strange experience. He remembers he was standing half-way up a short ladder when he heard the sound of a trumpet. For several seconds he thought nothing of the sound other than it must have been some odd acoustic effect; but then he heard it again, and this time it sounded nearer; then again, nearer still this time; and then, to his astonishment, he saw the figure of a horse come through the wall! Huge and lumbering it came, bearing a man on its back, a soldier dressed in Roman costume! The young plumber promptly fell off the ladder, confused and shocked, but to his amazement he watched the mounted soldier pass, to be followed by a group of foot-soldiers, carrying lances and short-bladed swords and wearing Roman helmets. They did not seem to notice the young lad leaning on one elbow on the floor with his mouth open, hardly able to believe what he was seeing. He noticed that they did not seem to be marching in any sort of formation, but were rather shuffling along with their heads down in a dispirited and dejected manner. The vision or appearance or whatever it was made a great impression on Harry Martindale, who took in every detail, and it is all as clear to him today as it was when he saw it. Archaeologists later discovered evidence suggesting the presence of a Roman headquarters in the vicinity of the Treasurer's House, and where the ghostly soldiers walked there had once been a Roman road.

York Minster has been the scene of several ghostly mani-festations, including a ghostly naval officer in full uniform – seen by three people simultaneously – an appearance that apparently took place at the exact hour and day that the officer (who was known to the witnesses) had died at sea; while the ghostly form of Dean Gale, who died in the Minster in 1702 and is buried there in a lead coffin, has been seen sitting in his old pew.

The Church of the Holy Trinity, Micklegate, is another well-known York haunting, perpetuated by Sabine Baring-Gould (1834–1924) in his *Yorkshire Oddities*, concerning three ghostly figures that were 'often' seen, always in daylight and generally during the morning church service. They consisted of a tall and graceful young woman, usually referred to as 'the mother', and a young nursemaid with a child which she brought to the older woman. Legend has it that the child, with her father and mother, lived near the church; that the father died and was buried near the east window, but the child, dying later of the plague, had to be buried outside the city walls. Soon afterwards the mother died and was buried beside her hus-band, but 'her restless spirit seeks their child and bemoans the separation'. Within living memory these unquiet ghosts have been reportedly seen and sensed, although the church is in fact much altered since the time of the ghost story; even the east window has been renewed and is not even in its original position.

The Theatre Royal is thought to occupy a monastic site, lending credence to the so-called Grey Lady apparition seen thereabouts, and the sound of chanting that has been heard there occasionally by a number of visitors and nearby residents; while the City Library was thought to be haunted in 1953 when the form of an old man with side whiskers and wearing a frock coat and drainpipe trousers was seen on several occasions, usually shuffling along between the rows and seeming to examine some of the volumes closely.

St William's College has the ghost of an unidentified woman who sits on the steps and smiles at passers-by. She was seen as recently as 1978 when two Dutch students walked into the college brass-rubbing centre and asked about the 'nice old lady sitting outside'; they were told she did not exist and they hurried outside to find she had completely disappeared. Nearby in a narrow cobbled alley called Bedern a nineteenth-century workhouse beadle is said to have starved to death fifteen children, whose voices are still heard there occasionally.

A local history teacher, John Mitchell, has chronicled the ghosts of York; and among the interesting hauntings he has written about is the ghost story associated with an ancient property almost opposite York Minster, where an entire family was walled up alive when they caught the plague in the seventeenth-century. Only one daughter recovered, it is said, and even though the citizens could hear her cries they refused to go near the house, and eventually the cries stopped. John Mitchell told me that he had heard about a nanny who had lived in the house and had thought the crying she heard was from the two children in her care, but one night, after the weeping, one of her children said sleepily to her, 'Please don't let the little girl come in and sit on my bed any more; she just keeps crying all the time.'

Several public houses in York can boast a ghost. There is the Cock and Bottle where I remember being told about the ghost of George Villiers, the evil Duke of Buckingham, whose ghost has been seen in the building he knew so well. The Black Swan, York's oldest inn, is said to be haunted by a partial manifestation: a pair of disembodied male legs that have, reportedly, been seen descending the staircase in the landlord's private quarters. The Windmill Hotel has some haunted steps, and once an assistant mayor heard distinct footsteps sounding on the wooden stairs although the room was in fact carpeted, and at the same time he felt that he was surrounded by an 'icy mist'.

In 1960 a policeman was passing St Crux's Church Hall late one night when he glanced through the window and saw a coffin resting on a trestle table, surrounded by mourners all dressed in black. Seeing no hearse and finding the hall door fastened, he suspected a student hoax, for it was an odd time for a funeral, and he called for a patrol car. It arrived within minutes, but on investigation there was no sign of any coffin or any mourners.

Other hauntings in York include a headless Cavalier; a dying Roundhead; a ghostly coachdriver; a mysterious figure in a ragged cloak and, by way of a change, a ballroom with a 'cold spot'!

Pluckley in Kent is generally considered to be the most haunted village in England, although Bramshott in Hampshire has also been awarded that doubtful honour. Pluckley I have visited several times, including a lengthy visit in 1976 with The Ghost Club, when we toured all the allegedly haunted sites and talked with all the local people who claimed to have seen ghosts or experienced ghostly phenomena.

We visited the site of the manor house of the Derings, still haunted by a ghostly White Lady on occasions; the Black Horse inn where furniture has moved by itself; the lane where a schoolmaster hanged himself, and his ghost form has been seen swinging from an overhanging branch; a house near the Black Horse where the occupants had seen 'a translucent apparition with dark curly hair'; a haunted tree where once a highwayman died in agony; the church of St Nicholas where the lonely Lady Dering is said to walk on certain nights of the year; the churchyard where the Red Lady searches the gravestones for her lost child and where a 'huge white phantom hound' was reportedly seen on Hallowe'en a few years ago.

There was also a house where one room was haunted by the sound of whispering; another where a ghost monk walked; a farm where objects moved by themselves, footsteps sounded that had no natural origin and smells that could not be explained were reported; there was an old ruined mill where a former owner walks on nights of the full moon; a ghost gypsy or watercress woman who smokes a smelly pipe beside a little stone bridge on autumn nights; a soldier who committed suicide; and a ghost that walks through one house and into the next!

Bramshott, too, I have visited on a number of occasions, but I have yet to see any of the reputed ghosts; although I enjoyed the atmosphere at the old manor house where there are said to be three ghosts – an Elizabethan priest, an early Quaker, and a White Lady, thought to be Lady Hole, a former owner.

Another Elizabethan ghost at Bramshott is that of a gamekeeper named Adams whose ghost is said to have been seen on occasions sitting outside his cottage enjoying a clay pipe of tobacco – a new-found pleasure in those days, surely. Ghostly pipe music has been heard in a nearby lane for centuries and is supposed to have its origin in a pipe-playing shepherd boy; while in the lush green meadows beside the slow-flowing stream the ghost of Mistress Elizabeth Butler, who drowned herself here in 1745, still walks; and at the nearby church there is another ghostly girl, wearing a poke bonnet, who disappears through the churchyard wall.

Bramshott also has a Grey Lady who is seen beside a wall where she is said to have committed suicide; and a ghostly pot-boy who hurries past as he would have done in the days of stage coaches. There is a leafy lane where a host of Tudor ghosts have been seen and the unmistakable figure of tall and bow-legged Boris Karloff (who lived at Bramshott) has, I have been told, been seen in the vicinity of the cottage he loved. Then there is the ghostly group of women and several children seen near a lodge house; a phantom coach and horses that clatters through the village; a mounted Cavalier who rides through a hedge; a murdered highwayman whose faithful horse carries the body of its master; a white calf-like creature about the size of a large cat; a black pig that grunts and then disappears; and yet another victim of suicide.

Finally, in this look at Britain's reputedly most haunted places, there is Borley where once stood the 'most haunted house in England'. We have already looked briefly at this remarkable haunting, so I will merely say here that Borley is still worth a visit. Although the haunted rectory has long vanished, the rectory cottage is still there, much as it always was from the front but much altered at the back. The church is still there and the churchyard where many of the chief actors in the Borley drama lie buried. From a historical viewpoint it is a fascinating place, but please do not worry the local people with questions and enquiries; they have had more than enough of the Borley ghosts and understandably they now tend to 'play down' the whole story. And if you do go to Borley, as every ghost hunter should at least once in his life, you will let me know if you encounter anything unusual at that strange place, won't you?

10 · Ghost Hunting in Europe

Europe is virtually unexplored as a hunting ground for ghost enthusiasts, although Professor Hans Bender of Freiburg has made extensive, important and exciting investigations into poltergeist phenomena. He is among the dedicated researchers who seek to explain what is at present inexplicable wherever it may be found and whatever form it may take.

Germany has an honoured place in the history of psychical research with investigators like von Schrenck-Notzing (1862–1929), Professor J.C.F. Zollner (1834–82), Professor Hans Driech (1867–1941) and Professor Karl Gruber (1881–1927), and it has produced such outstanding mediums as Willi and Rudi Schneider. It is a country full of legend and mystery, and when I was contemplating an *International Ghost Register* a few years ago I had prepared more than forty entries for Germany.

One of the best-known ghosts of Germany is the White Lady of Berlin, a phantom that has allegedly haunted the Old Palace at the end of the Unter den Linden for three hundred years. The palace was built by the cruel Frederick, first King of Prussia, and the formidable Iron Maiden instrument of torture was once housed in the Tower of the Green Hat. This was used by Frederick to pierce and crush many innocent people. However, the well-authenticated ghost does not appear to be one of these victims, although there are those who maintain that the White Lady was a model for the Iron Maiden – a beautiful woman who apparently reappeared many times after her death to warn the descendants of King Frederick of their own approaching ends. Others believe she is the ghost of an early Hohenzollern, Countess Agnes of Orlemundx, who murdered her two children. The ghost was first reported in 1619 and was immediately associated with a royal death. Subsequently she is said to have been seen by, among others, King Frederick William II in 1792; by Prince Louis of Prussia in 1806; by Napoleon Bonaparte when he was staying at the

Old Palace and reported by Marshall Ney; by Kaiser-Wilhelm II in June 1914; and again in April 1945 she was seen as Berlin burned. Today the great open space where once the Old Palace stood is reportedly haunted from time to time by a phantom lady in white.

The 900-year-old Wartburg Castle at Eisenach is the centre of many German legends. Here minstrels like Tannhauser and de Vogelweide sang of noble lords and lovely ladies. J.S. Bach was born in Eisenach. Martin Luther, who translated the New Testament into German, was imprisoned here, in the sixteenth-century, in a room where, it is said, he was visited one night by no less a person than his Satanic Majesty himself. Indeed, the actual room where the visitation took place is, or was, open to visitors, and the stone wall of the apartment is said to bear witness to the occurrence by showing a big black stain caused by the ink of Luther's ink-pot which was used by the great man as a hand-grenade when the apparition showed itself! Whether Luther did really see the Devil is of course open to argument, but letters he wrote at the time of his incarceration show that he undoubtedly believed that he was visited by apparitions and phantoms.

More recently a German correspondent tells me that the castle at Alsbach, in southern Germany, long having the reputation of being haunted, has been the scene of strange happenings. The old castle is visited by many people during the hours of daylight but it is shunned when darkness falls. One witness claims to have heard the sound of someone crying bitterly late at night when he passed close to the castle. He heard the same sound on several occasions; each time the sounds lasted about ten minutes and appeared to originate from the main tower. One April night he set out to record the sounds but all was quiet until, a little before midnight, he thought he saw something thrown down from the tower. At the same moment he had a vivid impression of the face of an Earl of Alsbach who had died in 1880. Later, during the course of local research, he discovered that the Earl of Alsbach had been murdered by two of his enemies. They had killed him and thrown his body out of the castle tower, on an April night a century earlier.

The Burg Falkenstein in the Harz Mountains is reputedly haunted by the White Lady of Falkenstein, and the castle contains a so-called 'haunted bed' which Harry Price found 'rather unexciting'. Nevertheless, he enjoyed the antiquities in one of the most beautiful and undamaged examples of mediaeval castles in existence – when he visited it. At that time there was a door leading out of the chapel, which was sealed with a massive iron lock. The story was that the door had not been opened for 500 years and no one knew what the room contained; a room which had no windows. The White Lady, an ancestress of the then owner, had been seen, Harry Price was told, many times by the resident staff, always at dusk and always in the vicinity of the 'haunted bed' – as if she were protecting someone or something in it. Harry Price and his two companions tried to get the owner to open the door of the 'curse room' and/or allow them to sleep in the haunted bed, but they were informed that the owner would not allow the room – or the White Lady – to be disturbed.

Some years ago an apartment of four rooms on the second floor of a building in the Augusta Strasse in Munich was the scene of curious happenings. I cannot do better than reproduce Harry Price's account of the case.

'The flat had for many years been occupied by an elderly lady, the widow of a doctor. She had let one room to a chemical student and, eight days before the commencement of the extraordinary events I am about to relate, she had dismissed her servant on account of "malevolence", and had engaged as a new maid a girl of fourteen years.

'The lady went out for a little while one afternoon and only the maid and the lodger were left at home. Suddenly the front door bell rang. The girl opened the door and saw a tall man with a dark cloak and blue hat standing before her. For some reason she could never explain, she no sooner set eyes on him than she felt afraid. The girl answered the door perhaps twenty times a day, but this man was "different" from all other visitors. It seemed to her that there was something uncanny about him. She was a little frightened by his dark and old-world clothes and his staring eyes, though he merely asked politely for the servant who had just been dismissed. At this the girl began to tremble, and when she informed the stranger that the person he wanted was no longer in the house, he became abusive. The maid plucked up sufficient courage to close and lock the door in his face, and then reported the incident to the lodger, who at once went to look for the mysterious intruder. He could not be found.

'Two hours later, after the widow had returned, strange things began to happen in the flat. At first, the door bell rang violently. The ringing lasted an hour, yet no one was to be seen at the door. There followed a violent "drumming" on the door, though the drummer remained invisible. This continued for some time, and then the family were thrown into a state of panic, for it seemed as if the disturbing entity had entered the flat. Glasses, plates, vases, tumblers, spoons and various other articles were flung in all directions by an unseen hand. Doors and windows opened by themselves, and the wardrobe mirror was smashed to pieces by some invisible object. A reel of thread was thrown through the letter-box of the door and as suddenly disappeared.

'Furniture moved of its own volition. Nothing would stay in its place for five consecutive minutes. Overcoats hanging in the hall were mysteriously transported to other rooms. The maid would close a drawer one moment, and it would be opened and the contents turned out by unseen hands the next. The manifestations became so alarming that finally the police were summoned.

'During the examination of the rooms and their contents, the manifestations went on without interruption. In the widow's bedroom a tumbler of water filled itself, flew across the room, and the contents splashed on her bed. When she picked up the tumbler and placed it on a table, it flew off and smashed itself against the wall. In the student's bed were found a bowl filled with water, shoes and plates; in the maidservant's bed were found a bottle of water and a sprig of fir tree which belonged to a bunch in the hall. In her trunk was discovered the missing reel of thread which had so mysteriously found its way through the letter-box. Behind a curtain were found several valuable vases which in some inexplicable manner had been removed from their usual positions. Whilst these discoveries were being made the strange displacement of objects continued.

'On another occasion, when the police were actually in the flat, a fire broke out in one of the rooms without any apparent cause. A knife was thrown at and struck one of the policemen, and a glass fell on his head. It is said that the mysterious stranger was again seen at the flat early in the morning on the day after his first visit, but quickly disappeared on being detected. No explanation of the extraordinary occurrences was forthcoming. The spiritualists claimed that the stranger was a ghost who was seeking some object. Whether there was any truth in this, I cannot say. A more likely explanation is that the manifestations were caused by the maidservant. Even the police had to confess themselves baffled, which, to say the least of it, is very unusual in such affairs. Eventually, as in most poltergeist cases, the mainifestations completely subsided.'

Other well-known German haunted properties include the ruins of Hohenratier Castle, Slawensick Castle, Cologne Cathedral and a host of reported haunted houses, offices, taverns and chalets throughout the length and breadth of that beautiful country.

The historic French town of Versailles was the scene of a very famous ghost story. In 1901 two ladies of distinguished academic standing walked through the gardens of the Palace of Versailles and seemed to encounter people, places and buildings as they had been in 1789, on the eve of the French Revolution. For ten years they painstakingly researched the period and the circumstances of their experience and came to the conclusion that they had stepped back in time and seen, among others, Queen Marie Antoinette, in the garden of the Petit Trianon, awaiting her arrest. Their book, *An Adventure*, published in 1911, caused a sensation, and the case was long considered to be the best-authenticated ghost story of all time; and although Dame Joan Evans, the distinguished historian, was convinced that the ladies had walked into a rehearsal of a *tableau vivant* enacted by the Comte Robert de Montesquiou-Fezenzac and his friends, a Society for Psychical Research investigator, Andrew MacKenzie, has shown that the Comte had moved back to Paris several years before the visit by Miss Moberley and Miss Jourdain. In fact it is not easy to explain the whole affair in rational terms, and this curious story remains something of a ghostly mystery.

Many of the castles and great chateaux of France have historic ghostly associations. The now peaceful and residential castle at Azay-le-Rideau in the Loire Valley contains a wealth of superb Renaissance furniture and tapestries and one is inclined to wonder whether they may act as a storehouse for the occasional play-back of past events. In 1418 Charles VII, who was then Dauphin, fancied himself insulted by the Burgendian guard of Azay and, with regal arrogance, ordered the town to be burnt and the 350 soldiers in the castle to be executed on the spot. Such a terrible event does seem to have left something behind, for not only are there stories of unexplained screams and mysterious figures seen flitting about the castle once in a while, but sometimes, on starless nights, a strange glow, as of flames, rises up and seems to lick around the base of the castle.

One of the most beautiful of all the chateaux in the beautiful Loire Valley is Chenonceaux, approached along an avenue of plane trees, where Charles IX used to entrance his guests by having courtiers dressed as mermaids, nymphs and satyrs. There is the delightful garden of Catherine de Medici; royal apartments on the first floor; and a tiny convent for Capuchin nuns installed in the attic with a drawbridge of its own to separate the nuns from the rest of the castle's occupants. Two women are said to haunt this slumbering chateau that has seen days of happiness and nights of frightful revelry and debauchery. There is Diane de Poitiers, Mistress of Henry II, regarded as the most beautiful woman in France in her day; her ghost lingers pale and sad on nights of the full moon before the great mirror in her bedroom. Catherine de Medici, wife of Henry II, appears, it is said, every full moon without fail, and combs the lovely hair of her rival. When Henry died, his jealous wife exiled Diane from Chenonceaux, the one place on earth that she loved above all others, and the one place her ghost or spirit seems unwilling or unable to abandon.

The great chateau at Blois where the standards of Joan of Arc were blessed by the Archbishop of Rheims is, according to one authority, 'thronged with ghosts'. Certainly at least two ghosts walk the halls of this great chateau; ghosts that seem destined never to meet on their midnight rambles, for one is said to be the ghost of a murderer who was himself murdered and the other is the ghost of his victim. The murderer and royal ghost is that of Henry III of France, who feared the growing popularity of his witty and attractive rival Henri de Guise, and one day, while 500 supporters of de Guise waited to see him in the Grand Hall, Henry effectively disarmed them by murdering their leader in the royal bedroom on the second floor. After the killing Henry went to his mother, Catherine de

Medici, and said, 'I no longer have a colleague; the so-called King of Paris is dead.' 'God grant,' Catherine replied, 'that you have not just become the King of Nothing at All!' Her intuition was prophetic and a few months later Henry was himself stabbed to death.

For years the hulk of a luxury schooner lay rotting in the beautiful Riviera harbour of Villefranche, haunted, it was said, by the ghost of Errol Flynn; for the dilapidated shell of a ship was once the pride and joy of the swashbuckling and flamboyant film actor, whose last words were, 'I'll be back.'

The ghost of Flynn has been reported by harbour workers, by people who knew the actor, and by people in passing boats. For five years after the death of its owner the *Zaca*, better known as the *Black Witch*, was berthed at Palma, Majorca, looked after by Flynn's wife Patrice Wymore, but then there were legal problems with the estate and also rumours of the haunting. The yacht was moved to Villefranche, and there Bernard Voisin and his son Thierry took possession of what was left of the yacht in lieu of mooring fees, and they at once set about restoring it. Within days, two of their workmen, Jean Luc Lopez and Francis Guerrero, reported hearing sounds that they were totally unable to explain: doors banging and voices, and a 'misty' figure reflected in a mirror in Flynn's old cabin. Barry Floyd, a marine painter, went on board and encountered a 'spectral figure'. He said afterwards that he could see right through the figure. 'I don't frighten easily,' he added 'but this was unreal ...'.

Colonel John Samuelson, and his Brazilian wife Beatriz, toured the shell of the schooner on the anniversary of Errol Flynn's death, 14 October (1978) and they both suddenly 'saw' eight people, including a girl in a yellow dress, another girl in blue jeans and a white blouse and Flynn himself in a blue-and-white striped tee shirt. 'Flynn appeared to be handing out drinks and singing at the top of his voice,' Beatriz added. 'Whatever they were doing, they were enjoying themselves.'

Actor Jack Hawkins was among the guests on board the old *Zaca* who felt odd and uncomfortable aboard her. He told Mr and Mrs Puck Willan afterwards that the boat gave him a 'very strange feeling' and he was 'terribly unhappy' about it. In 1979 reports of things happening on the schooner became so numerous that a local archdeacon conducted a service of exorcism for the *Zaca* in a little church in Monte Carlo.

Sweden's Royal Palace at Stockholm has long been reputed to be haunted by the ghost of Sweden's soldier King, Charles XII, and by other unspecified ghosts. According to one Swedish periodical the ghosts of three kings have been seen at the Palace: King Haakon of Norway, King Frederick of Denmark and King Gustav of Sweden.

The house at The Hague, Westeinde 12, for years the British Embassy, has long had the reputation of having a ghost, and some years ago Sir Peter Garron, the British Ambassador to The Netherlands, was good enough to tell me something of the history of the house and detail many of the curious happenings there.

In the middle of the fifteenth-century, a man of substance, Garrit van Assendelft, lived at what was then known as the House of Assendelft. A counsellor of Charles the Bold, he married a wealthy heiress named Beatrix van Dalem. Garrit's son, Nicholas, who also made a good marriage with Alyt van Arckel, Lady of Kyeffhouck and Cralinghen, duly inherited the house and was survived by his wife for thirty years. She shared the inheritance with her son, Ridder Garrit van Assendelft, who, as a young man at the beginning of the sixteenth-century, went off to France to study law in Orleans, and there met and married a girl named Catherine de Chasseur, who is sometimes regarded as the source of the ghostly happenings that have since been reported from the House on the Westeinde.

The marriage was disastrous and led to tragedy. Catherine was the daughter of an innkeeper, an attractive girl, and young Ridder, discovered with her in a compromising situation by her father, married her under pressure. His mother, the proud Alyt van Arckel, must have been angry and disappointed with her son, and indeed Ridder tried to leave his wife behind when he returned home; but she followed him to The Hague and, when he refused to admit her to his house, the Court (the *Hof van Holland*, of which he was later to become president), taking no account of rank, state, or fortune, ordered him to take 'her to live with him in his house, at his table and in his bed'. But it was no good; his mother and his sister did all in their power to turn him against his wife and their child, Nicholaes or Claes, and, although his mother did not live to see the result of her intrigues (for she died in 1530), the marriage did in fact break up in 1532.

After the legal separation, Catherine left the house and settled at the corner of the Voorhout and the Nieuwstraat, while Ridder (now known by his patronymic as Garrit) prospered and became a man of considerable importance and influence: his full list of titles and dignities being 'Garrit of Assendelft, Heemskerk, Castricum, Cronenburg and Assumburg, Cralingen, Overschie and Achiebroek'. He became a favourite of the Emperor, Charles V, and from 1528 until 1558 was President of the Court. Catherine, for her part, is said to have lived up to the rank of her husband and very extravagantly. To make ends meet she seems to have taken to counterfeiting money, with the help of her French chaplain, Mathurin Alys, and two young Frenchmen. On 11 February 1541, she was caught red-handed with her accomplices and there was a public scandal ending with a trial at which she was condemned to death. The original sentence was that she should be burned at the stake in public but, by special mercy of the Queen of Hungary, then Regent of the Netherlands, her sentence was commuted to private execution; and on 11 April 1541 in the Genvengepoort prison she suffered the gruesome water death, being filled with water until she expired.

About 1754, the Spanish Ambassador of the day had the old house pulled down and built the existing residence, although it is a strange fact that apart from the arms of Philip V of Spain, which can still be seen over the archway, there is nothing Spanish about the house. It appears to be a typical Dutch town house of the period with French (Louis XV) influence, perhaps explained by the fact that the architect is believed to have been Pieter de Zwart, a Dutchman who had studied in Paris.

During the Napoleonic Wars the house was sold to Petrus Judocus van Oosthuysen, Lord of Rysenburg, one of the wealthiest men in The Hague and a pious Catholic. During his ownership, the house was occupied by a French and then a Dutch Minister, until, in 1832, it changed hands again and was bought by Chevalier de Gilles of Antwerp who, a few years later, presented it to the Jesuit fathers who own it to this day. The British Minister at The Hague in 1861, Sir Andrew Buchanan, took a lease of the house and this lease has been renewed again and again.

Although everyone who has lived at Westeinde 12 has found it a very pleasant house to live in, there have been persistent references over many years to the existence of a ghost in the house. Sir Horace Rumbold, who was Minister from 1888 to 1896, refers to these stories in his memoirs, in which he mentions one particular upstairs room as being haunted and where the occupants were plagued by vivid nightmares, 'though the recurrence in them of the same distinctive features, were singularly akin to spectral visitations'. His successor gave up using the room as a bedroom and turned it into a boxroom. 'Certainly', says Sir Horace, 'we were all of us from the first conscious of an indefinable atmosphere of creepiness and mystery pervading the entire rambling building after dark'. He goes on to say that it was only towards the end of his tenancy that he became aware of the gruesome and authentic tradition attached to the house which could well have accounted for the sense of mystery experienced there; none other than the unhappy story of the French girl from Orleans, Catherine de Chasseur.

The first known reference to a ghost at the house seems to be in a letter to John de Witt from his sister, Johanna, who had the task of preparing the house for her brother when he came to live there in 1653. On 16 August that year she wrote teling her brother that a maid she had engaged was unwilling to sleep alone in the house because she had heard that it was haunted.

There is a reference to the ghost, too, in a book by Meriel Buchanan, daughter of Sir George Buchanan, Minister from 1908 to 1910, where she states that two maids left in succession complaining that somebody, or something, 'had tried to pull the covers off their beds in the middle of the night', and goes on to say that she herself had once experienced the same sensation. She had immediately put on a light but no one was in the room, although she did hear the rustle of a dress, 'as if someone had hurriedly left the room'.

In the records of the haunting there are a number of references to 'watery manifestations' which could perhaps be significant in view of the manner of Catherine de Chasseur's death; and during the occupation of Sir Odo Russell, Minister from 1928 to 1933, there are many reports of poltergeist-like activity: doors opening unaccountably, articles removed from drawers and scattered about rooms, water lying about in unexpected places, and taps found inexplicably turned on. The Russell children had no doubt whatever about an unseen presence in the small room at the end of an upstairs passage (perhaps the same room that had provoked 'nightmares'), then known as 'the train room' because the youngest boy, David, had his train set laid out there. One day, David, alone in the room, was quite certain that the 'presence' was between him and the door and although he finally managed to make good his escape, he never wanted to play trains in that room again!

It was at this period, too, that the most remarkable manifestation of all occurred one evening in the dining-room where the table was laid for a large dinner party. Suddenly, just before eight o'clock, water poured from the ceiling, falling exactly in the place where the hostess was to sit. The table was hurriedly moved to the ballroom and reset, but the strange thing was that afterwards there was no sign of water damage to the ceiling.

There are reports too of a ghostly lady with her head covered, walking along the upstairs passage during the time of Sir Paul Mason (1954–60), and of the Masons' dog, an inveterate barker, suddenly crouching back in the same passage, all its hackles up, absolutely quiet but obviously very frightened, at the same time as an English girl then living at the house heard unexplained footsteps and saw the handle of the door to the 'haunted bedroom' slowly turn. The door was in fact locked but there was no sound of the footsteps retreating from it; and when the girl had sufficiently recovered herself to unlock it, she found nothing inside to explain what she had heard and seen. Sir Peter Garron told me that although he felt that these two 'manifestations' might possibly be explained, 'the other occurrences are less easily explicable'.

The obvious question to ask Sir Peter was had he, or his family, seen the ghost lady? He did not find this question easy to answer, and related how, one evening, and, strangely enough, the evening of a day when a Jesuit priest had been to tea, while he and his wife were sitting at dinner, something shadowy seemed to pass between them. He saw what looked like a waving line of smoke which moved slowly across the table, although his wife did not notice anything. Sir Peter said he could offer no logical explanation for this experience, but it could have been the misty outline of a full and flowing dress. Brinkman, the Garrons' butler, who had been at the Embassy over forty years, certainly believed he saw the ghost. When asked to describe it, knowing nothing of Sir Peter's experience, Brinkman said he had seen 'a shadowy figure with a grey and smokey skirt'. The haunting of Westeinde 12, the British Embassy at The Hague, is an enthralling story, a well-authenticated historical haunting that may well continue.

Among the true ghost stories from Italy there is the intriguing account of the news of the death of Napoleon Bonaparte. On 5 May 1821, while Napoleon was in exile on St Helena, his mother Madame Bonaparte was sitting in the first floor of her house in the Palazzo Bonaparte, Rome, when a strange-looking man appeared at the door downstairs and requested an audience with Madame. The hall servant was reluctant, but when the stranger, who wore a large cloak and a broad-brimmed hat drawn low over his face, insisted that the matter was urgent as he had news of her son, the servant took the man upstairs. There another servant asked the man his name and business, but the visitor replied that his message was so important that he must speak at once with 'La Signora Madre'. Madame Bonaparte was informed and she said she would see the stranger. Covering his face even more the man said to her, in a low voice, 'The Emperor is freed from his sufferings; today May 5, 1821, he died.' The mysterious stranger then retreated and quickly left the room. Madame Bonaparte was stunned ... her son dead! But how could the stranger know? It would take weeks for the news to travel that distance; and the man himself – she felt sure she had seen him before.

She rushed out of the drawing-room to speak further with the man but he had vanished. She hurried into the anteroom and asked the servant there, whose business it was to sit all day in the room, where the man had gone. He replied: 'Excellent Signora Madre, no one has passed through this room other than the servants and I have not left my post for a single moment.' An immediate search of the house, of the vicinity, and indeed of Rome, failed to locate any trace of the mysterious stranger. In the days that followed Madame Bonaparte spent long hours in her chair in the drawing-room, thinking about her son and the stranger with the bad news:

who could he have been and how could he have known what he said he knew? His whole bearing had been so familiar. Two and a half months later Madame Bonaparte received the news that her son had indeed died on St Helena on 5 May 1821, and always afterwards she believed that it was the ghost of her son who came to her: 'the same figure, the same voice, the same features, the same eyes, the same commanding presence,' she would say. A ghost that was seen by three people and not by others. A ghost that is said to return periodically to the Palazzo Bonaparte and to appear at dusk in the drawing-room.

The Old Opera House at Malta has long been reputed to be haunted by the apparition of a monk, possibly associated with the nearby Vittoria Church; while the village of Mosta once had a haunted house where groans apparently emanated from the vicinity of the front doorstep. It was established by the police that one of two brothers who had lived at the house disappeared just before the other emigrated overseas. The police themselves heard the groans and the front doorstep was taken up; underneath they found the bones of a man.

Isabelle, Countess of Paris, has revealed that she and her husband experienced strange happenings at the Agimont Castle in the Belgian Ardennes. Almost nightly they heard footsteps in the corridor outside their bedroom, and on investigation no one was ever there. Their pet dog acted as though he saw someone, went to welcome them, and then returned to his accustomed place to sleep. The count's brother, Christophe, was once aware of 'something' large and strong but invisible beside him at a first-floor window, a presence that seemed to put a comforting arm about his shoulders.

In 1985 Luciana Arretini, the wife of an engineer and mother of three teenage children, experienced a series of apparently paranormal incidents at her home in Florence. Mysterious fires seemed to dominate the case and there were reports of rooms becoming filled with smoke; a garment hanging in a cupboard caught fire during the night; a pullover and a broom were burned inexplicably; and after a number of other incidents the police and fire brigade were called in. The fire chief decided to keep the house under surveillance, and two firemen were detailed to keep watch in four-hour shifts; meanwhile the three children were sent to sleep at relatives' houses.

Just after midnight, while Luciana and her husband Casare were asleep upstairs, the watching firemen noticed the smell of smoke and then saw smoke emerging from a downstairs room; on investigation they found a cushion burning; a few hours later a wooden bedhead was found alight; later a nylon stocking began smouldering, and as Luciana was talking to one of the firemen her woollen sweater began to smoke and smoulder. Cushion covers and various garments were found alight and drawers and cupboards smoked and emitted fire. Many of the burnt items were taken away by the public prosecutor Adolfo Izzo for analysis but no answers were forthcoming; and, as so often happens in these cases, the disturbances became fewer and eventually ceased.

Spain, once the centre of attention for psychic researchers world-wide due to the activities of the famous Saragossa Ghost, the ghost that talked, has more recently attracted researchers to a mountain village in Andalusia where human faces have repeatedly appeared on the concrete floor. These curious manifestations have been photographed, and witnesses include Andrew MacKenzie of the Society for Psychical Research in London and Professor Hans Bender of Freiburg who has filmed the mysterious faces. My particular 'psychic' memory of Spain is being a representative from Britain at an international four-hour television discussion on Ghosts. The Italian representative, I recall, said that only people who believed in ghosts saw them; I said in fact the opposite was true – most people did not believe in ghosts until they saw one!

In fact ghost hunters will find hundreds of reported ghosts in every country in Europe and the area is indeed a hitherto unexplored hunting ground for ghost enthusiasts.

e puzzling photograph of the Greenwich Ghost taken by the Reverend R. W. Hardy. (Photo: The Ghost Club.)

A ghost hunter tests for traces of a ghost during a haunted house investigation (Photo: Peter Underwood.)

Part of the author's ghost hunting equipment.(Photo: Peter Underwood.)

The interior of haunted Langenhoe Church, Essex. (Photo: Len Sewell.)

The author visits a haunted church in
Hampshire. (Photo: The Ghost Club.)

'Mary Felicity', a sketch based on a
clairvoyant sighting of one of the ghosts
at haunted Langenhoe Church, Essex.
(Photo: The Ghost Club.)

Harry Price (1881-1948), one of the first scientific ghost hunters. His books contain a wealth of good advice for present-day ghost hunters. (Photo: The Ghost Club.)

Ghost Club Chairman Harry Price making a broadcast from a haunted manor in Kent in 1936. (Photo: The Times and Harry Price Library, University of London.)

A psychic investigator (R. Thurston Hopkins) examines an allegedly haunted skull. (Photo: The Ghost Club.)

The Combermere Ghost. The figure seated in the chair on the left is said to be Lord Combermere, but at the time the photograph was taken he was being buried some miles away. This was his favourite chair. Note that the figure appears to have no legs, a fairly common phenomenon in photographs of ghosts. (Photo: The Ghost Club.)

The fifteenth-century 'Crown' inn at Bildeston, Suffolk, where ghostly happenings have been reported in several rooms. (Photo: Peter Underwood.)

A photograph taken by a ghost hunter at a haunted house near Bristol, purporting to depict the ghost that haunted the house. (Photo: The Ghost Club.)

Borley Rectory, Essex, known as 'the most haunted house in England', and subject to a year's scientific examinati by ghost hunters. (Photo: The Ghost Club.)

Each 4 November the ghost of Catherine Howard is said to dash along the Haunted Gallery. This 'faked' photogr was sold as a postcard for many years. (Photo: The Ghost Club.)

11 · Ghost Hunting in North America

One of the most famous poltergeist cases in history took place at the neat two-storey cottage at the corner of Princess Street in the middle of Amherst, Nova Scotia, for twelve months from August 1878 to August 1879. The disturbances – written up by Walter Hubbell at the time – included interference with bedclothes, movement of objects, loud explosive reports, writings, sledge-hammer blows on the roof, the appearance of lighted matches and showers of potatoes, spontaneous fires, and the physical swelling of the person at the centre of the case, nineteen-year-old Esther Cox. The strange but well-authenticated disturbances began shortly after an attempted sexual assault on Esther. Once words in huge characters were deeply indented into the bedroom wall, words that said: 'Esther Cox, you are mine to kill.' The mysterious happenings ceased as inexplicably as they began, and in later years Esther (who always believed in the supernormal origin of the manifestations) would not talk about those dark days because she was 'afraid they would come back'.

Canada's most famous ghost is perhaps that of William Lyon Mackenzie (1795–1861), the first mayor of Toronto and grandfather of Mackenzie King (1874–1950), the spiritualist who was three times Prime Minister of Canada. The former home of William Lyon Mackenzie, himself a political reformer and something of a rebel, was situated at 82 Bond Street, Toronto, a property that is now a museum of early Canadian history run by the William Lyon Mackenzie Homestead Foundation, and it is a house, if we are to believe repeated reports, that the ghosts of William Lyon Mackenzie and some of his female relatives haunt to this day.

Successive caretakers and their families, including Mr and Mrs Charles Edmunds and Mr and Mrs Alex Dobban, have left comfortable apartments in the building because of footsteps and apparitions. Mrs Edmunds heard the footsteps on many occasions, as did her husband. One night Mrs Edmunds found herself suddenly awake around midnight, and she saw the form of a lady standing beside the bed and then leaning over her; although in fact there was no room for anyone to stand where she saw the figure since the bed was pushed up against the wall that side. Mrs Edmunds thought that a touch had awakened her; at all events she distinctly saw the figure which had long dark hair hanging down the front of her shoulders and a narrow face – the next moment the figure had disappeared.

On a later, similar occasion, as she woke up the figure seemed to hit her, and she had a bruised and bloodshot eye to show as a reminder of the encounter. Mrs Edmunds also saw, one night, the figure of a 'little bald man in a frock coat'. He too vanished after a few seconds. Interestingly enough all the pictures in the museum show William Mackenzie with hair, and Mrs Edmunds didn't know, at the time she saw the 'little bald man', that in fact Mackenzie had been completely bald and wore a wig.

On three occasions Mrs Edmunds' son and his wife heard the piano playing when they were staying in the house. Twice Mr Edmunds and his son went to investigate, but as soon as they moved the music stopped. Several times both Mr and Mrs Edmunds said the whole property seemed to 'shake with a rumbling noise', almost like an underground train passing nearby, except that the subway was nowhere near the house.

When they left Mrs Edmunds said, 'I did not believe in ghosts when I went to stay at the Mackenzie Homestead; but I do now, its the only explanation . . .'. Her husband refused to accept the possibility of ghosts but admitted to 'something peculiar about the place'. Once, soon after they moved in, two of their grandchildren, aged three and four years, went down to the second floor bathroom and a few moments later there were screams. Mr Edmunds found both children huddled in a corner of the bathroom, terrified. They said they had seen a lady in the bathroom, a lady who disappeared. Mr Edmunds admitted that he and his wife often heard footsteps on the stairs, like someone thumping about wearing boots, and this would happen when there was no one in the house but themselves. 'The fact is,' he said when they left, 'I am not an imaginative man and I do not believe in ghosts, but we experienced so many strange happenings there that we had to leave.'

Mrs Dobban had not long moved in when she heard heavy footsteps going up the stairs. She called to her husband but he wasn't there; in fact there was no one else in the house at the time. 'But I heard footsteps on the stairs,' Mrs Dobban stated, 'and I heard the press going in the basement.' This printing press was purchased by Mackenzie in 1825 and is still in working order, although it is kept locked up. Mrs Dobban also heard the piano playing when she and her husband were in bed and there was no one else in the house.

An all-night investigation was carried out at the haunted house on Bond Street but it was quite uneventful and perhaps suggested once again that a certain lack of intense interest and expectancy is necessary for psychic phenomena to occur. Time after time, tense waiting and watching has resulted in nothing happening, but when attention is relaxed and the watchers decide nothing is going to happen – that is just when something *does* sometimes occur.

The large and historic house on Mountain Hill, Quebec City, once the home of Dr James Douglas and later the Mountain Hill Hotel, counted among its visitors Admiral Sir George Cockburn, who had conveyed Napoleon to St Helena; Charles Dickens; Lord Charles Wellesley and the Count d'Orsay.

When he first occupied the house, Dr Douglas used a room in the basement for dissecting the bodies of waifs and strays who died in the city without relatives or friends to claim their remains. Later a room in the attic was used for this purpose, and the room in the basement was used as a kitchen. The doctor's genial Irish cook, Kitty, slept in a cupboard bed in her kitchen and often, she said, she 'held communion with many of the sad spirits of those whose bodies had been subjected to indignities in the interests of science'. Be that as it may, one Sunday morning one of Dr Douglas's students, Dr Edward Worthington, later a much honoured and local physician in the area, knowing he was alone in the house, went down to the cellar for a light – Dr Douglas having a strong aversion to smoking in any form.

In the cellar Dr Worthington saw a man sitting on a chair in front of the coal stove, his feet on its hearth, his elbows on his knees and his face in his open palms. Dr Worthington had been certain that the manservant was out – but there sat someone. He passed behind the figure and, coming to his left side, stooped down to open the door of the stove to get a light. The figure made no attempt to move and there was not room to open the stove door. Dr Worthington asked politely. 'Will you please have the goodness to move your foot, I want to open the door'. There was no reply and the figure did not move or show any sign of having heard. Dr Worthington repeated his request and when this also produced no response he lost his patience and opened the door forcibly. It opened back on its hinges but the feet of the figure never moved; the stove door went right through them!

Dr Worthington stood up and looked steadily at the figure. It had not moved. The good doctor forgot all about the purpose for which he had come down to the basement, he backed away from the figure until he reached the foot of the stairs and then he turned and raced up them three at a time! Subsequently he learned that a similar figure had been seen by Kitty and other occupants of the house.

What seems to have been a ghost train has been reported from time to time at Quarry in the middle of Newfoundland. The railway agent on duty at Quarry, on one occasion, saw an unscheduled train pass through – ignoring his signal to stop. He noted the number '10' on the engine and tender and hurriedly sent a warning message to Howley, the next station down the line, to warn them, and he also telegraphed Millertown, on the up line, to ask why he had not been informed of the train. Millertown told him that no train had passed through and at that time there wasn't a train within a hundred miles of Quarry! The reply from Howley, when it came, was no less puzzling: nothing had appeared. Anxious messages were sent along the line and a pilot engine set off from Millertown to Howley, but of the missing train there was no sign.

The railway authorities wrote the Quarry agent a sympathetic letter and they gave him two weeks' leave, but they were not sceptical of his story. They knew that some years earlier such a train as he described – and numbered '10' – had been in service on that line; it had burst its boiler near St John's station, killing the driver and fireman.

The Old City Hall at Toronto has long been said to be haunted and in 1980 two judges were among those who testified to encounters there with some of the 'resident ghosts'. Judge S. Tupper Bigelow said, 'When I take the private judges' staircase, this thing catches my gown or gives me a gentle push every once in a while', yet nothing was ever visible to account for the experiences. Judge Peter Wilch reported similar incidents; he also said he had heard footsteps on the same staircase, and once he had followed them. They went up to the attic but there was no one there, although the sound of footsteps continued.

A maintenance worker, Joe Bonett, also claimed to hear mysterious footsteps when he was alone in the building and because of his experiences there he was reluctant to venture upstairs. Another employee, Joe Felgueiras, a janitor, said he once found himself 'rooted to the floor' by an invisible force. He was descending the back stairs at two o'clock one morning when he felt 'something' grip his ankles. The lights were on but he saw nothing to explain what happened on that occasion, although several times he had seen the dark outline of someone standing in the courtroom when no human was present.

A reporter on the *Toronto Star*, Agatha Bardoel, and her sister Frannie, decided to spend a night at the City Hall, although neither believed in the possibility of ghosts. They sat in Courtroom 33, where some of Canada's most notorious murderers were convicted, and when they experienced a definite and sudden drop in temperature at one time, the air becoming icy cold and clammy, they fled from the courtroom and sat on the judges' staircase. There Agatha Bardoel reported seeing a thin mist form around a light bulb and at the same time the temperature dropped ten degrees. After five hours in the Old City Hall, they left. Judge Bigelow said at the time: 'There's just no rational explanation for these strange experiences.'

The farmhouse of James Quinn at Burgess Township on the shores of Black Lake was at one time the scene of well-attested curious happenings as Richard Lambert MA, supervisor and broadcaster with the Canadian Broadcasting Corporation and former editor of *The Listener*, himself told me.

When James Kinlock (sent by a Toronto newspaper to investigate the disturbances) arrived at nine o'clock one evening he found about sixty people milling about the one-and-a-half storey log structure. All ten windows of the house had been broken and the apertures stuffed with sacks and blankets to keep out the cold.

Inside James Kinlock found the Quinn family, Mr and Mrs Quinn and their two small sons Michael and Sidney, together with Provincial Police Inspector Sidney Oliver from Perth and a group of men, sitting about talking in a room dimly lit with a kerosene lamp. The Quinns told the newcomer that they had lived in the house for about two and a half years before experiencing anything odd; then, about two weeks previously, Mr Quinn had found some pieces of beef, that he had cut up and stored in a closed barrel, strewn around on the floor of his barn. Shortly afterwards, a window of the house started to break with a loud bang. The first crash occurred one night at eleven o'clock, and he immediately got up and searched the house but found no one. The next night the same thing happened, and on the third night a number of panes of glass were broken, seemingly by stones, 'thrown by no human hand', that came whizzing through the windows. Soon pieces of firewood jumped out of the kitchen woodbox without anyone being near; a mirror shattered by itself; and a foot-long bone repeatedly flew in through one of the windows; no matter how often it was put outside, it flew back into the house.

The Quinns' story was corroborated by Andrew Burke, a neighbouring farmer, who had seen windows in the Quinns' household smash and stones drop to the floor just inside the window, 'with a queer thud, as if there was no force behind them...'. He had also seen dishes jump, and confirmed the mysterious re-entry into the house of the beef bone. No one, he asserted most positively, had been anywhere near any of the objects he had seen move.

Another neighbour, William Cordick, said he had witnessed three flat irons move by themselves down the stairs, one step at a time, 'just like someone walking'; he was upset and frightened when he saw this. The Rev. Father Whelan, whose parish of Stanleyville included the Quinns' house, had heard a window-pane crash and seen one of the apparently paranormally propelled stones. He could offer no explanation, but described the missiles as common field stones; he noticed that, while some of them were quite dry, others were coated with ice. Once again, as with many similar cases, the affair came to an unsatisfactory end. Amid accusations of fraud, which were strongly denied and never proved, the Quinns left the area, and whatever caused the disturbances seemed to leave with them.

Ghost stories from the United States of America seem to have been dominated for the last ten years by the so-called Amityville Horror; a purported record of some eighty-five incidents experienced in the twenty-eight days' residence of George and Kathleen Lutz and the latter's three children at a colonial-style house in Amityville, Long Island, New York; a house that had stood empty for over a year. Subsequently they discovered that about a year earlier Ronald DeFeo had murdered his father, his mother, two brothers and two sisters in the house.

Less than a month after they had moved into the house, the Lutz family moved out – driven out, they said, by evil forces. On the first night they spent in the house inexplicable noises had disturbed them. Soon doors and windows, carefully closed and locked on the inside, were found wrenched open; bright red eyes looked in at them through a window and in the snow outside they found prints of cloven hooves, like those of some enormous pig. Thick green slime oozed out of a ceiling and black slime dropped out of a keyhole. One night George awoke to find his wife floating above the bed and drifting away from him; he pulled her back and switched on the light; instead of his young blond wife he saw a horrible old hag. Kathleen, too, says she saw herself in this form in a mirror and she and her husband say it was six hours before Kathleen's skin and hair returned to normal.

Experienced psychical researchers were immediately sceptical, and any critical examination of the reported incidents shows that most of them *could* have had a normal explanation, but such interpretations were not sought. The Ghost Club instituted enquiries at an early stage, alerted by, among other aspects, the fact that a number of people were making a lot of money out of the story, and it was soon found that enquiries in and around the affluent avenue on Long Island where the property stands elicited less colourful explanations and quite different opinions as to the truth of the matter.

After the Lutzes left Amityville, to settle in San Diego where they reported strange events occurring, the new owners, James and Barbara Cromartz, said the house was not haunted and they brought a legal action against the former owners, claiming that their lives had been made intolerable by sightseers, and eventually the claim was settled out of court.

The house was sold again and bought by a man who, it has been said, planned to exploit the tourist attraction value of the property. Other lawsuits followed while various investigators failed to produce evidence that neighbours, police or Roman Catholic diocese officials were in fact consulted about the 'horrors' as was claimed. There are a few interesting aspects of the case, but in general, from a serious psychical researcher's point of view, there is much that is unsatisfactory about the Amityville case.

Jay Anson wrote the book, his first book, mainly from twenty tapes the Lutzes made recalling their experiences, and from interviews with a priest (whose name he refused to reveal), and with relatives of the couple and Suffolk County police. Does he really believe the couple's story? 'I never commit myself in the book', Jay Anson told me, smiling slightly, 'I leave it up to the reader to decide.' He and the Lutzes split the advance and considerable proceeds from the book.

The White House, Washington, official residence of the American presidents, apparently harbours several ghosts, but in particular the form of Abraham Lincoln has been seen and sensed by many of the successive occupants and by some distinguished visitors, including Queen Wilhelmina of the Netherlands.

Franklin Delano Roosevelt had an open mind on the subject of ghosts and the possibility of contact with the spirit world. He once told his wife: 'I think it is unwise to say you do not believe in anything when you can't prove that it is either true or untrue. There is so much in the world which is always new in the way of discoveries that it is wiser to say that there may be spiritual things which we are simply unable to fathom.' When Carl Sandburg was preparing his biography of Lincoln he went to see Roosevelt and asked him whether he knew in which room of the White House Lincoln had spent most of his time. The president replied that he didn't know for sure, but he had always felt that it had been the Blue Room, overlooking the Washington Monument. Sometimes, when he had been there alone, he could have sworn that Lincoln was present.

When the show *Watch on the Rhine* was performed at the White House, the negro actor Frank Wilson had a private chat with the president after supper and they talked about the ghost of Abraham Lincoln. 'Mr Wilson,' the president had said, 'the spirit of Lincoln still lives on here.' On another occasion a group of Broadway entertainers were being shown the various famous rooms at the White House by the president's wife, Mrs Eleanor Roosevelt, and when they reached the Lincoln Room, Patricia Bowman, the ballet dancer, said she felt that the room was haunted. Mrs Roosevelt admitted that she had always felt so too, and just a few days previously a maid, Mary Eban, had seen the ghost of Lincoln in the room. Mrs Roosevelt was downstairs in her study working late when the maid burst in on her in a state of great excitement. She said, 'He's up there – sitting on the edge of the bed, taking off his boots!' When Mrs Roosevelt asked who was upstairs, taking off his boots, Mary Eban had replied 'Mister Lincoln!'

At one time Mrs Roosevelt commented on the Lincoln legend during the course of her New York *Daily News* column, 'My Day', and she suggested that any place where someone had lived *hard* would be quite likely to be haunted by their personality. One night when Queen Wilhelmina was staying at the White House, she was awakened by a knock at her bedroom door. No one entered in response to her permission to enter, and when the knock was repeated she got out of bed and opened the door – and promptly fainted! Next morning when the president heard of the incident he expressed concern and asked for details. 'I know it sounds ridiculous,' Queen Wilhelmina replied, 'but when I opened the door I saw Abraham Lincoln standing there ... then everything went black and I fell to the floor ...'.

In 1956 ex-president Harry Truman revealed that when he was at the White House he got up several times in the middle of the night to answer raps upon his bedroom door, but he never found anything there; his daughter Margaret said she too had heard unexplained raps in one of the bedrooms during the middle of the night. On one occasion Katurah Brooks was working late at night in the Rose Room on the second floor when she was startled by a sudden burst of laughter, loud and booming. When she looked up she saw, just for a moment, the figure of Abraham Lincoln. The ghost of the great American president has also been seen walking through the East Room where his body lay in state, and standing thoughtfully at the window of the Oval Room, looking out towards Virginia. Mrs

Coolidge, wife of the 13th president, was one more dependable witness for the apparition of Abraham Lincoln at the White House.

The ghost of Lincoln's dead son, Willie – whose spirit the president believed was constantly with him – was seen by several members of the White House staff during Grant's presidency; and after Lincoln's assassination on 14 April 1865 (an event the president had foreseen in a dream) a phantom train is reported to have appeared each April on the New York Central Railway at Albany, New York, for some years. It was the funeral train retracing its slow and melancholy journey from Washington to Illinois. The event was reported in the *Albany Evening Times* where it was stated that railway workers would make a point of sitting along the track in the early evening of 27 April waiting for the train that appeared for several consecutive years.

It may be significant that both Abraham Lincoln and Franklin Roosevelt held seances at the White House. Soon after Lincoln became president he was shown an article in *The Cleveland Plaindealer* suggesting that he accepted the possibility of spirit return. He said in reply: 'This article does not begin to tell the wonderful things I have witnessed. Half of it has never been told.'

During the presidency of Franklin Roosevelt a medium was flown regularly from the West Coast to the White House during the anxious war years; many seances were held and both presidents seem to have sought the guidance of the spirit world in affairs of state.

Other ghosts at the White House include those of William Henry Harrison, 9th president of the United States, who died only a month after inauguration. His ghost was frequently seen wandering about the attic area in the days before the White House was rebuilt during Theodore Roosevelt's administration.

The ghost of the once all-powerful head of Columbia Pictures, tough movie boss Harry Cohn, is thought to haunt his old studios and offices which are now occupied by business firms. The man responsible for such film successes as *From Here to Eternity*, *Born Yesterday* and *On the Waterfront* died in the late 1950s and he was buried near his beloved Columbia Pictures Studios.

In 1978 a market research company occupied Cohn's old

office suite and president Michael Kellerman said he felt 'cold spots and chilly breezes' in the room when all the windows were closed. He reported strange noises including tapping on walls, unexplained footsteps and the clinking of glasses. Doors also opened and closed by themselves. 'I have a feeling the presence doing all this is Cohn's ghost', he reportedly said at the time, and when he moved his office downstairs the odd happenings did not cease. 'A figure watches by my door. It used to startle me. When I go to look for him he's heading for a door which is locked – and there he disappears.' The figure was said to be that of a man of fifty, five feet eight inches tall, and wearing his hair collar-length; an accurate description of the late Harry Cohn.

Phyllis Michael, President of California Actors and Models for Equal Opportunity, occupied the Cohn suite for three months. 'It's the weirdest place I've ever worked in my life,' she said afterwards. Candles suddenly went out, curtains billowed inexplicably and 'spine-chilling' tappings were heard. 'Once we tried to track where the tappings came from. We tapped the wall ourselves and back came a tapping from the other side – a sealed-up passage.' Cohn, it seems, had this secret exit to his office. Phyllis Michael is among those who saw a door slowly swing open and heard footsteps approach. When she got up to see who was there, 'there would be nobody. It would send a chill of panic through me. I'd think "It's Harry Cohn's ghost".'

At the Hollywood home of actress Elke Sommer and writer Joe Hyams furniture moved and doors flew open and the figure of a middle-aged man was seen. After three years the couple put the house up for sale. The next night they were awakened by the sound of knocking on their bedroom door; when they opened the door there was nobody there but the whole dining-room was ablaze.

Another Hollywood actor with first-hand experience of ghosts and hauntings is Glenn Ford, whose house on a broad boulevard in Beverly Hills apparently harbours the ghosts of Hollywood's past. Sometimes, as he and his wife Cynthia lie in bed at night, they hear what could be the echo of an old Hollywood party going on in the garden – the site of a Red Indian burial ground. 'There is laughter as though someone has just told a joke and glasses clink,' the actor says. 'When we go outside we find all the garden furniture placed in a circle, like somebody has had a party. The nice thing is that it's a happy party ... Once I even smelled cologne that's not made any more – the sort Valentino once used. Things certainly happen here which I can't explain: pictures in the house change places and sometimes fall off walls, and cushions are moved; little things like that but quite inexplicable.'

Rather more puzzling perhaps have been the reports of a spectral visitor in full-dress regimental uniform, complete with shako, the old-fashioned military dress hat, and a nineteenth-century musket, seen at the U.S. Military Academy at West Point. Reports of the apparition centred on Room 4714 of the 47th Division barracks, and two cadets reported seeing the form emerge from a solid wall and later disappear through the same wall. Captain Keith Bakken decided to investigate at one stage and the ghost 'promptly appeared but receded into the wall again; its point of exit was reported by the investigators to be icy to the touch.' Later, those who had seen the ghost believed that they identified it from a print preserved at West Point.

The historic Bell Witch Ghost is sometimes known as America's greatest ghost story but there are many fascinating accounts of spontaneous paranormal activity in the United States, perhaps especially California and North Carolina. Both states have been the subject of books devoted to their ghostly inhabitants.

12 · Ghost Hunting in Australasia and the Far East

Australia's best known unearthly appearance must be a ghost that appeared in the open air. Off the highway between Sydney and Melbourne, at Campbelltown, there stands a roadsign with the arresting inscription: Fisher's Ghost Creek. It commemorates a ghost story that has become part of the legend of the country, a story of a ghost that returned for a purpose.

The story goes that one evening in 1826 a prospector and farmer named Fred Fisher disappeared under mysterious circumstances, and soon afterwards there was a report of the sighting of a ghostly figure resembling Fisher, sitting on a bridge pointing to a spot in the creek below. When the same figure was reportedly seen by different people on different occasions and, as far as could be established, without previous knowledge of the figure (which always seemed to be pointing to the same spot) having been seen by other people, questions began to be asked.

Eventually it was decided to dig at the place seemingly indicated by the phantom figure, and the murdered remains of Fred Fisher were eventually unearthed. Soon news of the bizarre discovery of Fisher's body resulted in a hunt for the killer and the eventual confession by his murderer. After justice had been done and the murderer had been hanged, the ghost of Fisher was rarely, if ever, seen again, but the event was commemorated in the renaming of the creek, and for many years there was an annual gathering at the spot.

Some years ago a haunted farm at Boyup Brook, 180 miles from Perth in Western Australia, resulted in poltergeist activity being seen by television viewers. Two men, one a sceptical feature writer and the other an experienced cameraman, spent a night at the farm, and during the course of a six-hour tour of the farm both men saw and filmed a wealth of apparently inexplicable phenomena. A small stone seemingly passed through the iron roof of the dairy and landed in a milk bucket; no one was in a position to throw it. A pair of rubber boots, missing for two days, were retrieved from the top of a lemon tree; thirty points of rain had fallen the previous night but the boots were bone dry. Five stones fell from nowhere into the orchard. The visitors were pelted with bones, stones, tins and pieces of bark as they watched some pigs being fed. Stones fell around their cars as they travelled at forty miles an hour with all the windows shut. During previous incidents heavy milkchurns were flung considerable distances.

There was an eleven-year-old son of the farmer living on the farm, but on many occasions when strange things happened he was under observation. As with most 'poltergeist' hauntings, the disturbances began gradually, mounted to a crescendo, continued for a while, and then ceased with no complete explanation.

Much-travelled Ghost Clubber Alasdair Alpin MacGregor, a former Private Secretary to the Chancellor of the Duchy of Lancaster, spent two years in Australia. On his return he regaled his fellow Ghost Club members with accounts of the ghost stories he had encountered, including the haunting associated with the Prince Alfred Hospital at Sydney where the ghostly figure of a nurse was reportedly seen on many occasions.

MacGregor first heard about the case from David Barnes, an *Australian Post* reporter, but he subsequently checked out the story for himself and found that 'she' was not in the least frightening and was usually referred to as the Good Ghost Sister. One trainee nurse said, 'Don't get the idea that she is a terrifying or nasty ghost. She's quite beautiful and always kind and helpful. She appears at the most unexpected times, usually when we are exceptionally busy. She is mostly seen in one ward but she has been seen going into operating theatres when important operations were about to be performed. She has been seen so clearly that one sister even spoke to her – although she got no reply! She somehow drew attention to something important by her presence, and it gave the sister quite a shock for a few days.'

'I saw her,' this trainee nurse continued, 'and followed her into a room to ask a question thinking she was the Sister in charge. When I got into the room – it was empty. There wasn't another door or any open window in the room, and I thought I must have been mistaken about the room, although I knew I wasn't. I did not say anything to anybody about it until, three nights later, the same thing happened again.'

Another trainee nurse also told MacGregor of her experiences: 'I saw "Sister" reading the duty report and was on my way towards her when suddenly she was no longer there! I did not like to say anything about it but it came out at breakfast one day that a friend had followed this "Sister" into the day room and found she had been following a ghost; then it all came out.

'When I was at the hospital nearly all the girls had seen the "Ghost Sister" but they were afraid to say much for fear of ridicule. One of the older Sisters heard about the stories and told us we weren't seeing things; she said there was nothing to worry about because the "Ghost Sister" was well-known and had been doing the rounds for nearly thirty years.'

The general belief at this hospital was that the ghost was that of a one-time member of the hospital nursing staff. She is supposed to have contracted tuberculosis. There was no hope of her recovery, but she died as a result of a fall from a high verandah. After her death, she came back to help with the work. On one occasion, according to other nurses, the 'spirit' rattled a door to gain entrance. The solarium doors were locked each night and the nurse on duty had just fixed them when one began to rattle as though somebody were trying to get in. There was no wind that night and the doors fitted so well that they never rattled.

This nurse went to see what was the trouble with the rattling door and could not see anything wrong. She tried to shake the door to see if it moved, and was just about to walk away when it rattled again. She went back and undid the door, and as she opened it the 'Sister' walked through. Nurse began to apologize for not seeing 'Sister' before and turned to lock the door. When she turned back, only a second later, the figure had vanished. A few minutes later the Ghost Sister was seen by another nurse, seemingly reading the reports. The nurses were so casual about this presence that, when the nurse who saw the Sister reading the reports mentioned it, the other nurse said: 'Yes, I knew she was there. I let her in through the solarium.'

MacGregor also spoke to Sister Jacqueline Bull at her home in Elizabeth Bay. She confirmed what had been told to him.

175

She knew the nurses concerned and had a high opinion of them. She said the ghost had been well known for about thirty years. 'There is nothing sinister or frightening about it, although she appears at the most unexpected times,' said Sister Bull. 'Nobody gets scared,' she went on. 'Of course you must take into account that the girls in training these days are not the types to get themselves hysterical or scared.' She added that the ghost once drew her attention to a sudden change in a patient's condition. 'I was working in one section of the ward when I saw what I thought to be the night Sister bending over a patient in another part of the ward. I finished what I was doing and went over to see what the sister had discovered, but she disappeared while I was on the way. When I got to the patient I found that immediate attention was necessary, and I had to get a doctor quickly.

'When the night Sister arrived I said I didn't know whether she had gone for the doctor or not, and had taken it upon myself to get him. The Sister looked puzzled and asked how she would know the patient was worse when I hadn't told her before. I said I had seen her bending over the patient, and then she told me she hadn't been in the ward.'

On another occasion Sister Bull also followed the ghost nurse into another room, only to find that she had vanished. Despite the fact that she had become used to the ghostly presence, when she saw it on this occasion the form seemed so real that once again she mistook 'her' for a real Sister. 'I had got a bit used to the presence of the "Sister" by this time,' she said. 'But I mistook her for a real Sister and called her by name. She half-turned but kept walking and disappeared into the room; I was puzzled and followed her in. I knew it was not the Sister I had thought it was, and it was none of the other Sisters in the place either. I thought it was a chance to find out who this strange woman was, and finish the myth once and for all. She seemed very real to me at the time and I was positive it was somebody alive.'

Alasdair MacGregor asked her to describe exactly what happened. 'I went straight into the room', Sister Bull replied, 'the room she had just walked into, and I switched on the light. There was nobody there. There was no other way out except the door where I stood. She must have gone through the wall to disappear. So she couldn't have been a real person. It must either have been my imagination or it was a ghost. I decided it was my imagination until practically the same thing happened to another nurse. Nobody knew about this happening to me, until the other girl mentioned her own experience to me in confidence. There are dozens of incidents that can be checked, for there is simply no explanation for the appearance of the "Good Ghost Sister".'

MacGregor ended his account of this haunting by saying, 'There are too many frightening ghost stories. The purpose of some ghosts may be to help, not frighten, and here is a case of a woman returning after death to continue her chosen profession – that of tending the sick; and she is welcomed by those who see her; they regard her as an angel rather than as a "ghost".'

The Princess Theatre in Melbourne has the reputation of being haunted by the ghost of opera singer Frederick Baker, known professionally as Frederic. He died in 1888 immediately after a performance of Gounod's *Faust* in which he played Mephistopheles! In 1974 an hour-long documentary re-enacted the tragedy and included interviews with many theatrical people, including June Bromhill, who claimed to have personally seen the ghost.

Moving to the Far East, it is interesting to recall that the troops of General Orde Wingate of Burma were nicknamed 'Chindits' by him after a mythical creature which is believed to protect Burmese pagodas against evil spirits.

Gerald Pooler, a Royal Signals corporal in Burma during the last war decided to rest behind a pagoda at a village called Schwebb while under heavy artillery fire during service with the 19th Indian Division. Suddenly he became aware of a figure standing over him, and he saw a Sikh soldier who seemed to imply that the captain wanted to see him at once. When he reported to the Signals Office the captain said he had not sent for him and Pooler returned to the pagoda – to find that a ton of solid stone had crashed down onto it. Corporal Pooler, in relating this experience, said: 'The most astonishing thing was that later I was told there were no Sikh soldiers at Headquarters . . . the nearest were fighting twenty miles away.'

In 1985, in response to some correspondence in the columns of *The Daily Telegraph*, that newspaper printed a letter from me headed 'Isolated Remnants' in which I said: 'Further to the recent correspondence in your columns regarding "spirits" or ghosts, it is generally accepted among the more scientific-minded investigators of such phenomena that far from being "mostly sad, lost souls," most ghosts are in fact "atmospheric photographs" or "thought forms" projected on to the atmosphere by some tragic or traumatic event and reappearing under certain climatic conditions and in the presence of certain people. This is perhaps evident from the fact that most so-called ghosts appear in one particular place, doing one particular thing, and they do not appear ever to be aware of the presence of human beings. Whatever ghosts are, and the evidence for them is overwhelming, from every part of the world and in every civilisation, it seems certain that they are *not* the departed spirits of unhappy people but rather an isolated remnant of a personality, happy or sad, that has become impinged on to the atmosphere at a particular place which, after a time, disappears.'

Shortly after my letter appeared I received a most interesting letter from a lady in Bristol who wrote to tell me of her experiences in Singapore in the 1960s. My correspondent's husband had been seconded to the BBC to be Chief Executive of the newly-formed television service in Singapore, and remembering those wonderful days when she and her husband and their two small boys and three-year-old daughter lived in a palatial house in tropical sunshine, she says she remembers in particular their beloved Chinese cook, 'Cookie', as he liked to be called. He was an old man, a grandfather, but a great character, and the family soon grew to love him.

Cookie became a kind of deputy grandfather to the three children; he allowed them to sit with him when he was eating, offering them delicacies from his chopsticks and entertaining them on his flute . . . the only thing that somewhat alarmed the English people was when they learned that Cookie insisted on sleeping with a revolver under his pillow. 'I not like the hantu-hantu (*ghost*)! This house haunted! The dog always howl at night!' he explained. My correspondent tells me that she too had felt something strange in the atmosphere of the enormous, rambling, barracks of a house, but they put thoughts of ghosts out of their minds; until one day they decided to move some heavy furniture away from the walls in the bedroom. There they discovered dozens of indelibly-pencilled names, all ending with the words 'Prisoner of the Japanese'. They could not help wondering what had happened in that room, and they learned that it had been used as a temporary prison by the Japanese. The atmosphere was, it seems, 'something almost tangible', and my correspondent continued: 'I had been used to living on my own, apart from my small children, when my husband was away making films and I was never nervous until I went to Singapore. The house in Adam Park was one of those huge "Colonial piles" and I tried to rationalise my fear by telling myself it was merely the size and age of the house. I always used to wake in the early hours of the morning and, in a rather horrible way, used to feel my husband's chest to make sure he was breathing; I confided this to a friend and she was horrified! Nothing would have persuaded me to sleep there alone, and one night when my husband was called out by a neighbour to deal with a snake, I stood in the garden, rather than remain in the house.

'Perhaps nothing really terrible had happened in that house, apart from the prisoners of the Japanese being confined there; perhaps their homesickness and fear transmitted itself to that room. I am not sure. Suggestions that I should note the names of the prisoners (they were very clearly written) filled me with horror, just in case they had been cruelly treated. In a way I think I preferred to remain in ignorance.

'The sequel to this story is that only eight months after we returned from Singapore, my husband died of a totally unexpected coronary. I still don't know whether the feelings I had in that house in Singapore came from the atomsphere of sadness transmitted from the Australian POWs or whether, in a strange way, I was being given some inkling of my husband's tragic death.'

Another correspondent, this time from Auckland, New Zealand, tells me of a strange experience he had in 1974. '. . . We were coming home from the City at about 11.10 p.m. through Dominion Road to reach Mt Albert Road. All of a sudden we had company; a young man, I would say in his early twenties, was walking right behind us for quite a number of yards, and the wife said he was going to attack us. I said if he was going to he would have done so before now. All right, I said, this is where good will conquer evil, and I turned round quickly – but he had disappeared. He could not have gone in the front garden of any of the houses because there were long gardens and all the gates were shut; one of us must have seen him. Later we learned that the year before a tall young man was run over at that spot on the path and was killed; this was in August 1973.'

A policeman is among witnesses for a White Lady who haunts Levuka, the one-time capital of Fiji. Sometimes she is seen sitting on a bench near the Masonic Hall, sometimes near a water fountain, and sometimes running along the beach. The policeman paid little attention to the figure when he first saw a woman dressed in white, sitting near the Masonic Hall, but a few moments later he saw the same figure beside a water fountain some distance away. Back home he opened his door and there was the same woman. The constable fainted.

An investigating team discovered that the White Lady reportedly appeared frequently for several months at a time. On one occasion when she was seen running along the beach another police officer followed her down a back alley, 'where she simply disappeared'. Another man claimed to see the form on three occasions and described her as having shoulder-length blonde hair and wearing a long white dress. A doctor at Levuka Hospital once found himself face to face with the same figure; and several residents claimed that the appearance seemed to indicate that she wanted her grave repaired.

The investigators came to the conclusion that there was overwhelming evidence that such a form had been seen by different people on different occasions. The most likely theory seemed to be that she was a German woman who died in Levuka early this century and had been buried in a tomb that had been severely damaged. The tomb was repaired and the ghostly White Lady was reported less frequently. Unfortunately the grave bears no name so the White Lady remains unidentified.

Herbert Johnson was a flight sergeant in the Royal Air Force in 1946 and he was posted from Italy to Karachi on the West Coast of India. Enjoying a fortnight's leave as guests of the Maharajah of Datia, Johnson and his friend Flight Sergeant Charlie Stone explored some ruins on the hill that dominated the area. One night he decided to explore these ruins on his own, and taking a torch he made his way through the town and climbed to the shrub-covered top of the hill. There he came across a heap of crumbling masonry and some steps. He gingerly made his way down and found himself in a long underground passage with apartments that looked like dungeons ranged along each side. Wedging his torch into a recess in the wall he sat down to soak up the atmosphere.

After a while the cries of hundreds of bats was drowned by the unmistakable thud of horses' hooves galloping nearer and nearer; the air seemed to quiver, and he seemed to hear the clash of weapons and arms. Then he experienced the revolting stench of blood and sweat and smoke. After a few moments the hoofbeats faded and the smell of battle disappeared. Johnson made his way, somewhat shakily, out of the darkness of the passage and into the bright moonlit night. There was nothing to be seen.

Back in Karachi at the end of his leave Johnson discovered that the ruins at Datia were those of a fortress used by the eighteenth-century warlord Bir Singh, and the hill had been a battlefield many times and must have been almost drenched in blood. Forty years later he is still convinced that he lived through one of those ancient battles and always regrets that he did not make enquiries as to other possible witnesses for the sounds and smells he experienced.

Everest, in common with many mountains, has the reputation of being haunted, and Chris Bonington told me about a curious happening during the Everest climb in 1975. One bright moonlit night, as mountaineer Nick Estcourt plodded along from expedition Camp Four up to Camp Five, he suddenly realized that he was not alone. Someone was following him: a black figure against the snow, the arms and legs distinctly visible. Estcourt was not the kind of man to imagine things and he assumed that the figure plodding after him, some two hundred yards behind, was one of the Everest team. Then, when he again looked round, the mystery climber had vanished; and when he arrived at Camp Five and telephoned Camp Four, he was told, 'Nobody was following you.' Later the same day another member of the team, BBC cameraman Mick Burke, died in a blizzard on a lone climb towards the summit. Months before the tragedy a clairvoyant had warned that a ghost would walk on Everest during the expedition and that death would strike. The prediction was made by a retired photographer Clement Williamson who said he received the message in 'automatic writing' from Andrew Irvine, one of two mountaineers who disappeared on Everest in 1924. Williamson wrote to Chris Bonington and simply asked him to keep a look-out for anything odd. The details of the prediction he wrote out separately, dated it, sealed it in an envelope and put it in a vault in the Bank of Scotland. When Bonington returned from the expedition, Williamson got in touch with Dr John Beloff at Edinburgh University (a past president of the Society for Psychical Research) and arranged for the bank to send him the unopened letter by registered post. No one saw the contents between Williamson writing it and the recipient opening it. Dr Beloff says: 'I can testify to the authenticity of the document. The predictions were remarkable.'

Chris Bonington told me: 'Mr Williamson wrote to me some months before the expedition. I never mentioned it to anyone. Looking back the closeness of the predictions was quite remarkable.' Nick Estcourt would never discuss the experience; he died in 1978, killed by an avalanche during another Bonington expedition to the world's second highest mountain, the 28,740-foot peak known as K2. Of that expedition Bonington says: 'On the approach march Nick had a very strong sense of foreboding and that was unusual.'

Many years ago in old Tokyo a cruel and violent man is said to have imprisoned a servant in a cupboard after she had broken a set of ten valuable plates, and each day he cut off one of her fingers. At length the girl managed to bite through her bonds and escape into the garden where, in her agony and grief, she threw herself down a well and drowned. Thereafter a voice was heard apparently emanating from the well and for years no servant would stay in the house. Things became so bad that a priest from a nearby temple was called in, and he prayed and admonished the ghost. Although the house was less haunted thereafter, the area where once the well stood is still occasionally the scene of unexplained phenomena, especially voices.

Another house in Tokyo was so haunted that no one would live in it, until a poor fencing master, recently arrived in Tokyo with very little money, saw the owner of the house who agreed to let the fencing master live in the house rent-free in return for fencing lessons. One night the fencing master's wife heard a frightful noise that seemed to come from a pond in the garden.

The fencing master sat up next night and heard the same noises and saw a 'kind of black cloud' floating on the surface of the pond. He made enquiries and discovered that a murder had taken place in the house and the head of the murdered man had been thrown into the pond. Emptying the pond, the fencing master duly found a skull. He buried this in the garden and the 'black cloud' was seen no more.

In 1959 the Rev. R.S. Blance visited Corroboree Rock, a hundred miles from Alice Springs, and a site known as a place where aborigines used to carry out horrifying and gruelling initiation ceremonies in the past. The place was completely deserted when the reverend gentleman took a snap, and on the resulting photograph there is a clear but ghostly figure that has never been explained.

These are just a few ideas for potential ghost hunters in Australasia and the Far East. A few enquiries and a little digging will undoubtedly uncover a number of reported ghosts and haunted houses in your area – wherever you may live.

13 · A Ghost Calendar

A number of reported ghosts seem to be cyclic in their appearance, and there may be something logical in the possibility that whatever is necessary for such an apparition takes around 365 days to build up before it can again be seen. However, it has to be said that other cyclic ghostly appearances recur every five years, others every ten years, some every twenty years, and there are even some that are supposed to appear only every hundred years. But the commonest are those reported annually and such appearances are reportedly seen with unerring regularity, even surmounting the obstacle of a change in the calendar in 1752 (in Britain) when twelve days were 'lost', but still these recurring phantoms retain the dates long associated with their appearances; even an extra day during leap years or extra hours during 'summer time' has not, apparently, succeeded in breaking the cycles of such ghosts.

Other haunting incidents always seem to occur at a definite time but on no particular date. At a hotel at Birchington in Kent, for example, it has been suggested that a suicide two hundred years ago possibly triggered the disturbances that are said to take the form of a beautiful young lady with long blonde hair who suddenly appears in 'the haunted bedroom' at three am; perhaps the time of the original tragedy. A famous daytime ghost is the Man in Grey at Drury Lane theatre, London, a ghost that has been seen by scores of people, and always between nine am and six pm but on no special dates.

Other haunting activities always seem to occur on certain nights. At printing premises at 44, Penny Lane, Liverpool (a street made famous by a Beatles song), pacing footsteps were repeatedly heard on Friday, Saturday or Monday nights. Still other ghosts are active according to climatic conditions such as stormy nights, when, for example, the White Horse of Clumly and its rider may be seen at Clumly Farm, Hestwall, Mainland, Orkney; or the terror-stricken cries of two children can be heard echoing beneath a bridge at Farndon in Cheshire, thought to be those of the two sons of Prince Madoc, drowned there for political reasons in the fourteenth century. Still other ghosts appear *only* during periods of the full moon as at Lorton

Hall, Cockermouth, Cumbria, haunted by a Grey Lady, thought to be a lunatic member of the family that occupied the property 200 years ago.

Some ghosts are reported on the dates of certain ancient festivals, or indeed on several such anniversaries, as at the sixteenth-century Reform Cottage at Prestbury in Gloucestershire, where inexplicable footsteps, attributed to a Black Abbot, are regularly heard at Easter, Christmas and on All Saints Day.

Charles Dickens popularised Christmas ghosts; his writings, more than those of any author, are associated in the public mind with the festive season and the appearance of ghosts, and Christmas is still a popular time for reports of ghosts. Yuletime hauntings seem to have gathered momentum year by year at Poplar Farm Inn, Abbots Ann, near Andover in Hampshire (according to my records), and at the Hall-i'-th'-Wood, Bolton, Lancashire, and at the partly ruined church of St John the Baptist at Boughton Green, Northamptonshire, where spine-chilling moans and the shadowy figure of a large man (thought to be a ruffian hanged there in 1825) have been reported at Christmastime.

Other ghosts favour a certain month, such as the phantom children of Bramber Castle ruins, near Steyning in Sussex, who are only seen during the cold days of December, and Glamis Castle where Earl Beardie is heard on stormy nights in the month of November. A number of cyclic ghosts put in an appearance every seven years, as at some stepping-stones across the River Ribble at Brungerley near Clitheroe in Lancashire, where an evil spirit is said to materialise every seven years and drag any unwary traveller to a watery grave; and at the Kilkea Castle Hotel, Castledermot, County Kildare, where the sixteenth-century Earl of Kildare is thought to revisit his former castle every seven years (he is due again in 1991).

Let us look now at the days of the year where ghosts and ghostly manifestations are said to appear each year; the first time, incidentally, that anything like such a calendar has been attempted.

6 January (Old Christmas Day)
The ghost monks walk and the Holy Thorn blossoms at Glastonbury.

11 January

A mid-winter fire festival is conducted at Burghead, Moray; a ceremony that goes back to Druidic and Norse fire-worship as a charm against the evil forms that manifest this night on a hill that is called Doorie.

19 January

On this date in 1643 Cromwell's army suffered a rare defeat at Braddock Down, near Lostwithiel, Cornwall, and on each anniversary the thunder of horses' hooves is said to be heard.

1 February

The ancient serpent cult was associated with the Celtic Goddess Bride, later called St Brigid, and on this one day in the year the sacred serpent queen is said to emerge from a mound at Glenelg, near the Scalassig farm at Inverness. This is the night too when Bride's Beds are constructed from rushes on Barra, in the Outer Hebrides, so that the saint would be invoked and enter the house. The spirit is summoned by the words: 'Bride, come in, your bed is ready.'

12 February

The day of the execution of Lady Jane Grey (1537–54) at the Tower of London, and each anniversary her ghost is said to reappear in the form of a 'white shape', usually in the vicinity of the thirteenth-century Bloody Tower.

13 February

Every fifty years, it is said, the three-masted schooner, *Lady Luvibond*, lost with all hands on 13 February, 1748, on the treacherous Goodwin Sands off Deal, re-enacts her last journey. She was seen in 1798 by the master of the *Edenbridge* who entered the sighting in his log-book, and by the crew of a fishing vessel. In 1848 Deal long-shoremen saw the phantom ship aground and took part in a rescue operation, but no trace of any ship was found. In 1898 shore watchers again saw a schooner sailing straight for the sands, and in 1948 there were claims that she had been seen yet again and dead on schedule. The original *Lady Luvibond* sailed for Oporto out of London with the captain's new wife aboard and a first mate who had been a rival for the affections of the bride. It seems that in a fit of jealousy the mate killed the helmsman and deliberately sailed the *Lady Luvibond* onto the sands. Her next appearance is due in 1998.

15 February

In 1815, the year of Waterloo, a young Norfolk drummer boy from Hickling Green and a girl from Potter Heigham were deeply in love but the girl's father objected to a soldier for a son-in-law. The couple used to meet in secret on the Heigham side of Hickling Broad, on the marshy islet known as Swim Coots. All through that bitter winter the boy would skate across the ice-covered Broad. By the middle of February the ice was beginning to thaw, and on the foggy night of 15 February, in the centre of the Broad, the ice suddenly gave way beneath him and he disappeared to a watery and cold grave. Ever since, at seven o'clock on misty February evenings, in the middle of the month, the roll of a solitary drum is heard across the quiet water and the phantom figure of a drummer boy appears through the gloom, still seeking his long-dead sweetheart.

26 February

The Old Court House, Hampton Court, was the home of Sir Christopher Wren for the last five years of his life, and he died in the low dining-room at the front of the house on 26 February 1723. Every year, on the anniversary of his death, phantom footsteps are heard hurrying to and fro on the stairs of this mellow house.

17 March

900 years ago a girl named Juliet was disappointed in love and hanged herself from a tree by the river at Holywell in Cambridgeshire. A suicide could not be buried in the church-yard in those days so she was buried where she died and a simple stone marked the spot. Years later an inn was built on the river bank and the stone that marks Juliet's grave can be seen forming a flagstone in the bar of the Ferry Boat Inn. Year after year, on 17 March, the date of her death, generations of people have collected here, hoping to see the ghost of a heart-broken girl rise from the grave and drift towards the river bank.

29 March

Cheriton Battlefield near Alresford in Hampshire is reported to be haunted every fourth year since the battle on this day in 1664.

2 April

A ghostly band of marauding Norsemen, mounted and blowing

horns and armed with long whips, are said to thunder down from the trees and high ground towards Ludham Bridge, Norfolk, at dead of night each 2 April; some strange psychic echo perhaps of a raid from overseas in the days when East Anglia was young.

4 April

On Good Friday, 1264, Lady Blanche de Warren died at Rochester Castle from an arrow shot from the bow of her betrothed who saw her struggling with his enemy Gilbert de Clare. The arrow sped true to its mark but glanced off the knight's armour and entered the heart of the Lady Blanche. That same night her ghost walked the battlements dressed in white, her black hair streaming in the wind and the fatal arrow still embedded in her bosom. Each 4 April the scene is said to be re-enacted.

5 April (or Easter Saturday)

A Nutlers' Dance is performed over the seven miles from one side of Bacup in Lancashire to the other, in which a team of eight Morris dancers with blackened faces are led by a 'whipper-in' who drives off evil spirits. Obviously then there must have once been evil spirits abroad on this day at Bacup to be driven off – and some say evil spirits are still abroad each 5 April.

6 April (or Easter Sunday)

Rostherne Mere, Cheshire, has long been said to harbour a mermaid, and once a year on this date she is said to be heard singing and ringing a sunken bell on the bed of the lake.

7 April

Acle Bridge over the River Bure in Norfolk is said to be re-visited each year on this date by the ghost of a man who was murdered by his mother-in-law in the early part of the seventeenth century, after the man had been acquitted of the murder of his wife for which he had been responsible. The apparition only appears, it is said, if the night is dark and wet. According to tradition the first cuckoo is also heard each year on this day, singing from the top of the Celtic cross at Nevern in Dyfed.

12 April

On this day each year the tomb of Richard Smith at Hinckley in Leicestershire is said to sweat blood. A 20-year-old saddler, Richard, in 1727, annoyed a recruiting sergeant who lost his temper and ran his pike through the astonished lad. There is evidence that the leaning gravestone has exuded a red liquid on this day in recent years.

24 April

Each St Mark's Eve the churchyard of St Mary's, Scarborough, is said to be haunted by those who are about to die. A moving shadow is seen near the remains of the abbey's great east window and a procession of those who will die during the following twelve months is said to pass slowly through the main door of the church. A similar tradition is associated with Whittlesford in Cambridgeshire, but those who are destined to be buried in the churchyard during the next twelve months are said to be seen examining their burial places. When they find the spot where they are to be buried, they lie down on the ground and vanish. On a happier note those who are to be married appear and walk arm-in-arm around the church.

27 April

Burgh Castle in Norfolk was once an important Roman fort and on this date each year its massive walls reverberate at dawn to the clang of arms and the wild cries of men in battle, distant yet distinct sounds that seem to quiver on the tranquil spring air.

30 April

Walpurgis Night, when the forces of evil hold sway over the earth, sees deformed and ugly primitive forms, people of the hills, manifesting on the Isle of Man, while at Birse, Aberdeenshire, Beltane or May Day Eve fire festivals connected with Belenus, the Celtic pastoral god, survived for many centuries with stories of shadowy pagan forms joining in the festivities. The Irish hero O'Donoghue, mounted on a white horse, is said to ride round Lough Leane, Killarney, on the evening of each 30 April (some say dawn on 1 May) to the sound of ghostly music.

1 May

At dawn a phantom army fights desperately but silently on the shores of Loch Ashie, Inverness-shire; it was the one day of the year that a secret door near Llyn Cwm Llwch in the Brecon Beacons opened to admit mortals to fairyland; and girls dressed in white offered garlands to the fairies of a well on the slopes of Schiehallion, the Fairy Hill of the Caledonians, at the east end of Rannoch Moor, Perthshire. On South Walsham Broad, Norfolk, a Viking funeral is said to take place, with the

Vikings' boat in the middle of the Broad, piled high with faggots, blazing against the night sky. As the ship burns to the water-line, the whole vision vanishes.

2 May

A skeleton-like form is reputed to haunt the ancient little church of St Mary's at Burgh St Peter, Norfolk, on this one day in the year; a presence that has been sensed and seen in various parts of the churchyard but especially in the vicinity of the church porch.

4 May

On this day in 1471 the battle of Tewkesbury was fought. One can imagine the great activity and urgent messengers and couriers galloping along the lanes of the surrounding country-side, including Shaw Green Lane at Prestbury, Gloucester-shire. Early on this one morning in the year there have been many reports of the shadowy form of a horse and rider, possibly a Cavalier on a white horse, riding at breakneck speed; while other visitors or passers-by have seen nothing, but have heard the fast 'clip-clop, clip-clop' of horses' hooves pass them in the deserted lane.

8 May

The nearest Saturday to the day of the Apparition of St Michael the Archangel sees Helston in Cornwall holding its annual Furry Dance, an event that has its origin in a pagan spring festival. A large stone built into the wall of the Angel Hotel in Coinagehall Street is said to be the stone, destined for blocking the entrance to Hell, dropped by the Devil during his fight with St Michael; a stone that gave the town its name. There are those who say that a winged form is to be seen near the stone at dawn on each anniversary.

12 May

A ghostly procession walks down a grassy slope in front of an old farmhouse on the bank of Salthouse Mere in Norfolk and the rites and rituals of a Roman mass are performed in the open air at midnight, according to a number of witnesses.

15 May

Once, in the far past, a mill stood beside Ormsby Broad in Norfolk, and there are those who believe that the mill can be seen again in all its glory, each 15 May soon after midnight, when it seems to be on fire as perhaps it was one 15 May long, long ago.

17 May

Five hundred years ago the beautiful Lady Edona from Lewes Castle watched for the ship carrying her betrothed, Lord Manfred, sailing home after a year's voyaging. She saw it strike a submerged rock, keel over on its side and sink with all hands. Each 17 May at midnight a ghost ship is said to sail towards the harbour and seem to founder ... an ancient plinth in the churchyard of St Nicholas marks the grave of the heartbroken Lady Edona.

One of the fiercest battles of the Greek War of Independence was fought on 17 May 1828, in a small plain on the south coast of Crete. Near the Venetian fortress of Frangocastello, 385 Greeks were attacked by a Turkish force 9000 strong and slaughtered to the last man. This phantom army is said to materialise at dawn on each anniversary of the battle.

19 May

Blickling Hall in Norfolk was built 200 years after Anne Boleyn was executed on Tower Green, but an earlier house occupied the site and Anne may have been born in that house; at all events she enjoyed her childhood thereabouts. On each 19 May, the anniversary of her death, a phantom coach drives towards the hall, so goes the story, drawn by headless horses, and vanishes into thin air. Inside the coach the figure of a slim young woman has been glimpsed, recognizably Anne, although her head rests on her lap.

22 May

This day, in 1455, the Battle of St Albans was fought, and on each anniversary the houses and properties standing on the supposed site of the battle, in the centre of the town, are said to resound with the clash of armies in combat.

25 May

The ruins of St Benedict's Abbey, Norfolk, were once the scene of a murder, an event which some people say is re-enacted each year on 25 May when the ghostly form of a figure wearing an abbot's cope and mitre, and with a rope around his neck, is seen swinging in mid-air from the ruins of this former abbey.

27 May

The aged Margaret, Countess of Salisbury, daughter of George, Duke of Clarence, was executed on Tower Green at the Tower of London on 27 May, 1541. That morning the reluctant victim was forcibly taken to the scaffold, screaming and fighting every inch of the way, and the actual execution, according to reports, consisted of the executioner chasing her round and round the scaffold until with repeated blows he finally succeeded in hacking off her head; and it is this dreadful and harrowing scene that is reputed to be re-enacted each 27 May.

29 May

At midnight on this ancient 'feast day' a great wolf-like creature is said to emerge from Southery Fen near Littleport in Cambridgeshire, a beast that then prowls the area and kills every living thing that it meets.

31 May

This night each year a ghostly coach is said to career towards the old bridge at Potter Heigham in Norfolk and, exactly at midnight, sparks flying from the wheels, it crashes into the side of the bridge and plunges over the low wall to disappear with a terrifying hiss into the River Thurne beneath. Also, on this one night in the year, a black phantom coach drawn by four horses is said to gallop down from Antrim Castle in Northern Ireland and disappear into the depths of Long Pond, the re-enactment of an eighteenth-century tragedy when a drunken coachman mistook the moonlit waters of the lake for the surface of the road and drove his coach and its occupants to a watery grave. Yet another phantom coach, a mustard-coloured one this time, is reputed to trundle down the drive at Elizabethan Hill Hall, Theydon Bois, Essex, at midnight on this last day of May. Driving the coach is thought to be a ghostly 'Duke de Morrow', an eccentric who lived at the Hall from 1900 to 1908.

Among the ghosts at St James's Palace, London, is that of a small man, his throat slit from ear to ear, who apparently returns to the room in which he was murdered (some say by the Duke of Cumberland, son of George III) on the anniversary of the crime that took place on 31 May 1810.

1 June

Hickling Broad, Norfolk (already boasting a recurring phantom in the shape of a drummer boy, see 15 February) is reputed to be the scene of a ghost voice once a year. If the evening of 1 June is a fine and quiet summer evening, as it usually is, visitors to the peaceful banks of this marshlined stretch of water have reported hearing a woman's voice, soft and caressing, rising and falling on the gentle breeze that hardly stirs the surface of the water. The voice has even been recorded on tape, or so I have been told.

4 June

During the hours of daylight a phantom sailor has been repeatedly seen on this day in Ballyheigue Bay below the ruins of Ballyheigue Castle. It seems that in 1730 a Danish ship was wrecked off Ballyheigue strand and the crew rescued by Sir Thomas Crosbie and his men who also managed to salvage much of the ship's cargo of silver bars and coins. Shortly afterwards Sir Thomas died, his end hastened, said his wife Lady Margaret, by his labours and exertions on the night of the wreck, and she put forward a claim for salvage and the loss of her husband. The captain, fearing for his cargo, had the treasure removed to the castle cellars and mounted guard over it, but before he could ship the bullion to Denmark the castle was raided and the silver stolen; less than a quarter of it was ever recovered. The raid on the castle took place on 4 June 1731 and it has been suggested that the unrecovered treasure may still lie somewhere among the crumbling walls of Ballyheigue Castle and that the phantom sailor who has been seen on this day may be some kind of ghostly guardian of the treasure.

13 June

The ides of June is nearly always beautiful and still, a perfect summer day, and those who have found themselves at Horsey Mere, Norfolk, on 'Childer's Night' have said that they have seen and heard children playing, children who were buried there, years ago. Once it was the custom when a little child died hereabouts for it to be brought to Horsey Mere, the little body weighted with stones and lowered to the bottom of the mere. The spirits of these children still seem to haunt Horsey Mere and many people say they return on 'Childer's Night'.

15 June

Hitchin Priory in Hertfordshire is reputedly visited each year on this day by the ghost of a Cavalier named Goring, who was wounded in a skirmish during the Civil War and sheltered in a house called High Down at nearby Pirton. When the Round-heads began to search the house he changed his hiding place (a small chamber over the porch) to a hollow elm near the gate, and there he was discovered and killed on the spot. Perhaps his ride to Hitchin Priory and safety is what he had in his mind or hoped to do before he was discovered and hastily dispatched.

19 June

Long ago there lived at Lochlee, Glen Esk, Angus, a popular piper whose playing used to give much pleasure to his fellow men. One summer evening, 19 June to be exact, he was playing his pipes near Dalbrack Bridge, when a troupe of little men dressed in green led him to their boat. They sailed away upstream and he was never seen again, but sometimes the faint sound of pipes can be heard near Dalbrack Bridge on summer evenings, and especially on 19 June.

20 June

Midsummer Eve is the date that the fairies are reputed to be very active and when they can sometimes be seen, it is said, especially on the Isle of Man, in the vicinity of Ballona Bridge, where they invariably make themselves seen, heard or felt if they do not receive a polite greeting from everyone crossing this bridge. Spirits and fairies and goblins are supposed to abound on this ancient feast-day. One recipe for seeing spirits at midnight on Midsummer Eve consists of putting a pint of salad oil into a glass which has been washed out with rosewater; to this add hollyhock buds, marigold petals, hazel leaves and the tops of wild thyme; add grass from a fairy ring and leave for three days in the sun.

Every seven years, on Midsummer Eve, a door is said to open inside Cadbury Castle, near Yeovil in Somerset, and King Arthur and his men appear and ride down the hill to water their horses at a spring near Sutton Montis Church. Recent excavations have established that, where the hill has long been said to open, on this night once every seven years, there was indeed once a gateway. At Purse Caundle Manor in Dorset King John's hounds are said to be seen and heard on Midsummer Eve; they were heard in 1959, although some people say the date is 23 June. An earlier house that occupied the site of the present Tudor building was often visited by the unpopular king who used it as a hunting-lodge. At Chantonbury Ring in Sussex the Devil can be made to appear, so it is believed, if you run seven times backwards round the clump of beech trees at midnight on Midsummer Eve.

21 June (some say 24 June)

Midsummer Day, when the famous but unidentified White

Lady of Hampton Court haunts the vicinity of the landing-stage and has been reported by many anglers over the years; and a ghost wherry visits Oulton Broad in Suffolk. In 1851 the huge vessel left Yarmouth with a fortune aboard; the skipper's evil plans went wrong and the *Mayfly* became a ship of death – to sail each Midsummer Day through Oulton Broad making no sound except a weird creaking that seems to come from the mast and sail of the deserted ghost ship.

3 July

At Burgh Castle (where we have already noted that the sounds of primitive battle is heard each 27 April) 3 July brings the annual sight, it is said, of a dead body with a white flag tied tightly round the neck; a body that is thrown from all that remains of a once proud fortress on to the foreshore, where it lands with a sickening thud, and disappears.

5 July

On this night in the year 1685 was fought the battle of Sedgemoor, and the vanquished Duke of Monmouth fled from his foes; as his ghost flees each year, on horseback, on the anniversary of the annihilating defeat. Furthermore the aftermath of that bitter struggle has been thought by some to be manifested on the night of 5 July in the shape of balls of light over the marshy battlefields, while strange shadows, phantom horsemen and ghostly troops flee silently through the neighbouring lanes towards the banks of the River Cary where they disappear. Other visitors to this spot say they have heard the sounds of battle during the long night hours of 5 July.

6 July

Ashdown House, Forest Row, near East Grinstead in Sussex, has associations with Lord Heathfield, although he neither lived nor died there, but it is said to be his faltering footsteps that are heard once a year on this date, echoing along the main staircase of what is now a boys' school.

10 July

Whiddon Park Guest House, Chagford in Devon, has the ghost of a bride who was shot on her wedding day, 10 July, more than 300 years ago. She is thought to be Mary Whiddon, who was shot by a jealous suitor as she stood at the altar of the local church. The inscription on her tombstone refers to 'a Matron yet a Maid' and her ghost was reportedly seen in 1971, standing in the doorway of a bedroom, dressed in black.

11 July

Breydon Water by Great Yarmouth in Norfolk is reputed to harbour a phantom fleet of sailing galleons that appear just before midnight each 11 July – and take more than an hour to pass!

15 July

Thurne Mouth, where the rivers Thurne and Bure meet, north of Acle in Norfolk, has the ghost of a murdered man looking for the man who killed him one St Swithun's Day, long ago.

17 July

A ghostly giant is said to be abroad at Somerleyton, north of Lowestoft, Suffolk, each night of 17 July, a giant who lies quiet, buried a couple of miles north between Mill Hill and Bell Hill, for the other 364 nights of the year.

21 July

One of several days in the year when a ghostly Roman soldier is said to be seen on the banks of Wroxham Broad in Norfolk and a ghostly procession is said to make its silent way along the riverside at Horning, two miles to the west; a procession that disappears as it leaves the village in the direction of haunted St Benedict's Abbey; a procession that reappears on 21 July every five years. The next scheduled appearance is 1991.

28 July

Each year on this date the famous ghost nun of Borley Rectory, 'the most haunted house in England', is said to walk along a narrow grass path that became known as the Nun's Walk. Although the rectory has long disappeared and parts of the Nun's Walk have been built on, there are still occasional reports that the Borley nun has been seen in recent years by local people and by visitors to the neglected locale of the best-known ghost of all.

1 August

According to tradition each year on 1 August the statue of Queen Mary Tudor – Bloody Mary as she was called – steps down from the plinth in Queen Anne's Gate, Westminster, and wanders about the nearby streets.

2 August

Two stone effigies of knights in Stalham Church, Norfolk, have long been reputed to walk from the church down to Stalham Dyke and back again on this one night in the year: at midnight of course.

4 August

Haunted Barton Water in Norfolk has a unique ghostly spectacle: the face of a beautiful girl that is reflected in the dawn haze, clear and distinct before it fades, and one wonders whether it was ever there; yet the serene face has been reportedly seen by aeroplane pilots and their passengers and by sailors who have anchored there and have been awake and alert at dawn on 4 August. On the same day, between midnight and one o'clock in the morning, crowds have been known to gather on the shores of Loch na Naire near Strathnaver, Sutherland, for at that time the magic curative properties of the loch water are at their height and the ghost of a Gordon highlander has been glimpsed by the lochside.

11 August

Those who sleep at Beeleigh Abbey in Essex on this night hear 'a haunting wail around the house', according to the owner, Miss Christina Foyle. The date is a few days before Sir John Gate was executed and the wailing noises are thought to be some kind of echo of the doomed man's misery and moans at the thought of his approaching death.

17 August

On this day each year the ghost of a nun, Bertha Rosaca, is said to walk at Chicksands Priory, Clophill, Bedfordshire, in retribution for having become pregnant by a male superior. She was seen in 1960 disappearing through a wall in the picture gallery where two men at different times saw a female figure that disappeared in equally inexplicable fashion.

21 August

The ghost of a running man is said to race down the High Street at Reedham in Norfolk, his mouth distorted and his face full of fear, but not a sound is heard as he passes like a flash late at night on this date as he did in reality once long, long ago.

24 August

At Belaugh, Norfolk, there appears a curious phenomenon on this one day each year: a vivid red sunset heralds the appearance of a female form that is said to emerge from the churchyard, but where it goes or what it wants nobody knows.

31 August

Beccles, Suffolk, is said to have a ghostly skeleton-like form that manifests near the Quay on this night every year.

3 September

On this day in the year 1658 Oliver Cromwell died as a great storm raged through Brampton Bryan Park, Herefordshire, destroying many trees, and the superstitious said that the Devil had dragged Cromwell across the parkland on the way to Hell. Tradition asserts that each 3 September the Devil returns to Brampton Bryan to rampage through the park.

14 September

This evening, regularly once a year, according to some of the local people, a half-hour fight takes place between a great black barge and two smaller ships – a phantom fight that once really took place on peaceful Breydon Water, east of Great Yarmouth in Norfolk.

18 September

Charming little Brundall in Norfolk is the last place in the world that you would think is haunted yet, each 18 September, a ghostly bishop is said to bestow a ghostly blessing upon the River Yare from the grassy banks where buttercups grow.

25 September

On this date, once every twenty years, the ghost of a beautiful girl is said to appear at the Old Ferry Inn, downstream from Horning in Norfolk. The inn was once a meadhouse and one 25 September, centuries ago, a local girl was waylaid and raped by drunken monks; no wonder she returns every two decades. In 1936 the licensee of the inn saw her in the passage by the staircase. In 1956 a slim figure was seen to disappear outside the front of the inn. She is due again in 1996.

28 September

The ghost of Sir Walter Raleigh is said to return to his old home, Sherborne Castle, Dorset, each St Michael's Eve. Raleigh loved the Old Castle and he wished to be buried at Sherborne, but he lies at Westminster – is this why his ghost returns to the trees and gardens that he loved and to the stone seat known as 'Sir Walter Raleigh's seat' where his restless shade has most frequently been seen? On this day, the anniversary of the birth of Edward VI at Hampton Court Palace, the ghost of Jane Seymour is said to walk, clad in white and holding a lighted taper in her hand, mounting the stairs that led to the elusive Silver Stick Gallery.

20 October

A tall dark figure returns once a year on this date to Testwood

House, Totton, in Hampshire. It is usually seen in the drive at the front of the house and is thought to be connected with a murder committed there many years ago. Also on this date each year, a ghost squad of sailors in out-of-date uniforms is said to return to the barracks that they once knew at Chatham in Kent.

23 October

Edgehill, a hilly ridge in Warwickshire, was the scene of the first major battle of the Civil War in 1642 when 14,000 Englishmen fought one another – and left behind psychic emanations that, if reports are to be believed, are to be encountered every anniversary of the battle, notwithstanding alterations to the calendar which would make the present date 12 October. There are many convincing accounts of curious experiences on the site of the battle, but each 23 October, it is said, visitors have glimpsed a spectral band of soldiers, or seen lights over the battlefield, or heard the sound of men and horses, of hoofbeats and neighing, of the jingle of harness and the grind of wheels ... the phantoms of Edgehill are among the more interesting instances of alleged recurring psychic phenomena.

31 October

Hallowe'en – All Saint's Eve – has long been traditionally associated with ghosts, and certainly there are more cyclic ghosts reputed to appear on this date than on any other day in the year. They include a soldier of the 1914–18 War who appears to take a drink of water at Bournemouth Town Hall; a doe, a hound and a ghostly huntsman (Lord William Towneley) haunt the Eagle's Crag at Cliviger Gorge near Burnley, Lancashire; ghost bells ring and a phantom dog swims in Thirlmere Lake at Armboth Fell in Cumbria; the original bells of Whitby Abbey can be heard ringing under the sea where they have been since the Dissolution of the Monasteries; six hooded figures are seen in the choir loft of St Rita's Church, South Fairfield Avenue, Chicago; and a ghost monk walks the ruins of Minsden Chapel near Hitchin in Hertfordshire.

1 November

The squire of Hyde Hall, Sawbridgeworth, Hertfordshire (now a school) was once Sir John Jocelyn, and in accordance with his wishes he and his favourite white horse were buried on his land instead of in the village churchyard. Each 1 November, the anniversary of the burial, the ghost of Sir John, mounted on his white steed, rides furiously down the old carriage drive.

3 November

Bruce Castle, Tottenham, once a Jacobean mansion and now a museum, has a screaming ghost: Costantia, Lady Coleraine, who rushes through the chamber where once her jealous husband kept her under lock and key. Once every year on this date, the anniversary of the day on which the poor demented creature threw herself from a balcony to her death, she appears.

4 November

On this day in 1541 Queen Catherine Howard escaped from her room at Hampton Court Palace and tried to make a last appeal for her life to the king, Henry VIII, only to be led back, sobbing, to her room. Next day she was removed to the Tower where she was executed 100 days later. Each 4 November a distraught and sobbing figure dashes along what has become known as the Haunted Gallery, if we are to believe occasional reports; certainly cards depicting a 'ghostly' Catherine Howard were sold at Hampton Court for years.

11 November

Haroldslea House, Horley, Surrey, is said to be haunted on this one night in the year when, at twilight, a bell is heard tolling. The sound gets gradually louder until midnight when there is a sound of marching men. The sounds approach the old oak kitchen door of the eighteen-century house and unarmed grey figures appear and disappear as the sounds of footsteps die away, leaving a cold silence – or so they say. The present owner has seen and heard nothing.

13 November

A 'grey lady' is reputed to walk through some of the wards of the Royal National Orthopaedic Hospital at Stanmore each 13 November, and while many hospitals have reputed ghosts this particular hospital is built on part of a former nunnery and the 'grey lady' is thought to be a nun.

23 November

The downland village of Pyecombe, Sussex, is haunted each St Clement's night by groans and shrieks that are said to be a psychic echo of supernatural happenings associated with the village smithy; occurrences that are celebrated by a procession and a ceremonious fire festival.

21 December

At the Stiper Stones near Bishops Castle, Shropshire, all the ghosts in Britain are said to meet on the longest night of the year!

24 December

Christmas Eve is the only night in the year to vie with Hallowe'en for recurring ghosts. They include Hever Castle in Kent, where the ghost of Anne Boleyn walks across the bridge over the River Eden; a ghost monk tries to restore the altar among the ruins of Strata Florida Abbey in Dyfed; a phantom coach and four horses draws up at the door of Roos Hall, Beccles in Suffolk, with a headless groom on the box; the ghost of Charles Dickens wanders about the graveyard in the shadow of Rochester Castle in Kent where he wished to be buried; and a lost sanctus bell is heard ringing from the depths of Bomere Pool near Shrewsbury in Shropshire.

25 December

Rochfort Hall, one of the reputed birthplaces of Anne Boleyn and now a golf club, has a formless white apparition that flits through the grounds on Christmas Day.

28 December

On the anniversary of the Tay Bridge disaster of 1879 a ghost train has been seen on the Tay Bridge, around midnight, its lights blazing – before it disappears.

31 December

The last day of the year is a popular one for recurring ghosts and those interested can take their pick from King John's hounds that have been seen by some witnesses and heard by others at Purse Caundle Manor in Dorset; a ghost carriage that crosses the frozen Loch of Skene, west of Aberdeen; a spectral pig at Andover in Hampshire; and a huge black horse with a shrieking rider that races out of the drive of the Old Hall, Ranworth in Norfolk – surely an arresting collection of spectacles by any standards and a fitting finale to this calendar of ghosts.

Many of these reports sound as though they do not merit serious consideration, but in ghost hunting we seek to eliminate by experimentation; so, if there is any chance of recording or photographing a ghostly cyclic recurrence, we need to know.

201

Useful Addresses

The enthusiastic ghost hunter will find a great deal of help is available to him if he seeks for it. The various spiritualist organisations are usually very helpful, as are the College of Psychic Studies, 16 Queensberry Place, London SW7 2EB, and *Psychic News*, 20 Earlham Street, London WC2H 9LW; the latter will supply without charge (except for postage) a copy of their Yearbook and Catalogue containing addresses of spiritualist centres throughout the world and other helpful material from the spiritualist's viewpoint.

Membership of a responsible organisation concerned with the study of the paranormal is likely to prove invaluable. Many of these organisations have excellent libraries and helpful members who are able and willing to guide you round the many pitfalls that await all investigators; but always remember to enclose a stamp or International Reply Coupon with any enquiry, especially when writing to an individual. Many authors and private investigators are quite prepared to help with reasonable queries, but their outlay on postage can be enormous, and correspondents should not expect a reply unless they enclose a stamped and addressed envelope or the equivalent.

The following list of some useful societies – worldwide – which I have prepared with the help of Miss Eleanor O'Keeffe of the English Society for Psychical Research, may prove helpful in selecting a suitable society or organisation.

EUROPE

Austria

Institut fur Grenzgebiete der Wissenschaft – Imago Mundi, Maximilianstrasse 8, Postfach 8, A-60lol, Innsbruck.

United Kingdom

Association for the Scientific Study of Anomalous Phenomena, 30, South Row, London, SE3 ORY.
British Society of Dowsers, Sycamore Cottage, Tamley Lane, Hastingleigh, Ashford, Kent TN25 5HW.

The College of Psychic Studies, 16 Queensberry Place, London, SW7 2EB.

Churches' Fellowship for Psychical and Spiritual Studies, St Mary Abchurch, Abchurch Lane, London EC4N 7SA.

The Ghost Club (founded 1862), Peter Underwood, c/o The Savage Club, Berkeley Square, London W1X 6JD.

Institute of Psychophysical Research, 118 Banbury Road, Oxford.

Paraphysical Laboratory, Downton, Wiltshire.

Paraphysical Study Group, International Parascience Institute, Cryndir, Nantmel, Llandrindod Wells, Powys LD1 6EH.

Society for Psychical Research, 1 Adam and Eve Mews, Kensington, London W8 6UG.

Society of Metaphysicians (Metaphysical Research Group), Archers Court, Stonestile Lane, Hastings, Sussex.

The Spiritualist Association of Great Britain, 33 Belgrave Square, London SW1X 8QL.

The Theosophical Society, 50 Gloucester Place, London W1H 3HJ.

Unitarian Society for Psychical Studies, 20 Wetherill Road, London N10 2LT.

Finland

Sallskapet for Psykist Forskning i Finland, Fanrik Stalsgaten 8 A7, Helsingfors.

France

Institut Metapsychique International, 1 Place Wagram, 75017 Paris.

Group d'Etudes et de Recherches en Parapsychologie, 8 Rue Octave Dubois, 95150 Taverny.

Germany

Institut fur Grenzgebiete der Psychologie und Psychohygiene, Eichhalde 12, D 7800 Frieburg, im-Breisgau, West Germany.

Italy

Associazione Italiana Scientifica di Metapsichica, Via S. Vittore 19 – 20123 Milano.

Netherlands

Parapsychology Laboratory, University of Utrecht,

Sorbonnelaan 16, 3584 CA Utrecht.
Research Institute for PSI Phenomena and Physics,
Akexanderkade 1, 1018 CH Amsterdam.
Studievereniging voor Psychical Research, Antwoordnummer
81, 3500 ZH Utrecht.

Poland

Instytut Wydawniczy Zwiazkow Zawodowych.
Towarzystwo Psychotroniczne, ul. Noakowskiego 10 m 54
Warszawa.

Spain

Sociedad Espanola de Parapsicologia, Belen 15, 1 Derecha,
Madrid 4.

SOUTH AFRICA

The South African Society for Psychical Research, PO Box
23154, Joubert Park, Johannesburg 2044.

UNITED STATES OF AMERICA

American Society for Psychical Research, 5 West 73rd Street,
New York, NY 10023:
Academy of Religion and Psychical Research, PO Box 614,
Bloomfield, Connecticut 06002.
Centre for Scientific Anomalies Research, PO Box 1052, Ann
Arbor, Michigan 48103
Central Premonitions Registry, Box 482, Times Square
Station, New York, NY 10023.
Division of Parapsychology, Box 152, Medical Centre,
University of Virginia, Charlottesville, Virginia 22908.
Foundation for Research on the Nature of Man, Box 6847,
College Station, Durham, N. Carolina 27708.
International Association for Near-death Studies, Dept. of
Psychology, University of Connecticut, Storrs, Connecticut
06268.
Mind Science Foundation, 8301 Broadway, Suite 100, San
Antonio, Texas TX 78209.
Parapsychological Association, Inc., PO Box 12236, Research
Triangle Park, NC 27709.
Parapsychology Division, Department of Psychiatry,

University of Virginia School of Medicine, Charlottesville, Virginia 22901.
Parapsychology Foundation Inc., 228 East 71st Street, New York, NY 10021.
Parapsychology Institute of America, 42–47 78th Street, Elmhurst, New York.
Psychical Research Foundation, Psychology Department, West Georgia College, Carrollton, Georgia 30118–0001.
Psychophysical Research Laboratories, 301 College Road East, Princeton, NJ 08540.
Spiritual Frontiers Fellowship, 10189 Winner Road, Independence, MO 64052–0519.

CANADA

Institute of Parapsychological Studies, 5740 Yonge Street, Toronto, Ontario, M2N 5S1.
Spiritual Science Institute of Toronto, 801 St Clair Avenue West, Toronto, Ontario M6C 1C2.

AUSTRALASIA AND THE FAR EAST

Australia
Australian Institute of Psychic Research, PO Box 445, Lane Cove, NSW 2066.

India
Indian Foundation for Parapsychology, Andhra University, Waltair, A.P.

Japan
Japan Psychic Science Association, Inc., No. 161 1 12–12 Kamiochiai, Shinjuku-Ku, Tokyo.

Recommended Books

The Reference Department at almost any Public Library can prove invaluable in the ghost hunter's search for knowledge of local history, and in the recommendation of suitable and helpful books. The study of the right books is an excellent way of acquiring knowledge and experience from other people in a short time. Perusal of the following volumes as appropriate will help the ghost hunter to look for ghosts in the right places and explore reliable evidence for the subject in general, and individual cases in particular. Not all of these books may be regarded by everyone knowledgeable on the subject as 'the best books to read' but the majority are the best books in the field and the others are of special interest because they represent local research or a particular case, such as *The Amityville Horror* and *The Bell Witch*. Still others are personal favourites of many years' standing. Some of the books that some people might recommend are in fact completely unreliable and these I have omitted. On a personal note readers may like to know that the list has been compiled from books in my library which are destined one day for the Harry Price Library at the University of London.

Abbott, Geoffrey, *Ghosts of the Tower of London*, London 1980.
Alexander, Marc, *Haunted Houses You May Visit*, London 1982.
Alexander, Marc, *Phantom Britain*, London 1975.
Alexander, Marc, *Haunted Churches and Abbeys of Britain*, London 1978.
Alexander, Marc, *Ghostly Cornwall*, Kingsley 1977.
Alexander, Marc, *Haunted Inns*, London 1973.
Alexander, Marc, *Haunted Castles*, London 1974.
Anson, Jay, *The Amityville Horror*, New Jersey 1977.
Archer, Fred, *Ghost Writer*, London 1966.
Archer, Fred, *Ghosts, Witches and Murder*, London 1972.
Armstrong, Warren, *The Authentic Shudder*, London 1965.
Armstrong, Warren, *Sea Phantoms*, London 1963.
Atkins, Meg Elizabeth, *Haunted Warwickshire*, London 1981.

Baird, A.T., *One Hundred Cases for Survival After Death*, London 1943.

Bardens, Dennis, *Mysterious Worlds*, New York 1970.

⅄ Bardens, Dennis, *Ghosts and Hauntings*, London 1965.

Bell, Charles Bailey, *The Bell Witch*, Nashville, 1934.

Bell, Harry, *Guide to the Haunted Castles of Scotland*, East Kilbride 1981.

Bennett, Sir Ernest, *Apparitions and Haunted Houses*, London 1939.

Bolton, Gambier, *Ghosts in Solid Form*, London 1914.

⋇Branden, Victoria, *Understanding Ghosts*, London 1980.

Braddock, Joseph, *Haunted Houses*, London 1956.

Branston, Brian, *Beyond Belief*, London 1974.

Brown, Christopher, *Haunted Sherborne*, Sherborne 1975.

Brown, Theo, *Devon Ghosts*, Norwich 1982.

Brooks, J.A., *Ghosts and Witches of the Cotswolds*, Norwich 1981.

Brooke, A.O'S., *Legends of Bruges*, Bruges 1910.

Brown, Raymond Lamont, *A Casebook of Military Mystery*, Cambridge 1974.

Blashford-Snell, John, *Mysteries*, London 1983.

Brown, Raymond Lamont, *Phantoms of the Theatre*, London 1978.

Brown, R.L., *Phantoms, Legends, Customs and Superstitions of the Sea*, London 1972.

Boyd, Elizabeth, *A Strange and Seeing Time*, London 1969.

Campbell, John L. and Hall, Trevor H., *Strange Things*, London 1968.

Carrington, Hereward and Fodor, Nandor, *The Story of the Poltergeist Down the Centuries*, London 1953.

Chambers, Aidan, *Great Ghosts of the World*, London 1974.

Chambers, Aidan, *Ghosts and Hauntings*, London 1973.

'Cheiro' (Hamon, Count), *True Ghost Stories*, London n.d.

Christopher, Milbourne, *Seers, Psychics and ESP*, London 1970.

Chilcott-Monk, J.P., *Ghosts of South Hampshire and Beyond*, Southampton 1980.

Christian, Roy, *Ghosts and Legends*, Newton Abbot 1972.

Clarke, Stephan, *Ghosts and Legends of Monmouth*, Monmouth 1965.

Coates, James, *Photographing the Invisible*, London 1911.

Cohen, David, *Poltergeists and Hauntings*, London 1965.

Cohen, David, *Price and His Spirit Child Rosalie*, London 1965.

Collins, B. Abdy, *The Cheltenham Ghost*, London 1948.

Cox, W.L. and Meredith, R.D., *Haunted Cheltenham*, Gloucester 1982.

Coxe, Antony Hippisley, *Haunted Britain*, London 1973.

Crowe, Catherine, *The Night Side of Nature*, London 1848.

Currie, Ian, *You Cannot Die*, London 1978.

Daniel, Clarence, *Ghosts of Derbyshire*, Clapham (N. Yorks) 1973.

Davis, Richard, *I've Seen a Ghost!*, London 1979.

Day, James Wentworth, *Ghosts and Witches*, London 1954.

Day, J.W., *A Ghost Hunter's Game Book*, London 1958.

Day, J.W., *In Search of Ghosts*, London 1969.

Day, J.W., *The Queen Mother's Family Story*, London 1967.

Day, J.W., *Essex Ghosts*, Bourne End (Bucks) 1973.

Dingwall, Eric J. and Hall, Trevor H., *Four Modern Ghosts*, London 1958.

Dingwall, Eric J, Goldney, Kathleen M., and Hall, Trevor H., *The Haunting of Borley Rectory*, London 1956.

Dixon, Jeanette, *Welsh Ghosts*, St Ives (Cornwall) 1975.

Dunne, John J., *Haunted Ireland*, Belfast 1977.

Ellis, Keith, *Science and the Supernatural*, London 1974.

Ebon, Martin, *True Experiences with Ghosts*, New York 1968.

Eyre, Kathleen, *Lancashire Legends*, Clapham (N. Yorks) 1975.

Eyre, K., *Lancashire Ghosts*, Clapham (N. Yorks) 1976.

Farquharson-Coe, A., *Devon's Legends and Folklore*, St Ives (Cornwall) 1974.

Findler, Gerald, *Lakeland Ghosts*, Clapham (N. Yorks) 1984.

Finucane, R.C., *Appearances of the Dead*, London 1982.

Flammarion, Camile, *Haunted Houses*, London 1924.

Fodor, Nandor, *On the Trail of the Poltergeist*, New York 1958.

Fodor, N., *Between Two Worlds*, New York 1964.

Fodor, N., *Mind Over Space*, New York 1962.

Forman, Joan, *Haunted East Anglia*, London 1974.

Forman, J., *The Haunted South*, London 1978.
Fuller, John G. *The Ghost of Flight 401*, London 1976.
Francis, Di, *Cornish Ghosts*, St Ives (Cornwall) 1977.

Gauld, Alan, and Cornell, A.D. *Poltergeists*, London 1979.
Godwin, John, *Unsolved: The World of the Unknown*,
New York 1976.
Goodrich-Freer, A., *The Alleged Haunting of B-House*,
London 1899.
Gray, Affleck, *The Big Grey Man of Ben MacDhui*, Aberdeen
1970.
Green, Celia and McCreery, Charles, *Apparitions*, London
1975.
Greenhouse, Herbert B., *In Defense of Ghosts*, New York
1970.

Haining, Peter, *A Dictionary of Ghosts*, London 1982.
Haining, Peter, *Ghosts – The Illustrated History*, London 1974.
Halifax, Lord, *Ghost Book*, London 1936.
Hall, Trevor H., *New Light on Old Ghosts*, London 1965.
Hallam, Jack, *Ghosts of London*, London 1975.
Hallam, Jack, *Ghosts of the North*, Newton Abbot 1976.
Hallam, Jack, *The Ghost Tour*, London 1967.
Hallam, Jack, *The Ghosts' Who's Who*, Newton Abbot 1977.
Hallam, Jack, *The Haunted Inns of England*, London 1972.
Harper, Charles G., *Haunted Houses*, London 1907.
Harries, John, *The Ghost Hunter's Road Book*, London 1968.
Herbert, W.B., *Railway Ghosts*, Newton Abbot 1985.
Hole, Christina, *Haunted England*, London 1940.
Holzer, Hans, *Best True Ghost Stories*, New Jersey 1983.
Holzer, Hans, *The Lively Ghosts of Ireland*, London 1968.
Holzer, Hans, *Psychic Photography*, London 1970.
Holzer, Hans, *The Great British Ghost Hunt*, London 1975.
Hopkins, R. Thurston, *Ghosts Over England*, London 1953.
Hopkins, R.T., *Adventures with Phantoms*, London 1946.
Hopkins, R.T., *Cavalcade of Ghosts*, Kingswood 1956.
Hurley, Jack, *Legends of Exmoor*, Dulverton (Somerset)
1973.
Hurwood, Bernhardt J., *Haunted Houses*, London 1974.

Inglis, Brian, *Science and Parascience*, London 1984.

Ingram, John H., *The Haunted Homes and Family Traditions of Great Britain*, London 1912.
Iremonger, Lucille, *The Ghosts of Versailles*, London 1957.

Lambert, R.S., *Exploring the Supernatural*, London n.d.
Lamont, Stewart, *Is Anybody There?*, Edinburgh 1980.
Lang, Andrew, *The Book of Dreams and Ghosts*, London 1899.
Lang, Andrew, *Cock Lane and Common-sense*, London 1894.
Legg, Rodney, Collier, Mary, and Perrott, Tom, *The Ghosts of Dorset, Devon and Somerset*, Sherborne 1974.
Leslie, Shane, *Ghost Book*, London 1955.
Lethbridge, T.C., *Ghost and Ghoul*, London 1961.
Lewes, Mary L., *The Queer Side of Things*, London 1923.
Ludlam, Harry, *The Mummy of Birchen Bower and Other True Ghost Stories*, London 1966.
Ludlam, Harry, *The Restless Ghosts of Ladye Place and other True Hauntings*, London 1967.
Lytton, Lord, *The Haunted and the Haunters*, London 1925.

MacGregor, Alasdair Alpin, *The Ghost Book*, London 1955.
MacGregor, A.A., *Phantom Footsteps*, London 1959.
MacKenzie, Andrew, *Apparitions and Ghosts*, London 1971.
MacKenzie, A., *Frontiers of the Unknown*, London 1968.
MacKenzie, A., *Hauntings and Apparitions*, London 1982.
MacKenzie, A., *The Unexplained*, London 1966.
Macnaghten, Angus, *Windsor Ghosts and Other Berkshire Hauntings*, Slough 1976.
Macnaghten, A., *More Berkshire Ghosts and Other Stories*, Slough 1977.
Macterlinck, Maurice, *The Unknown Guest*, London 1914.
Maple, Eric, *The Realm of Ghosts*, London 1964.
Maple, Eric, *Supernatural England*, London 1977.
Marryatt, Florence, *There is no Death*, London 1891.
Martin, Stuart, *Ghost Parade*, London n.d.
May, Clarence, *The World His Stage*, London 1972.
Mercer, T.S., *Tales and Scandals of old Thames Ditton*, Thames Ditton 1965.
Mercer, T.S., *More Thames Ditton Tales and Scandals*, Thames Ditton 1965.
May, Antoinette, *Haunted Houses and Wandering Ghosts of*

California, San Francisco 1977.

Middleton, Jessie Adelaide, *The White Ghost Book*, London 1916.

Mitchell, Anne, *Ghosts Along the Thames*, Bourne End 1972.

Mitchell, John V., *Ghosts of an Ancient City*, York 1975.

Moberley, Anne E., and Jourdain, Eleanor F., *An Adventure*, London 1931 edn.

Moss, Peter, *Ghosts Over Britain*, London 1977.

Nicholls, Jeff, *Our Mysterious Shire*, Slough 1985.

Norman, Diana, *The Stately Ghosts of England*, London 1963.

O'Donnell, Elliott, *Family Ghosts and Ghostly Phenomena*, London 1933.

O'Donnell, E., *The Hag of the Dribble and Other True Ghosts*, London 1971.

O'Donnell, E., *Haunted Britain*, London 1949.

O'Donnell, E., *Haunted Churches*, London 1939.

O'Donnell, E., *Haunted People*, London 1955.

O'Donnell, E., *Haunted Waters*, London 1957.

O'Donnell, E., *Phantoms of the Night*, London 1956.

O'Donnell, E., *Rooms of Mystery*, London 1931.

O'Dornell, E., *Some Haunted Houses*, London 1908.

Owen, A.R.G., *Can We Explain the Poltergeist?*, New York 1964.

Oxley, C.T., *The Haunted North Country*, Harrogate n.d.

Paine, Lauran, *A Gaggle of Ghosts*, London 1971.

Pearsall, Ronald, *The Table-Rappers*, London 1972.

Pearson, Margaret M., *Bright Tapestry*, London 1956.

Permutt, Cyril, *Beyond the Spectrum*, Cambridge 1983.

Playfair, Guy Lyon, *This House is Haunted*, London 1980.

Playfair, G.L., *The Flying Cow*, London 1975.

Poole, Keith B., *Ghosts of Wessex*, Newton Abbot 1976.

Price, Harry, *Cold Light on Spiritualistic "Phenomena"*, London 1922.

Price, H., *Confessions of a Ghost Hunter*, London 1936.

Price, H., *Fifty Years of Psychical Research*, London 1939.

Price, H., *The Haunting of Cashen's Gap*, London 1936.

Price, H., *Leaves from a Psychist's Case-Book*, London 1933.

Price, H., *'The Most Haunted House in England'*, London 1940.

211

Price, H., *Poltergeist Over England*, London 1945.
Price, H., *Search for Truth*, London 1942.
Price, H., *The End of Borley Rectory*, London 1946.

Randles, Jenny, *Beyond Explanation?*, London 1985.
Redesdale, Lord, *Tales of Old Japan*, London 1910.
Reynolds, James, *Ghosts in Irish Houses*, New York 1947.
Rhys, Ernest (editor), *The Haunters and the Haunted*, London 1921.
Rice, Hilary Stainer, *Ghosts of the Chilterns and Thames Valley*, Slough 1983.
Roberts, Nancy, *An Illustrated Guide to Ghosts*, Charlotte N.C. n.d.
Roll, William G., *The Poltergeist*, London 1972.
Rosenthal, Eric, *They Walk in the Night*, London n.d.
Royal, Margaret, and Girvan, Ian, *Local Ghosts*, Bristol 1976.
Royal, M., and Girvan, I., *Bristol Ghosts and their Neighbours*, Bristol 1977.
Ruland, Wilhelm, *Legends of the Rhine*, Cologne 1937.
Russell, Eric, *Ghosts*, London 1970.

St Clair, Sheila, *Psychic Phenomena in Ireland*, Dublin 1972.
St Leger-Gordon, Ruth, *The Witchcraft and Folklore of Dartmoor*, London 1965.
Salter, W.H., *Ghosts and Apparitions*, London 1938.
Sampson, Charles, *Ghosts of the Broads*, London 1931.
Sergeant, Philip W., *Historic British Ghosts*, London n.d.
Seymour and Neligan, *True Irish Ghost Stories*, Dublin 1969.
Seymour, Deryck, and Hazzard, Jack, *Berry Pomeroy Castle*, Torquay 1982.
Shepard, Leslie, *How to Protect Yourself against Black Magic and Witchcraft*, Secaucus N.J. 1978.
Singer, Kurt, *Ghost Book*, London n.d.
Sitwell, Sacheverell, *Poltergeists*, London 1940.
Smith, Susy, *Haunted Houses for the Millions*, New York 1967.
Squires, Patricia, *The Ghost in the Mirror*, London 1972.
Steedman, Gay, and Anker, Ray, *Ghosts of the Isle of Wight*, Newport I.W. 1977.
Steiger, Brad, *Real Ghosts, Restless Spirits and Haunted Minds*, London 1968.
Stevens, William Oliver, *Unbidden Guests*, London 1949.

Stirling, A.M.W., *Ghosts Vivisected*, London 1957.

Sturge-Whiting, J.R., *The Mystery of Versailles*, London n.d.

Tabori, Cornelius, *My Occult Diary*, New York 1966.

Tabori, Paul, *Beyond the Senses*, London 1971.

Tabori, Paul, *Pioneers of the Unseen*, London 1972.

Tabori, Paul, *Harry Price: the Biography of a Ghost Hunter*, London 1950.

Tackaberry, Andrew, *Famous Ghosts, Phantoms and Poltergeists*, New York 1967.

Taillepied, Noel, *A Treatise of Ghosts*, London n.d.

Thompson, Francis, *Ghosts, Spirits and Spectres of Scotland*, Aberdeen 1973.

Thurston, Herbert, *Ghosts and Poltergeists*, London 1953.

Travis, Peter, *In Search of the Supernatural*, London 1975.

Turner, James, *Ghosts in the South West*, Newton Abbot 1973.

Tweedale, Violet, *Ghosts I Have Seen*, London 1920.

Tyrrell, G.N.M., *Apparitions*, London 1953 (ed).

Uhler, Alfred, *Cast Out Your Devils*, London 1939.

Underwood, Peter, *A Gazetteer of British Ghosts*, London 1971. (See next entry.)

Underwood, Peter, *A Gazetteer of Scottish & Irish Ghosts*, London 1973 (re-published with above in one volume, New York 1985).

Underwood, Peter, *A Host of Hauntings*, London 1973.

Underwood, Peter, *Into The Occult*, London 1972.

Underwood, Peter, *Deeper Into the Occult*, London 1975.

Underwood, Peter, *Haunted London*, London 1973.

Underwood, Peter, *The Ghosts of Borley*, Newton Abbot 1975.

Underwood, Peter, *Dictionary of the Supernatural*, London 1978.

Underwood, Peter, *Ghosts of North West England*, London 1978.

Underwood, Peter, *Hauntings: New Light on 10 Famous Cases*, London 1977.

Underwood, Peter, *Ghosts of Devon*, St Teath (Cornwall) 1982.

Underwood, Peter, *Ghosts of Cornwall*, St Teath (Cornwall) 1983.

Underwood, Peter, *Ghosts of Somerset*, St Teath (Cornwall) 1985.

Underwood, Peter, *Westcountry Hauntings*, St Teath (Cornwall) 1986.

Underwood, Peter, *Ghosts of Kent*, Rainham (Kent) 1985.

Underwood, Peter, *Ghosts of Hampshire & the Isle of Wight*, Farnborough (Hants) 1983.

Underwood, Peter, *This Haunted Isle*, London 1984.

Underwood, Peter, *The Ghost Hunters*, London 1985.

Underwood, Peter, *No Common Task*, London 1983.

Underwood, Peter, *Ghosts of Wales*, Swansea 1978.

Walker, Danton, *Spooks Deluxe*, New York 1956.

Waring, Edward, *Ghosts and Legends of the Dorset Countryside*, Tisbury (Wilts) 1977.

Watson, Lyall, *Supernature*, London 1973.

Whitaker, Terrence W., *Lancashire's Ghosts and Legends*, London 1980.

Whitaker, Terrence W., *Yorkshire's Ghosts and Legends*, London 1983.

Wickwar, J.W., *The Ghost World*, London n.d.

Williams, Margo, *Ghostly Gifts*, Ventnor (Isle of Wight) 1980.

Wilson, Colin, *Mysteries*, London 1978.

Wilson, Colin, *The Occult*, London 1971.

Wilson, Colin, *The Psychic Detectives*, London 1984.

Wilson, Colin, *Poltergeist!*, London 1981.

Wilson, Colin, *Afterlife*, London 1985.

Winer, Richard and Osborn, Nancy, *Haunted Houses*, New York 1979.

Winer, R., and Osborn, N., *More Haunted Houses*, New York 1981.

Wood, G. Bernard, *Secret Britain*, London 1968.

Index

A

Abbots Ann, Hampshire 185
Aberdeen, Scotland 201
Acle, Norfolk 188, 196
Airlie Drummer 19
Airline, Eastern (Flight 401) 17
Albany, New York 170
Albany Evening News 170
Alice Springs, Australia 74, 183
Allingham-Macguire, Mrs Trixi 116
Alresford, Hampshire 187
Alsbach, Germany 148
Amberst, Nova Scotia 161
Amityville, Long Island, New York
   167–8
'Amityville Horror' 167–8
An Adventure 151
Andalusia, Spain 160
Andover, Hampshire 185, 201
Anne of Denmark, Queen 68
Anson, Jay 168
Antrim Castle, N. Ireland 192
Appley Bridge, Lancashire 19
Armboth Fell, Cumbria 199
Arretini, Luciana 159–60
Arthur, King 194
Ashdown House, Forest Row,
   Sussex 195
Assendelft family 154–5
Auckland, New Zealand 179–80
Australia 74, 173–7, 179, 183
Australian Post 174
Azay-le-Rideau, France 151

B

Bach, Johann Sebastian 148
Bacup, Lancashire 188
Baker, Frederick 177
Bakken, Captain Keith 172
Ballona, Isle of Man 194
Ballyheigue, Kerry, Eire 193
Banshee 19
Bardens, Dennis 67
Bardoel, Agatha and Fannie 165
Baring-Gould, Sabine 142
Barlow, Fred 65
Barnes, David 174

Barra, Outer Hebrides 186
Barrett, Sir William 11
Barrie, J. M. 134
Barton Water, Norfolk 197
Beardie, Earl 185
Beatles, The 184
Beattie, John 63
Beaufort, Cardinal 130
Beccles, Suffolk 197, 201
Bedfordshire 197
Beeleigh Abbey, Essex 197
Belaugh, Norfolk 197
Belgium 159–60
'Bell Witch Ghost' 172
Beloff, Dr John 182
Bender, Proffessor Hans 103–4,
   147, 160
Bernadotte family 19
Berry Pomeroy Castle, Devon 19
Bettiscombe Manor, Dorset 19–20
Bigelow, Judge S. Tupper 164–5
Bigelow, Kennard and Company 61
Bir Singh 181
Birch, John 129
Birchington, Kent 184
Birse, Aberdeenshire 189
Bishops Castle, Shropshire 201
Bjerre, Dr Paul 100
Black Witch 153
Blance, Rev. R.S. 183
Blickling, Norfolk 191
Blois, France 152
Boleyn, Queen Anne 191, 201
Bolton, Lancashire 185
Bomore Pool, Shropshire 201
Bonett, Joe 164
Bonnington, Chris 181–2
Borley, Essex 35–6, 89–94, 104–5,
   110, 112, 113, 129, 145–6, 196
Born Yesterday 170
Boston, Massachusetts 61, 62
Boughton Green, Northants 185
Bournemouth, Dorset 199
Boursnell, Richard 64
Bowman, Patricia 169
Boyup Brook, Perth, W. Australia,
   173–4

Braddock Down, Lostwithiel, Cornwall 186
Bramber Castle, Sussex 185
Brampton Bryan, Herefordshire 198
Bramshott, Hampshire 144, 145
Breydon Water, Norfolk 196, 198
Bristol, Somerset 74, 178
British Broadcasting Corporation 35, 178, 181
British Journal of Photography 63
Bromhill, June 177
Brooks, Katurah 169
Bruce Castle, Tottenham 200
Brundall, Norfolk 198
Brungerley, Lancashire 185
Buchanan, Meriel 156
Buchanan, Sir Andrew 155
Buchanan, Sir George 156
Buguet, Edouard 63
Bull, Sister Jacqueline 175–7
Bull, Rev. H.D.E. 104–5
Bull, Rev. Henry Foyster 104–5
Bure, River 188, 196
Burgess Township, Canada 165–6
Burgh Castle, Norfolk 189, 195
Burgh St. Peter, Norfolk 190
Burghead, Moray, Scotland 186
Burke, Andrew 166
Burke, Mike 181
Burma 177
Burnett family 19
Burnley, Lancashire 199
Burton Agnes Hall, Humberside 19
Busby Stoop Inn, Yorkshire 20
Butler, Elizabeth 145
Byfork, Mrs E. 129

C

Cadbury Castle, Somerset 194
California, USA, 170–2
California Actors and Models for Equal Opportunity 171
Cambridgeshire 187, 189, 192
Campbell, Donald 11
Canadian Broadcasting Corporation 165
Carnegie family 19
Carrington, Dr Hereward 65
Cary, River 195
Castledermot, C. Kildare 185
Catherine de Medici 152–3
Centre for International Briefing, Farnham, Surrey 130–1

Chagford, Devon 195
Chantonbury Ring, Sussex 194
Charles I, King 68, 129, 141
Charles II, King 132
Charles V, Emperor 155
Charles VII, King of France 151
Charles IX, King of France 152
Charles XII, King of Sweden 154
Chatham, Kent 199
Chenonceux, France 152
Cheriton, Hampshire 187
Cheshire 184, 188
Chicago, USA 199
Chicksands Priory, Bedfordshire 197
Chilton Cantello, Somerset 19
'Chindits' 177
Church of England 117, 118, 119
Civil War (1642) 199
Clarendon, Quebec 101
Cleveland Plaindealer 170
Clitheroe, Lancashire 185
Cliviger Gorge, Lancashire 199
Clophill, Bedfordshire 197
Clumly, Orkey 184
Cobbett, William 129
Cockburn, Admiral Sir George 163
Cockermouth, Cumbria 184–5
Cohn, Harry 170–1
College of Psychic Studies 32, 82, 107
Colley, Archdeacon Thomas 64–5
Cologne, Germany 151
Columbia Pictures Studios 170–1
Combermere Abbey, Cheshire 74
Corbett, Tom 115–6
Cordick, William 166
Cornell, Tony 37
Cornwall 186, 190
Corroboree Rock, Australia 74, 183
Costantia, Lady Coleraine 200
County Kildare 185
Country Life 67
Cowper-Coles, Sherrard 73
Cox, Esther 161
Cox, Mrs Elizabeth, 131–2
Crathes Castle, Scotland 19
Crete 191
'Crewe circle' 64–5
Cromartz, James and Barbara 167
Cromwell, Oliver 138, 186, 198
Crookes, Sir William 12
Crosbie, Sir Thomas 193
Crown Inn, Bildeston, Suffolk 115-6

Cubitt, Miss 109–14
Cumberland, Duke of 192
Cumbria 185, 199
Cuncliffe, the Hon. Anne 131
Cutten, John 39

D

Daily Telegraph 177–8
Dalbrack, Angus, Scotland 194
Davis, Andrew Jackson 61, 62
de Chasseur, Catherine 154–6
de Clare, Gilbert 188
de Gilles, Chevalier 155
de Montesquiou-Fezenzac, Comte
    Robert 151
de Morrow, Duke 192
de Vogelweide 148
de Warren, Lady Blanche 188
de Witt, John and Johanna 156
Deal, Kent 186
Deane, Mrs Ada, 65–6
Dening, Rev. John C. 109–14
Denmark 193
Dering family 144
Devon 195
Diane de Poitiers 152
Dickens, Charles 12, 163, 185, 201
Dingwall, Dr Eric John 107–8
Dobban, Mr and Mrs Alex 161–3
Donegall, Lord 66
d'Orsay, Count 163
Dorset 194, 198, 201
Douglas, Dr James 163
Dowding Air Chief Marshall Lord 12
Doyle, Sir Arthur Conan 12, 65
Driech, Professor Hans 147
Drury Lane Theatre, London 184
Duchy of Lancaster 174
Dyfed 188, 201

E

East Grinstead, Sussex 195
Eban, Mary 169
Eden, Rover 201
Edenbridge 186
Edgehill, Warwickshire 199
Edmunds, Mr and Mrs Charles
    161–2
Edona, Lady 191
Edward VI, King 198
Eglinton, William 64
Eisenbud, Professor Jule 66
Elizabeth I, Queen 119, 130

Elizabeth Bay, Australia 175
Enfield poltergeist case 96, 104
Essex, 35–6, 89–94, 104–5, 110,
    112, 113, 129, 145–6, 192, 196,
    197, 201
Estcourt, Nick 181–2
Ethelbald, King 130
Evans, Dame Joan 151
Everest, Mount 181–2
Exorcism 116–20, 154
Extra-Sensory Perception (ESP) 28,
    84, 87

F

Falkenstein Castle, Germany 148–9
Farnham, Surrey 129–41
Faust 177
Felgueiras, Joe 165
Ferndon Cheshire 184
Ferry Boat Inn, Holywell,
    Cambridgeshire 187
Fiji Island Group 180
Fisher, Fred 173
Fisher's Ghost Creek, Australia 173
Florida, USA 17
Floyd, Barry 153
Flynn, Errol 153–4
Ford, Glenn and Cynthia 171–2
Forest Row, Sussex 195
Fox Sisters 61
Foyle, Miss Christina 197
Foyster, Rev. Lionel A. 104–5
France 151–4
Frangocastello, Crete 191
Fraser, Mrs Joyce 68
Frederick, King of Denmark 154
Frederick, King of Prussia 147
FrederickWilliam II, King 147
Freiburg, W. Germany, University
    of 103
From Here to Eternity 170
Fuller, John 17
Furry Dance 190
Fyvie Castle, Scotland 19

G

Gale, Dean 142
Garrett, Mrs Eileen 114
Garron, Sir Peter 154–8
Gate, Sir John 197
Gauld, Dr Alan 37
Gazetteer of British Ghosts 46, 138

Gazetteer of Scottish and Irish Ghosts 46
George, Duke of Clarence 191
George III, King 130, 192
George IV, King 19
George V, King 20
Germany 147–151
Ghost Club, The 11, 18, 32, 38, 41, 65, 66, 67–73, 75, 79, 87, 88–9, 96, 109, 114, 121, 123, 125, 126–7, 128, 131, 137, 144, 167, 174
Ghost Hunters, *The* 39
Ghost ships 20
Ghost trains 164, 170
Ghosts, aerial phenomena 22–3
Ghosts, animal 22
Ghosts, atmospheric photograph 14, 15, 24, 32
Ghosts, crisis apparitions 18, 24, 31
Ghosts, cyclic 15–16, 102, 116, 152, 170, 184–201
Ghosts, death-bed visions 18, 24, 31
Ghosts, false or fake 7, 20–21, 33, 66
Ghosts, family 19
Ghosts, haunted objects 19–20
Ghosts, historical 15, 24, 30–1
Ghosts, mental imprint manifestations 14
Ghosts, mixed hauntings 23
Ghosts, modern 16–17
Ghosts, psychic echoes 22
Ghosts, recurring (see also Ghosts, cyclic) 16
Ghosts, subjective 7–9, 24
Ghosts, survival hypothesis 22, 114
Ghosts, time-slips 22
Ghosts of the living 24, 31
Gibson, Lord 20
Glamis Castle, Scotland 19, 185
Glastonbury, Somerset 185
Glen Esk, Angus, Scotland 194
Gloucestershire 185, 190
Goldney, Kathleen M. 12
Goodwin Sands Kent 186
Gordon, Peter 134
Gordon family 19
Grant, 18th president of the USA 170
Great Yarmouth, Norfolk 195, 196, 198
Gregson family 105
Grenadier Inn, Wilton Row, London 116

Grenville-Grey, W.E. 131
Grey, Lady Jane 186
Gruber, Professor Karl 147
Guerrero, Francis 153
Guppy, Mrs Samuel 63
Gustav, King of Sweden 154

H

Haakon, King of Norway 154
Hague, The, Netherlands 154–8
Hall-i-th'-Wood, Bolton, Lancashire 185
Ham Common, Surrey 97
Hamilton family 19
Hampshire 185, 187, 199, 201
Hampton Court, Middlesex 187
Hampton Court Palace 130, 195, 198, 200
Hardy, Rev. R. W. 68–73
Haroldslea House, Horley, Surrey 200
Harris, Mrs 109–14
Harrison, William H.H. 9th president of the USA 170
Harz Mountains, Germany 148–9
Hauntings 105
Hawkins, Jack 153
Heathfield, Lord 195
Helston, Cornwall 190
Henri de Guise 152
Henry II, King of France 152
Henry III, King of France 152–3
Henry IV, King 130
Henry IV, King of France 72
Henry VIII, King 130, 200
Henry of Blois 130
Herald of Progress 62
Herefordshire 198
Hertfordshire 191, 193–4, 199–200
Hesse family 19
Hever Castle, Kent 201
Hickling Broad, Norfolk 187, 192–3
Hilton-Rowe, Dr Peter 70
Hinckley, Leicestershire 188–9
Hitchin, Hertfordshire 193–4, 199
Hohenratier Castle, Germany 151
Hohenzollern family 19, 147
Hole, Lady 145
Hollywood, USA 170, 171–2
Holywell, Cambridgeshire 187
Holzer, Hans 66, 114
Hope, William 64–5
Horley, Surrey 200

Horning, Norfolk 196, 198
Horsey Mere, Norfolk 193
Host of Hauntings, *A* 108
Howard, Catherine 200
Howard, Richard 70
Howitt, William 63
Howley, Newfoundland 164
Hubbell, Walter 161
Hudson, Frederick A. 63
Huxley, Six Julian 12
Hyams, Joe 171
Hyde Hall, Hertfordshire 199–200

I

Illinois, USA 170
Imperial Dry Plate Company 65
India 180–2
International Ghost Register 147
Inverness, Scotland 186
Isabelle, Countess of Paris 159–60
Italy, 158–60 180

J

James I, King 68, 130
Japan 182–3
Jenkins, Dr J.D. 100
Joan of Arc 130, 152
Jocelyn, Sir John 199–200
John, King 194, 201
John of Gaunt 130
Johnson, Herbert 180–1
Jonas, Air Commodore R.C. 122
Jones, Inigo 68
Jourdain, Miss Eleanor 151
Joy, Sir George 12, 87

K

Kaiser-Wilheim II 148
Karachi, India 180–1
Karloff, Boris 145
Kellerman, Michael 171
Kensington, London 17
Kent 184, 186, 188, 199, 201
Kildare, Earl of 185
Kilkea Castle Hotel, Castledermot,
   Co. Kildare 185
Killarney, Co. Kerry 189
King, Mackenzie 161
Kinlock, James 165–6
Kodak Photographic Ltd. 71
Koestler, Arthur 12
Kohn, Miss 100–1

L

Lady Luvibond 186
Lambert, Guy 41–2
Lambert, Richard 165
Lampard, Mrs 109–14
Lancashire 185, 188, 199
Langenhoe, Essex 108–14
Lauderdale, Earl of 118
Leicestershire 188–9
Leslie, Sir Shane 12
Levuka, Fiji 180
Lewes, Sussex 191
Lincoln, Abraham 168–70
Lincoln, Willie 170
Listener, The 165
Littleport, Cambridgeshire 192
Liverpool 184
Llyn Cwn Llwch, Wales 189
Loch Ashie, Inverness, Scotland 189
Loch na Naire, Scotland 197
Loch of Skene, Scotland 201
Lochlee, Glen Esk, Angus, Scotland
   194
Loft, Bob 17
Loire Valley, France 151–2
Lombroso, Professor Cesare 99
Lopez, Jean Luc 153
Lorton Hall, Cockermouth,
   Cumbria 184–5
Lostwithiel, Cornwall 186
Lough Leane, Killarney 189
Louis, Prince of Prussia 147
Louis XV, King of France 155
Lowestoft, Suffolk 196
Ludham, Norfolk 188
Luther, Martin 148
Lutz, George and Kathleen 167–8
Lyon family 19

M

MacGregor, Alasdair Alpin 174–7
Mackenzie, Andrew 151, 160
Mackenzie, William Lyon 161–3
MacQueen, Mr and Mrs Hector 68,
   70
Madoc, Welsh Prince 184
Magic Circle 65
Maharajah of Datia 180
Malta 159
Man, Isle of 189, 194
'Man in Grey' 184
Margaret, Countess of Salisbury

191–2
Maria, Henrietta, Queen 68–72
Marie Antionette, Queen 151
Marryat, Captain 19, 67
Martindale, Harry 141–2
Mary I, Queen 130, 196
Mason, Sir Paul 157
May, Commander W.E. 69
Melbourne, Australia 173, 177
Michael, Phyllis 171
Middlesex 130, 187, 195, 198, 200
Millertown, Newfoundland 164
Minsden Chapel, Hertfordshire 199
Mitchell, John 143
Moberley, Miss Annie 151
Monmouth, Duke of 195
Moore, Admiral W. Usborne 73
Moray, Scotland 186
Morley, Bishop 132
Moses, William Stainton 63
Mountain Hill Hotel, Quebec 163
Mumler, William 61–2
Munich, Germany 149–51
Myers, John 66

N

Napoleon Bonaparte 147–8, 158–9,
   163
National Maritime Museum,
   Greenwich 68–73
National Portrait Gallery, London
   72
Netherfield, Sussex 21
Nevern, Dyfed 188
New York, USA 62, 63
New York Central Railway 170
New York Daily News 169
New Zealand 179–80
Newbury, Berkshire 22
Ney, Marshall 148
Nichols, Beverley 12
Norfolk 187, 188, 189, 190, 191, 192,
   193, 195, 196, 197, 198, 201
North Caroline, USA 172
North Vancouver, B.C. 68
Northamptonshire 185
Nutlers' Dance 188

O

O'Donoghue, (legendary chieftain)
   189
Old City Hall, Toronto 164–5

Old Court House, Hampton Court
   187
Old Ferry Inn, Norning, Norfolk 198
Old Hall, Ranworth, Norfolk 201
Oliver, Inspector Sidney 166
On the Waterfront 170
Oporto, Portugal 186
Ordnance Survey Office 123
Orkney 184
Ormsby Broad, Norfolk 190
Oulton Broad, Norfolk 195
Outer Hebrides 186
Owen, Dr A.R.G. 12, 96, 97
Oxford, New College 130

P

Palma, Majorca 153
Palmer, A.S. 74
Pearce-Higgins, Rev. Canon John 87
Peckham, London 102–3
Perth, Canada 166
Perth, Western Australia 173–4
Petitpierre, Dom Robert, OSB.
   117–8
Philip of Spain, King 130, 155
Pickford, John 35–6
Pinney, Michael 20
Pirton, Hertfordshire 193
Playfair, Guy 104
Pluckley, Kent 144–5
Poltergeist activity 24, 29–30, 41–2
   79–84, 95–106, 149–51, 153,
   156–7, 159–60, 161, 166, 172,
   173–4
Pomeroy family 19
Pontefract, Black Monk of 104
Pooler, Gerald 177
Poona, India 100–101
Pope Pius V 119
Potter Heigham Norfolk 187, 192
Prestbury, Gloucestershire 185, 190
Price, Harry 12, 65, 89–94, 149–51
Prince Alfred Hospital, Sydney,
   Australia 174–7
Princess Theatre, Melbourne 177
Provand, Captain H.C. 67
Psychic News 107
Psychic Photography 66
Purse Caundle, Dorset 194, 201
Pyecombe, Sussex 200

Q

Quarry, Newfoundland 164

Quebec, Canada 163–4
Queen's House, Greenwich 68–73
Quinn family 165–6

R

Raleigh, Sir Walter 198
Rannoch Moor, Perthshire 189
Ranworth, Norfolk 201
Raynham Hall, Norfolk 19, 67–8, 73
Redgrave, Sir Michael 134
Reedham, Norfolk 197
Repo, Don 17
Rheims, Archbishop of 152
Rhine, Dr J.B. 87
Ribble, River 185
Ringcroft case 104
Richester, Kent 188, 201
Rochfort Hall, Essex 201
Rockland County, USA 114
Rogers, John, CBE JP 87
Roman Catholic Church 117–120
Romanoff family 19
Rome, Italy 158–9
Roos Hall, Suffolk 201
Roosevelt, Mr and Mrs Franklin
    Delano 168–70
Roosevelt, Theodore 170
Rosaca, Bertha 197
Rose, Major W. Rampling 65
Rosenheim case 103–4
Rossel House, Sunbury-on-Thames
    73
Rostherne, Cheshire 188
Royal Air Force 20, 180
Royal National Orthopaedic
    Hospital, Stanmore 200
Rumbold, Sir Horace 156
Rupert, Prince 17
Russell, Sir Odo 156–7
Russia 19

S

St Albans, Hertfordshire 191
St Benedict's Abbey, Norfolk 191,
    196
St Botolph's Church, Bishopsgate 73
St Brigid 186
St Helena, Isle of 87, 158, 159, 163
St James's Palace, London 192
St Mary the Virgin, Woodford,
    Northants 73
St Michael 190
St Rita's Church, Chicago 199

Salhouse Mere, Norfolk 190
Samuelson, Colonel and Mrs 153
San Diego, USA 167
Sandburg, Carl 168
'Saragossa Ghost' 160
'Sawbridgeworth, Hertfordshire
    199–200
Scarborough, Yorkshire 189
Schneider, Willi and Rudi 147
Schrenck-Notzing, Baron Albert von
    147
Scott, Sheila 23
Sedgemoor, Battle of 195
Serios, Ted 66
Sesame Club, London 18
Sewell, Leonard 109–14
Seymour, Jane 198
Shrewsbury, Shropshire 201
Shropshire 201
Singapore 178–9
Sitwell, Sir Osbert 12
Skulls and ghostly phenomena
    19–20
Slawensick Castle, Germany 151
Smith, Rev. G. Eric 104–5
Smith, Richard 188–9
Society for Psychical Research 17,
    22, 32, 39, 41, 46–59, 65, 75, 87,
    107, 151, 160, 182
Somerleyton, Suffolk 196
Somerset 185, 194
Sommer, Elke 171
South Walsham, Norfolk 189
Southery Fen, Cambridgeshire 192
Spain 20, 160
Spiritualism 9, 40, 59–60, 61–66,
    107–116, 170
Stalham, Norfolk 196
Stanleyville, Canada 166
Stanmore, Middlesex 200
Stephen, King 130
Steyning, Sussex 185
Stiper Stones, Shropshire 201
Stockholm, Sweden 154
Stone, Charlie 180
Strata Florida Abbey, Dyfed 201
Strathnaver, Sutherland 197
Stringer, Graham and Vera 102–3
Suffolk 189, 195, 196, 197, 201
Surrey 200
Sussex 185, 191, 194, 195, 200
Sutherland, Scotland 197
Sutton Montis, Somerset 194

Sweden 19, 100, 154
Sydney, Australia 173 174–7

T

Tabori, Dr Paul 87
Talbot, Gulbert 129–30
Tannhauser 148
Tay Bridge, Scotland 201
Taylor, Professor John 35–6
Testwood House, Totton,
    Hampshire 198–9
Tewkesbury, Gloucestershire 190
Theydon Bois, Essex 192
Thirlmere Lake, Cumbria 199
Thurne, River 192, 196
Tokyo, Japan 182–3
Toronto, Canada 10–11, 161, 164–5
Toronto New Horizons Research
    Foundation, 10–11
Toronto Star 165
Tottenham, Middlesex 200
Totton, Hampshire 199
Tower of London 20, 186, 191, 200
Towneley, Lord William 199
Townshend family 19, 67
Tremain, Brian 71
Truman, Harry 169
Truman, Margaret 169
Turin, Italy 97
Tyrrell, G.N.M. 18

U

US Military Academy, West Point
    172

V

Valentino, Rudolph 172
Van Oosthuysen, Petrus Judocus 155
Versailles, France 151
Victoria, Queen 19, 130
Victoria and Albert Museum,
    London 72
Villefranche, France 153
Villiers, George, Duke of
    Buckingham 143
Voisin, Bernard and Thierry 153

W

Walker, Denton 114
Wallace, Dr Alfred Russel 63
Walpole, Lady Dorothy 19, 67
Walpurgis Night 189
Warbleton Priory, Sussex 19
Wardley Hall, Lancashire 19

Wartburg Castle, Eisenach,
    Germany 148
Warwickshire 199
Washington, D.C. 170
Watch on the Rhine 168
Waterloo, Battle of 187
Wellesley, Lord Charles 163
Wellington, Duke of 116
West Point Military Academy 172
Westminster, London 196, 198
Weston, Horace 62
Wheatley, Dennis 12
Wheeler, Rev. Allan 138
Whelan, Rev. Father 166
Whiddon, Mary 195
Whiddon Park, Chagford, Devon
    195
Whitby, Yorkshire 199
White House, The, Washington
    168–70
Whittlesfork, Cambridgeshire 189
Wijk, Hjalmar 100
Wilch, Judge Peter 165
Wilhelmina, Queen 168, 169
Wilkinson, Cyril 66
Willan, Mr and Mrs Puck 153
William Lyon Mackenzie
    Homestead Foundation, Toronto
    161–3
William of Wykeham 130
William the Conqueror 130–1
Williamson, Clement 181–2
Wilson, Frank 168–9
Winchester 130
Wingate, General Orde 177
Wolsey, Cardinal 130
Work-Association tests 28, 79, 84–6
Worthington, Dr Edward 163–4
Wren, Sir Christopher 187
Wroxham, Norfolk 196
Wymore, Patrice 153

Y

Yare, River 198
Yeats, W.B. 12
Yeovil, Somerset 194
York, 129, 141–4
Yorkshire 129, 141–4, 189, 199
Yorkshire Oddities 142

Z

Zaca 153
Zener cards 28, 30, 84, 87
Zollner, Professor J.C.F. 147